Saint THÉRÈSE OF LISIEUX

THE STORY OF A SOUL : THE AUTOBIOGRAPHY OF
ST. THÉRÈSE OF LISIEUX

WITH ADDITIONAL WRITINGS AND SAYINGS OF ST. THÉRÈSE

───────────────────

1912

© 2024, Sainte Thérèse de Lisieux, (domaine public)
Édition: BoD • Books on Demand GmbH, In de Tarpen 42, 22848 Norderstedt (Allemagne)
Impression: Libri Plureos GmbH, Friedensallee 273, 22763 Hamburg (Allemagne)
ISBN: 978-2-3225-5060-9
Dépôt légal : Octobre 2024

PREFACE

As we become acquainted with the histories of those in whom, in long succession, God has been pleased to show forth examples of holiness of life, it seems as if every phase of human existence had in the history of the Church received its consecration as a power to bring men nearer to their Maker. But there is no limit to the types of sanctity which the Creator is pleased to unfold before His Creatures. To many, on reading for the first time the story of Sister Teresa of the Child Jesus and of the Holy Face, it came almost as a shock to find a very youthful member of an austere Order, strictly retired from the world, engaged in hidden prayer and mortification, appearing before us to reveal to the whole world the wonders of the close intimacy of friendship to which her Divine Spouse had been pleased to call her. Certainly the way by which Soeur Thérèse was led is not the normal life of Carmel, nor hers the manner whereby most Carmelites are called to accomplish the wondrous apostolate of intercession to which their lives are given. But no less certain is it that, in her particular case, her work for God and her apostolate were not to be confined between the walls of her religious home, or to be limited by her few years on earth.

In the first place, we know that it was by obedience that the record of God's dealings with her soul were set down in writing. And again, the long tale of graces granted in such strange profusion through her intercession is proof sufficient that it was not without Divine permission and guidance that the history of her special and peculiar vocation has become the property of all Catholics in every land. It is for God to keep, and for Him to make known the secrets of His Love for men. And in the case of Soeur Thérèse it has been His Will to divulge His secrets in most generous consideration for our needs.

What are the hidden treasures which Our Divine Master thus reveals to us through His chosen little servant?

It is the old story of simplicity in God's service, of the perfect accomplishment of small recurring duties, of trustful confidence in Him who made and has redeemed and sanctified us. Humility, self-effacement, obedience, hiddenness, unfaltering charity, with all the self-control and constant effort that they imply, are written on every page of the history of this little Saint. And, as we turn its pages, the lesson is borne in upon our souls that there is no surer nor safer way of pleasing Our Father Who is in Heaven than by remaining ever as little children in His sight. Doubtless for many of her clients whose hearts are kindled as they read this book, Soeur Thérèse will obtain, as she has done so often in the past, wonderful gifts for health of soul and body. But may she win for all of us without exception a deep and fruitful conviction of the unchanging truth, that unless we become as little children in the doing of our Heavenly Father's Will, we cannot enter into our Eternal Home.

FRANCIS CARDINAL BOURNE, Archbishop of Westminster.

Feast of the Presentation of Our Blessed Lady, 1912.

PROLOGUE: THE PARENTAGE & BIRTH OF MARIE FRANÇOISE THÉRÈSE MARTIN

In the month of September, 1843, a young man of twenty climbed the mountain of the Great St. Bernard. His eyes shone with a holy enthusiasm as the splendour of the Alps stirred to the depths his responsive nature. Presently, accustomed as they were to discern God's beauty in the beauty of His handiwork, they glistened with tears. He paused for a space, then, continuing his journey, soon reached the celebrated monastery that like a beacon on those heights darts afar its beams of faith and magnificent charity.

The Prior, struck by the frank and open countenance of his guest, welcomed him with more than wonted hospitality. Louis Joseph Stanislaus Martin was the pilgrim's name. He was born on August 22, 1823, at Bordeaux, while his father, a brave and devout soldier, was captain in the garrison there. "God has predestined this little one for Himself," said the saintly Bishop of Bordeaux on the occasion of his baptism, and events have proved the truth of his words. From this town, by the banks of the Garonne, his parents went to Alençon in lower Normandy, and there in their new home, as in their old one, Louis was the cherished Benjamin.

It was not the loveliness of Swiss lakes and mountains and skies that had drawn the traveller from distant Alençon. He came to the monastery — and his journey was chiefly on foot — to consecrate his days to God. On learning his purpose the Prior questioned him upon his knowledge of Latin, only to discover that the young aspirant had not completed his course of studies in that language. "I am indeed sorry, my child," said the venerable monk, "since this is an essential condition, but you must not be disheartened. Go back to your own country, apply yourself diligently, and when you have ended your studies we shall receive you with open arms."

Louis was disappointed. He set out for home — for exile he would have said — but ere long he saw clearly that his life was to be dedicated to God in another and equally fruitful way, and that the Alpine monastery was to be nothing more to him than a sweet memory.

* * * * * *

A few years after the vain quest of Louis Martin, a similar scene was enacted in Alençon itself. Accompanied by her mother, Zélie Guérin — an attractive and pious girl — presented herself at the Convent of the Sisters of Charity in the hope of gaining admission. For years it had been her desire to share the Sisters' work, but this was not to be. In the interview that followed, the Superioress—guided by the Holy Ghost—decided unhesitatingly that Zélie's vocation was not for the religious life. God wanted her in the world, and so she returned to her parents, and to the companionship of her elder sister and her younger brother. Shortly afterwards the gates of the Visitation Convent at Le Mans closed upon her beloved sister, and Zélie's thoughts turned to the Sacrament of Holy Matrimony. "O my God"—she repeated constantly—"since I am unworthy to be Thy Spouse, like my dear sister, I shall enter the married state to fulfill Thy Holy Will, and I beseech Thee to make me the mother of many children, and to grant that all of them may be dedicated to Thee."

God gave ear to her prayer, and His Finger was visible in the circumstances which led to her becoming the wife of Louis Martin, on July 12, 1858, in Alençon's lovely Church of Notre Dame. Like the chaste Tobias, they were joined together in matrimony—"solely for the love of children, in whom God's Name might be blessed for ever and ever." Nine white flowers bloomed in this sacred garden. Of the nine, four were transplanted to Paradise ere their buds had quite unfolded, while five were gathered in God's walled gardens upon earth, one entering the Visitation Convent at Caen, the others the Carmel of Lisieux. From the cradle all were dedicated to Mary Immaculate, and all received her name: Marie Louise, Marie Pauline, Marie Léonie, Marie Hélène, who died at the age of four and a half, Marie Joseph Louis, Marie Joseph Jean Baptiste, Marie Céline, Marie Mélanie Therèse, who died when three months old, and lastly, *Marie Françoise Thérèse*.

The two boys were the fruit of prayers and tears. After the birth of the four elder girls, their parents entreated St. Joseph to obtain for them the favour of a son who should become a priest and a missionary. Marie Joseph soon was given them, and his pretty ways appealed to all hearts, but only five months had run their course when Heaven demanded what it had lent. Then followed more urgent novenas.

The grandeur of the Priesthood, glorious upon earth, ineffable in eternity, was so well understood by those Christian parents, that their hearts coveted it most dearly. At all costs the family must have a Priest of the Lord, one who would be an apostle, peradventure a martyr. But, "the thoughts of the Lord are not our thoughts, His ways are not our ways." Another little Joseph was born, and with him hope once again grew strong. Alas! Nine months had scarcely passed when he, too, fled from this world and joined his angel brother.

They did not ask again. Yet, could the veil of the future have been lifted, their heavy hearts would, of a surety, have been comforted. A child was to be vouchsafed them who would be a herald of Divine love, not to China alone, but to all the ends of the earth.

Nay, they themselves were destined to shine as apostles, and we read on one of the first pages of the Portuguese edition of the Autobiography, these significant words of an eminent Jesuit:

"To the Sacred Memory of Louis Joseph Stanislaus Martin and of
Zélie Guérin, the blessed parents of Sister Teresa of the Child
Jesus, for an example to all Christian parents."

They little dreamed of this future apostolate, nevertheless they made ready their souls day by day to be God's own instruments in God's good time. With most loving resignation they greeted the many crosses which the Lord laid upon them—the

Lord whose tender name of Father is truest in the dark hour of trial.

Every morning saw them at Mass; together they knelt at the Holy Table. They strictly observed the fasts and abstinences of the Church, kept Sunday as a day of complete rest from work in spite of the remonstrance of friends, and found in pious reading their most delightful recreation. They prayed in common—after the touching example of Captain Martin, whose devout way of repeating the *Our Father* brought tears to all eyes. Thus the great Christian virtues flourished in their home. Wealth did not bring luxury in its train, and a strict simplicity was invariably observed.

"How mistaken are the great majority of men!" Madame Martin used often to say. "If they are rich, they at once desire honours; and if these are obtained, they are still unhappy; for never can that heart be satisfied which seeks anything but God."

Her whole ambition as a mother was directed to Heaven. "Four of my children are already well settled in life," she once wrote; "and the others will go likewise to that Heavenly Kingdom—enriched with greater merit because the combat will have been more prolonged."

Charity in all its forms was a natural outlet to the piety of these simple hearts. Husband and wife set aside each year a considerable portion of their earnings for the Propagation of the Faith; they relieved poor persons in distress, and ministered to them with their own hands. On one occasion Monsieur Martin, like a good Samaritan, was seen to raise a drunken man from the ground in a busy thoroughfare, take his bag of tools, support him on his arm, and lead him home. Another time when he saw, in a railway station, a poor and starving epileptic without the means to return to his distant home, he was so touched with pity that he took off his hat and, placing in it an alms, proceeded to beg from the passengers on behalf of the sufferer. Money poured in, and it was with a heart brimming over with gratitude that the sick man blessed his benefactor.

Never did he allow the meannesses of human respect to degrade his Christian dignity. In whatever company he might be, he always saluted the Blessed Sacrament when passing a Church; and he never met a priest without paying him a mark of respect. A word from his lips sufficed to silence whosoever dared blaspheme in his presence.

In reward for his virtues, God showered even temporal blessings on His faithful servant. In 1871 he was able to give up his business as a jeweller, and retire to a house in the Rue St. Blaise. The making of point-lace, however, begun by Madame Martin, was still carried on.

In that house the "Little Flower of Jesus" first saw the sunshine. Again and again, in the pages of her Autobiography, she calls herself by this modest name of the *Little Flower,* emblematic of her humility, her purity, her simplicity, and it may be added, of the poetry of her soul. The reader will learn in the Epilogue how it was also used by one of her favourite martyr-saints—the now Blessed Théophane Vénard. On the manuscript of her Autobiography she set the title: "*The Story of the Springtime of a little white Flower,*" and in truth such it was, for long ere the rigours of life's winter came round, the Flower was blossoming in Paradise.

It was, however, in mid-winter, January 2, 1873, that this ninth child of Louis Martin and Zélie Guérin was born. Marie and Pauline were at home for the Christmas holidays from the Visitation Convent at Le Mans, and though there was, it is true, a slight disappointment that the future priest was still denied them, it quickly passed, and the little one was regarded as a special gift from Heaven. Later on, her beloved Father delighted in calling her his "Little Queen," adding at times the high-sounding titles—"Of France and Navarre."

The Little Queen was indeed well received that winter's morning, and in the course of the day a poor waif rang timidly at the door of the happy home, and presented a paper bearing the following simple stanza:

"Smile and swiftly grow; All beckons thee to joy, Sweet love, and tenderest care. Smile gladly at the dawn, Bud of an hour!—for thou Shalt be a stately rose."

It was a charming prophecy, for the bud unfolded its petals and became a rose—a rose of love—but not for long, "for the space of a morn!"

* * * * * *

On January 4, she was carried to the Church of Notre Dame to receive the Sacrament of Baptism; her eldest sister, Marie, was her godmother, and she was given the name of *Marie Françoise Thérèse*.[1]

All was joy at first, but soon the tender bud drooped on its delicate stem: little hope was held out—it must wither and die. "You must pray to St. Francis de Sales," wrote her aunt from the convent at Le Mans, "and you must promise, if the child recovers, to call her by her second name, Frances." This was a sword-thrust for the Mother. Leaning over the cradle of her Thérèse, she awaited the coming of the end, saying: "Only when the last hope has gone, will I promise to call her Frances."

The gentle St. Francis waived his claim in favour of the great Reformer of the Carmelite Order: the child recovered, and so retained her sweet name of Thérèse. Sorrow, however, was mixed with the Mother's joy, when it became necessary to send the babe to a foster-mother in the country. There the "little rose-bud" grew in beauty, and after some months had gained strength sufficient to allow of her being brought back to Alençon. Her memory of this short but happy time spent with her sainted Mother in the Rue St. Blaise was extraordinarily vivid. To-day a tablet on the balcony of No. 42 informs the passers-by that here was born a certain Carmelite, by name, Sister Teresa of the Child Jesus and the Holy Face. Fifteen years have gone since the meeting in Heaven of Madame Martin and her Carmelite child, and if the pilgrimage to where the Little Flower first saw the light of day, be not so large as that to the grave where her remains await their glorious resurrection, it may nevertheless be numbered in thousands. And to the English-speaking pilgrim there is an added pleasure in the fact that her most notable convert, the first minister of the United Free Church of Scotland to enter the True Fold, performs, with his convert wife, the courteous duties of host.

* * * * * *

It will not be amiss to say a brief word here on the brother and sister of Madame Martin. Her sister—in religion, Sister Marie Dosithea—led a life so holy at Le Mans that she was cited by Dom Guéranger, perhaps the most distinguished Benedictine of the nineteenth century, as the model of a perfect nun. By her own confession, she had never been guilty from earliest childhood of the smallest deliberate fault. She died on February 24, 1877. It was in the convent made fragrant by such holiness that her niece Pauline Martin, elder sister and "little mother" of Thérèse, and for five years her Prioress at the Carmel, received her education. And if the Little Flower may have imbibed the liturgical spirit from her teachers, the daughters of St. Benedict in Lisieux, so that she could say before her death: "I do not think it is possible for anyone to have desired more than I to assist properly at choir and to recite perfectly the Divine Office"—may it not be to the influences from Le Mans that may be traced something of the honey-sweet spirit of St. Francis de Sales which pervades the pages of the Autobiography?

With the brother of Zélie Guérin the reader will make acquaintance in the narrative of Thérèse. He was a chemist in Lisieux, and it was there his daughter Jeanne Guérin married Dr. La Néele and his younger child Marie entered the Carmel. Our foreign missionaries had a warm friend in the uncle of Thérèse—for his charities he was made godfather to an African King; and to the Catholic Press—that home missionary—he was ever most devoted. Founder, at Lisieux, of the Nocturnal Adoration of the Blessed Sacrament, and a zealous member of the Society of St. Vincent de Paul, he was called to his abundant reward on September 28, 1909. Verily the lamp of faith is not extinct in the land of the Norman.

The Father of Thérèse, after the death of his wife, likewise made his home in the delightful town which lies amid the beautiful apple orchards of the valley of the Touques. Lisieux is deeply interesting by reason of its fine old churches of St. Jacques and

St. Pierre, and its wonderful specimens of quaint houses, some of which date from the twelfth century. In matters of faith it is neither fervent nor hostile, and in 1877 its inhabitants little thought that through their new citizen, Marie Françoise Thérèse Martin, their town would be rendered immortal.

* * * * * *

"The cell at Lisieux reminds us of the cell of the Blessed Gabriel at Isola. There is the same even tenor of way, the same magnificant fidelity in little things, the same flames of divine charity, consuming but concealed. Nazareth, with the simplicity of its Child, and the calm abysmal love of Mary and Joseph—Nazareth, adorable but imitable, gives the key to her spirit, and her Autobiography does but repeat the lessons of the thirty hidden years."[2]

And it repeats them with an unrivalled charm. "This master of asceticism," writes a biographer[3] of St. Ignatius Loyola, "loved the garden and loved the flowers. In the balcony of his study he sat gazing on the stars: it was then Lainez heard him say: 'Oh, how earth grows base to me when I look on Heaven!' . . . The like imaginative strain, so scorned of our petty day, inhered in all the lofty souls of that age. Even the Saints of our day speak a less radiant language: and sanctity shows 'shorn of its rays' through the black fog of universal utilitarianism, the materiality which men have drawn into the very lungs of their souls."

This is not true of the sainted authoress of the chapters that follow—"less radiant," in the medium of a translation. In her own inimitable pages, as in those of a Campion or an Ignatius, a Teresa of Avila, or a John of the Cross—the Spirit of Poetry is the handmaiden of Holiness. This new lover of flowers and student of the stars, this "strewer of roses," has uplifted a million hearts from the "base earth" and "black fog" to the very throne of God, and her mission is as yet but begun.

The pen of Soeur Thérèse herself must now take up the narrative. It will do so in words that do not merely tell of love but set the heart on fire, and at the same time lay bare the workings of God in a soul that "since the age of three never refused the Good God anything." The writing of this Autobiography was an act of obedience, and the Prioress who imposed the task sought, in all simplicity, her own personal edification. But the fragrance of its pages was such that she was advised to publish them to the world. She did so in

1899 under the title of *L'Histoire d'une Âme*. An English version by M. H. Dziewicki appeared in 1901.

This new translation relates more fully the story of the childhood, girlhood, and brief convent days of Soeur Thérèse. It tells of her "Roses," and sets forth again, in our world-wide tongue, her world-wide embassy—the ever ancient message of God's Merciful Love, the ever new *way* to Him of "confidence and self-surrender."

The Editor. _____

[1] The baptismal entry, with its numerous signatures, is shown to visitors, and a tablet in the baptistry of the beautiful Gothic church tells the pilgrim that here the "Little Queen" was made a child of God. [Ed.]

[2] "*As Little Children*": the abridged life of Soeur Thérèse. Published at the Orphans' Press, Rochdale.

[3] Francis Thompson.

CHAPTER I EARLIEST MEMORIES

It is to you, dear Mother, that I am about to confide the story of my soul. When you asked me to write it, I feared the task might unsettle me, but since then Our Lord has deigned to make me understand that by simple obedience I shall please Him best. I begin therefore to sing what must be my eternal song: "the Mercies of the Lord."[1]

Before setting about my task I knelt before the statue of Our Lady which had given my family so many proofs of Our Heavenly Mother's loving care.[2] As I knelt I begged of that dear Mother to guide my hand, and thus ensure that only what was pleasing to her should find place here.

Then opening the Gospels, my eyes fell on these words: "Jesus, going up into a mountain, called unto Him whom He would Himself."[3]

They threw a clear light upon the mystery of my vocation and of my entire life, and above all upon the favours which Our Lord has granted to my soul. He does not call those who are worthy, but those whom He will. As St. Paul says: "God will have mercy on whom He will have mercy.[4] So then it is not of him that willeth, nor of him that runneth, but of God that showeth mercy."[5]

I often asked myself why God had preferences, why all souls did not receive an equal measure of grace. I was filled with wonder when I saw extraordinary favours showered on great sinners like St. Paul, St. Augustine, St. Mary Magdalen, and many others, whom He forced, so to speak, to receive His grace. In reading the lives of the Saints I was surprised to see that there were certain privileged souls, whom Our Lord favoured from the cradle to the grave, allowing no obstacle in their path which might keep them from mounting towards Him, permitting no sin to soil the spotless brightness of their baptismal robe. And again it puzzled me why so many poor savages should die without having even heard the name of God.

Our Lord has deigned to explain this mystery to me. He showed me the book of nature, and I understood that every flower created by Him is beautiful, that the brilliance of the rose and the whiteness of the lily do not lessen the perfume of the violet or the sweet simplicity of the daisy. I understood that if all the lowly flowers wished to be roses, nature would lose its springtide beauty, and the fields would no longer be enamelled with lovely hues. And so it is in the world of souls, Our Lord's living garden. He has been pleased to create great Saints who may be compared to the lily and the rose, but He has also created lesser ones, who must be content to be daisies or simple violets flowering at His Feet, and whose mission it is to gladden His Divine Eyes when He deigns to look down on them. And the more gladly they do His Will the greater is their perfection.

I understood this also, that God's Love is made manifest as well in a simple soul which does not resist His grace as in one more highly endowed. In fact, the characteristic of love being self-abasement, if all souls resembled the holy Doctors who have illuminated the Church, it seems that God in coming to them would not stoop low enough. But He has created the little child, who knows nothing and can but utter feeble cries, and the poor savage who has only the natural law to guide him, and it is to their hearts that He deigns to stoop. These are the field flowers whose simplicity charms Him; and by His condescension to them Our Saviour shows His infinite greatness. As the sun shines both on the cedar and on the floweret, so the Divine Sun illumines every soul, great and small, and all correspond to His care—just as in nature the seasons are so disposed that on the appointed day the humblest daisy shall unfold its petals.

You will wonder, dear Mother, to what all this is leading, for till now I have said nothing that sounds like the story of my life; but did you not tell me to write quite freely whatever came into my mind? So, it will not be my life properly speaking, that you will find in these pages, but my thoughts about the graces which it has pleased Our Lord to bestow on me.

I am now at a time of life when I can look back on the past, for my soul has been refined in the crucible of interior and exterior trials. Now, like a flower after the storm, I can raise my head and see that the words of the Psalm are realised in me: "The Lord is my Shepherd and I shall want nothing. He hath set me in a place of pasture. He hath brought me up on the water of refreshment. He hath converted my soul. He hath led me on the paths of justice for His own Name's sake. For though I should walk in the midst of the shadow of death, I will fear no evils for Thou are with me."[6]

Yes, to me Our Lord has always been "compassionate and merciful, long-suffering and plenteous in mercy."[7]

And so it gives me great joy, dear Mother, to come to you and sing His unspeakable mercies. It is for you alone that I write the story of the little flower gathered by Jesus. This thought will help me to speak freely, without troubling either about style or about the many digressions that I shall make; for a Mother's heart always understands her child, even when it can only lisp, and so I am sure of being understood and my meaning appreciated.

If a little flower could speak, it seems to me that it would tell us quite simply all that God has done for it, without hiding any of its gifts. It would not, under the pretext of humility, say that it was not pretty, or that it had not a sweet scent, that the sun had withered its petals, or the storm bruised its stem, if it knew that such were not the case.

The Little Flower, that now tells her tale, rejoiced in having to publish the wholly undeserved favours bestowed upon her by Our Lord. She knows that she had nothing in herself worthy of attracting Him: His Mercy alone showered blessings on her. He allowed her to grow in holy soil enriched with the odour of purity, and preceded by eight lilies of shining whiteness. In His Love He willed to preserve her from the poisoned breath of the world — hardly had her petals unfolded when this good Master transplanted her to the mountain of Carmel, Our Lady's chosen garden.

And now, dear Mother, having summed up in a few words all that God's goodness has done for me, I will relate in detail the story of my childhood. I know that, though to others it may seem wearisome, your motherly heart will find pleasure in it. In the story of my soul, up to the time of my entry into the Carmel, there are three clearly marked periods: the first, in spite of its shortness, is by no means the least rich in memories.

It extends from the dawn of reason to the death of my dearly loved Mother; in other words, till I was four years and eight months old. God, in His goodness, did me the favour of awakening my intelligence very early, and He has imprinted the recollections of my childhood so deeply in my memory that past events seem to have happened but yesterday. Without doubt He wished to make me know and appreciate the Mother He had given me. Alas! His Divine Hand soon took her from me to crown her in Heaven.

All my life it has pleased Him to surround me with affection. My first recollections are of loving smiles and tender caresses; but if He made others love me so much, He made me love them too, for I was of an affectionate nature.

You can hardly imagine how much I loved my Father and Mother, and, being very demonstrative, I showed my love in a thousand little ways, though the means I employed make me smile now when I think of them.

Dear Mother, you have given me the letters which my Mother wrote at this time to Pauline, who was at school at the Visitation Convent at Le Mans. I remember perfectly the events they refer to, but it will be easier for me simply to quote some passages, though these charming letters, inspired by a Mother's love, are too often full of my praises.

In proof of what I have said about my way of showing affection for my parents, here is an example: "Baby is the dearest little rogue; she comes to kiss me, and at the same time wishes me to die. 'Oh, how I wish you would die, dear Mamma,' she said, and when she was scolded she was quite astonished, and answered: 'But I want you to go to Heaven, and you say we must die to go there'; and in her outburst of affection for her Father she wishes him to die too. The dear little thing will hardly leave me, she follows me everywhere, but likes going into the garden best; when I am not there she refuses to stay, and cries so much that they are obliged to bring her back. She will not even go upstairs alone without calling me at each step, 'Mamma! Mamma!' and if I forget to answer 'Yes, darling!' she waits where she is, and will not move."

I was nearly three years old when my Mother wrote: "Little Thérèse asked me the other day if she would go to Heaven. 'Yes, if you are good,' I told her. 'Oh, Mamma,' she answered, 'then if I am not good, shall I go to Hell? Well, you know what I will do—I shall fly to you in Heaven, and you will hold me tight in your arms, and how could God take me away then?' I saw that she was convinced that God could do nothing to her if she hid herself in my arms."

"Marie loves her little sister very much; indeed she is a child who delights us all. She is extraordinarily outspoken, and it is charming to see her run after me to confess her childish faults: 'Mamma, I have pushed Céline; I slapped her once, but I'll not do it again.' The moment she has done anything mischievous, everyone must know.

Yesterday, without meaning to do so, she tore off a small piece of wall paper; you would have been sorry for her—she wanted to tell her father immediately. When he came home four hours later, everyone else had forgotten about it, but she ran at once to Marie saying: 'Tell Papa that I tore the paper.' She waited there like a criminal for sentence; but she thinks she is more easily forgiven if she accuses herself."

Papa's name fills me with many happy memories. Mamma laughingly said he always did whatever I wanted, but he answered: "Well, why not? She is the Queen!" Then he would lift me on to his shoulder, and caress me in all sorts of ways. Yet I cannot say that he spoilt me. I remember one day while I was swinging he called out as he passed: "Come and kiss me, little Queen." Contrary to my usual custom, I would not stir, and answered pertly: "You must come for it, Papa." He refused quite rightly, and went away. Marie was there and scolded me, saying: "How naughty to answer Papa like that!" Her reproof took effect; I got off the swing at once, and the whole house resounded with my cries. I hurried upstairs, not waiting this time to call Mamma at each step; my one thought was to find

Papa and make my peace with him. I need not tell you that this was soon done.

I could not bear to think I had grieved my beloved parents, and I acknowledged my faults instantly, as this little anecdote, related by my Mother, will show: "One morning before going downstairs I wanted to kiss Thérèse; she seemed to be fast asleep, and I did not like to wake her, but Marie said: 'Mamma, I am sure she is only pretending.' So I bent down to kiss her forehead, and immediately she hid herself under the clothes, saying in the tone of a spoilt child: 'I don't want anyone to look at me.' I was not pleased with her, and told her so. A minute or two afterwards I heard her crying, and was surprised to see her by my side. She had got out of her cot by herself, and had come downstairs with bare feet, stumbling over her long nightdress. Her little face was wet with tears: 'Mamma,' she said, throwing herself on my knee, 'I am sorry for being naughty—forgive me!' Pardon was quickly granted; I took the little angel in my arms and pressed her to my heart, smothering her with kisses."

I remember also my great affection for my eldest sister Marie, who had just left school. Without seeming to do so, I took in all that I saw and heard, and I think that I reflected on things then as I do now. I listened attentively while she taught Céline, and was very good and obedient, so as to obtain the privilege of being allowed in the room during lessons. She gave me many trifling presents which pleased me greatly. I was proud of my two big sisters; but as Pauline seemed so far away from us, I thought of her all day long. When I was only just learning to talk, and Mamma asked: "What are you thinking about?" my answer invariably was: "Pauline." Sometimes I heard people saying that Pauline would be a nun, and, without quite knowing what it meant, I thought: "I will be a nun too." This is one of my first recollections, and I have never changed my mind; so it was the example of this beloved sister which, from the age of two, drew me to the Divine Spouse of Virgins. My dearest Mother, what tender memories of Pauline I could confide to you here! But it would take me too long.

Léonie had also a very warm place in my heart; she loved me very much, and her love was returned. In the evening when she came home from school she used to take care of me while the others went out, and it seems to me I can still hear the sweet songs she sang to put me to sleep. I remember perfectly the day of her First Communion, and I remember also her companion, the poor child whom my Mother dressed, according to the touching custom of the well-to-do families in Alençon. This child did not leave Léonie for an instant on that happy day, and in the evening at the grand dinner she sat in the place of honour. Alas! I was too small to stay up for this feast, but I shared in it a little, thanks to Papa's goodness, for he came himself to bring his little Queen a piece of the iced cake.

The only one now left to speak of is Céline, the companion of my childhood. My memories of her are so many that I do not know which to choose. We understood each other perfectly, but I was much more forward and lively, and far less ingenuous. Here is a letter which will show you, dear Mother, how sweet was Céline, and how naughty Thérèse. I was then nearly three years old, and Céline six and a half. "Céline is naturally inclined to be good; as to the little puss, Thérèse, one cannot tell how she will turn out, she is so young and heedless. She is a very intelligent child, but has not nearly so sweet a disposition as her sister, and her stubbornness is almost unconquerable. When she has said 'No,' nothing will make her change; one could leave her all day in the cellar without getting her to say 'Yes.' She would sooner sleep there."

I had another fault also, of which my Mother did not speak in her letters: it was self-love. Here are two instances: —One day, no doubt wishing to see how far my pride would go, she smiled and said to me, "Thérèse, if you will kiss the ground I will give you a halfpenny." In those days a halfpenny was a fortune, and in order to gain it I had not far to stoop, for I was so tiny there was not much distance between me and the ground; but my pride was up in arms, and holding myself very erect, I said, "No, thank you, Mamma, I would rather go without it."

Another time we were going into the country to see some friends. Mamma told Marie to put on my prettiest frock, but not to let me have bare arms. I did not say a word, and appeared as indifferent as children of that age should be, but I said to myself, "I should have looked much prettier with bare arms."

With such a disposition I feel sure that had I been brought up by careless parents I should have become very wicked, and perhaps have lost my soul. But Jesus watched over His little Spouse, and turned even her faults to advantage, for, being checked early in life, they became a means of leading her towards perfection. For instance, as I had great self-love and an innate love of good as well, it was enough to tell me once: "You must not do that," and I never wanted to do it again. Having only good example before my eyes, I naturally wished to follow it, and I see with pleasure in my Mother's letters that as I grew older I began to be a greater comfort. This is what she writes in 1876: "Even Thérèse is anxious to make sacrifices. Marie has given her little sisters a string of beads on purpose to count their acts of self-denial. They have really spiritual, but very amusing, conversations together. Céline said the other day: 'How can God be in such a tiny Host?' Thérèse answered: 'That is not strange, because God is Almighty!' 'And what does Almighty mean?' 'It means that He can do whatever He likes.'

"But it is more amusing still to see Thérèse put her hand in her pocket, time after time, to pull a bead along the string, whenever she makes a little sacrifice. The children are inseparable, and are quite sufficient company for one another. Nurse has given Thérèse two bantams, and every day after dinner she and Céline sit by the fire and play with them.

"One morning Thérèse got out of her cot and climbed into Céline's. The nurse went to fetch her to be dressed, and, when at last she found her, the little thing said, hugging her sister very hard: 'Oh, Louise! leave me here, don't you see that we are like the little white bantams, we can't be separated from one another.'"

It is quite true that I could not be separated from Céline; I would rather leave my dessert unfinished at table than let her go without me, and I would get down from my high chair when she did, and off we went to play together. On Sundays, as I was still too small to go to the long services, Mamma stayed at home to take care of me. I was always very good, walking about on tip-toe; but as soon as I heard the door open there was a tremendous outburst of joy — I threw myself on my dear little sister, exclaiming: "Oh, Céline! give me the blessed bread, quick!"[8] One day she had not brought any — what was to be done? I could not do without it, for I called this little feast my Mass. A bright idea struck me: "You have no blessed bread! — make some." Céline immediately opened the cupboard, took out the bread, cut a tiny bit off, and after saying a Hail Mary quite solemnly over it, triumphantly presented it to me; and I, making the sign of the

Cross, ate it with devotion, fancying it tasted exactly like the real blessed bread.

One day Léonie, thinking no doubt that she was too big to play with dolls, brought us a basket filled with clothes, pretty pieces of stuff, and other trifles on which her doll was laid: "Here, dears," she said, "choose whatever you like." Céline looked at it, and took a woollen ball. After thinking about it for a minute, I put out my hand saying: "I choose everything," and I carried off both doll and basket without more ado.

This childish incident was a forecast, so to speak, of my whole life. Later on, when the way of perfection was opened out before me, I realised that in order to become a Saint one must suffer much, always seek the most perfect path, and forget oneself. I also understood that there are many degrees of holiness, that each soul is free to respond to the calls of Our Lord, to do much or little for His Love—in a word, to choose amongst the sacrifices He asks. And then also, as in the days of my childhood, I cried out: "My God, I choose everything, I will not be a Saint by halves, I am not afraid of suffering for Thee, I only fear one thing, and that is to do my own will. Accept the offering of my will, for I choose all that Thou willest."

But, dear Mother, I am forgetting myself—I must not tell you yet of my girlhood, I am still speaking of the baby of three and four years old.

I remember a dream I had at that age which impressed itself very deeply on my memory. I thought I was walking alone in the garden when, suddenly, I saw near the arbour two hideous little devils dancing with surprising agility on a barrel of lime, in spite of the heavy irons attached to their feet. At first they cast fiery glances at me; then, as though suddenly terrified, I saw them, in the twinkling of an eye, throw themselves down to the bottom of the barrel, from which they came out somehow, only to run and hide themselves in the laundry which opened into the garden. Finding them such cowards, I wanted to know what they were going to do, and, overcoming my fears, I went to the window. The wretched little creatures were there, running about on the tables, not knowing how to hide themselves from my gaze. From time to time they came nearer, peering through the windows with an uneasy air, then, seeing that I was still there, they began to run about again looking quite desperate. Of course this dream was nothing extraordinary; yet I think Our Lord made use of it to show me that a soul in the state of grace has nothing to fear from the devil, who is a coward, and will even fly from the gaze of a little child.

Dear Mother, how happy I was at that age! I was beginning to enjoy life, and goodness itself seemed full of charms. Probably my character was the same as it is now, for even then I had great self-command, and made a practice of never complaining when my things were taken; even if I was unjustly accused, I preferred to keep silence. There was no merit in this, for I did it naturally.

How quickly those sunny years of my childhood passed away, and what tender memories they have imprinted on my mind! I remember the Sunday walks when my dear Mother always accompanied us; and I can still feel the impression made on my childish heart at the sight of the fields bright with cornflowers, poppies, and marguerites. Even at that age I loved far-stretching views, sunlit spaces and stately trees; in a word, all nature charmed me and lifted up my soul to Heaven.

Often, during these walks, we met poor people. I was always chosen to give them an alms, which made me feel very happy. Sometimes, my dear Father, knowing the way was too long for his little Queen, took me home. This was a cause of grief, and to console me Céline would fill her basket with daisies, and give them to me on her return. Truly everything on earth smiled on me; I found flowers strewn at every step, and my naturally happy disposition helped to make life bright. But a new era was about to dawn.

I was to be the Spouse of Our Lord at such an early age that it was necessary I should suffer from my childhood. As the early spring flowers begin to come up under the snow and open at the first rays of the sun, so the Little Flower whose story I am writing had to pass through the winter of trial and to have her tender cup filled with the dew of tears.

---

[1] Ps. 88[89]:1.

[2] This statue twice appeared as if endowed with life, in order to enlighten and console Mme. Martin, mother of Thérèse. A like favour was granted to Thérèse herself, as will be seen in the course of the narrative.

[3] Mark 3:13.

[4] Cf. Exodus 33:19.

[5] Cf. Rom. 9:16.

[6] Cf. Ps. 22[23]:1-4.

[7] Ps. 102[103]:8.

[8] The custom still prevails in some parts of France of blessing bread at the Offertory of the Mass and then distributing it to the faithful. It is known as *pain bénit*. This blessing only takes place at the Parochial Mass. [Ed.]

CHAPTER II A CATHOLIC HOUSEHOLD

All the details of my Mother's illness are still fresh in my mind. I remember especially her last weeks on earth, when Céline and I felt like poor little exiles. Every morning a friend came to fetch us, and we spent the day with her. Once, we had not had time to say our prayers before starting, and on the way my little sister whispered: "Must we tell her that we have not said our prayers?" "Yes," I answered. So, very timidly, Céline confided our secret to her, and she exclaimed: "Well, well, children, you shall say them." Then she took us to a large room, and left us there. Céline looked at me in amazement. I was equally astonished, and exclaimed: "This is not like Mamma, she always said our prayers with us." During the day, in spite of all efforts to amuse us, the thought of our dear Mother was constantly in our minds. I remember once, when my sister had an apricot given to her, she leant towards me and said: "We will not eat it, I will give it to Mamma." Alas! our beloved Mother was now too ill to eat any earthly fruit; she would never more be satisfied but by the glory of Heaven. There she would drink of the mysterious wine which Jesus, at His Last Supper, promised to share with us in the Kingdom of His Father.

The touching ceremony of Extreme Unction made a deep impression on me. I can still see the place where I knelt, and hear my poor Father's sobs.

My dear Mother died on August 28, 1877, in her forty-sixth year. The day after her death my Father took me in his arms and said: "Come and kiss your dear Mother for the last time." Without saying a word I put my lips to her icy forehead. I do not remember having cried much, and I did not talk to anyone of all that filled my heart; I looked and listened in silence, and I saw many things they would have hidden from me. Once I found myself close to the coffin in the passage. I stood looking at it for a long time; I had never seen one before, but I knew what it was. I was so small that I had to lift up my head to see its whole length, and it seemed to me very big and very sad.

Fifteen years later I was again standing by another coffin, that of our holy Mother Genevieve, [1] and I was carried back to the days of my childhood. Memories crowded upon me; it was the same little Thérèse who looked at it, but she had grown, and the coffin seemed small. She had not to lift up her head to it, now she only raised her eyes to contemplate Heaven which seemed to her very full of joy, for trials had matured and strengthened her soul, so that nothing on earth could make her grieve.

Our Lord did not leave me wholly an orphan; on the day of my Mother's funeral He gave me another mother, and allowed me to choose her freely. We were all five together, looking at one another sadly, when our nurse, overcome with emotion, said, turning to Céline and to me: "Poor little dears, you no longer have a Mother." Then Céline threw herself into Marie's arms, crying: "Well, you will be my Mother now." I was so accustomed to imitate Céline that I should undoubtedly have followed her example, but I feared Pauline would be sad and feel herself left out if she too had not a little daughter. So, with a loving look, I hid my face on her breast saying in my turn: "And Pauline will be my Mother."

That day, as I have said, began the second period of my life. It was the most sorrowful of all, especially after Pauline, my second Mother, entered the Carmel; and it lasted from the time I was four years old until I was fourteen, when I recovered much of my childish gaiety, even though I understood more fully the serious side of life.

I must tell you that after my Mother's death my naturally happy disposition completely changed. Instead of being lively and demonstrative as I had been, I became timid, shy, and extremely sensitive; a look was enough to make me burst into tears. I could not bear to be noticed or to meet strangers, and was only at ease in my own family circle. There I was always cherished with the most loving care; my Father's affectionate heart seemed endowed with a mother's love, and my sisters were no less tender and devoted. If Our Lord had not lavished so much love and sunshine on His Little Flower, she never could have become acclimatised to this earth. Still too weak to bear the storm, she needed warmth, refreshing dew, and soft breezes, and these gifts were never wanting to her, even in the chilling seasons of trials.

Soon after my Mother's death, Papa made up his mind to leave Alençon and live at Lisieux, so that we might be near our uncle, my Mother's brother. He made this sacrifice in order that my young sisters should have the benefit of their aunt's guidance in their new life, and that she might act as a mother towards them. I did not feel any grief at leaving my native town: children love change and anything out of the common, and so I was pleased to come to Lisieux. I remember the journey quite well, and our arrival in the evening at my uncle's house, and I can still see my little cousins, Jeanne and Marie, waiting on the doorstep with my aunt. How touching was the affection all these dear ones showed us!

The next day they took us to our new home, *Les Buissonets*,[2] situated in a quiet part of the town. I was charmed with the house my Father had taken. The large upper window from which there was an extensive view, the flower garden in front, and the kitchen garden at the back—all these seemed delightfully new to my childish mind; and this happy home became the scene of many joys and of family gatherings which I can never forget. Elsewhere, as I said before, I felt an exile, I cried and fretted for my Mother; but here my little heart expanded, and I smiled on life once more.

When I woke there were my sisters ready to caress me, and I said my prayers kneeling between them. Then Pauline gave me my reading lesson, and I remember that "Heaven" was the first word I could read alone. When lessons were over I went upstairs, where Papa was generally to be found, and how pleased I was when I had good marks to show. Every afternoon I went out for a walk with him, and we paid a visit to the Blessed Sacrament in one or other of the Churches. It was in this way that I first saw the Chapel of the Carmel: "Look, little Queen," Papa said to me, "behind that big grating there are holy nuns who are always praying to Almighty God." Little did I think that nine years later I should be amongst them, that in this blessed Carmel I should receive so many graces.

On returning home I learnt my lessons, and then spent the rest of the day playing in the garden near Papa. I never cared for dolls, but one of my favourite amusements was making coloured mixtures with seeds and the bark of trees. If the colours were pretty, I would promptly offer them to Papa in a little cup and entice him to taste them; then my dearest Father would leave his work and smilingly pretend to drink. I was very fond of flowers, and amused myself by making little altars in holes which I happened to find in the middle of my garden wall. When finished I would run and call Papa, and he seemed delighted with them. I should never stop if I told you of the thousand and one incidents of this kind that I can remember. How shall I make you understand the love that my Father lavished on his little Queen!

Those were specially happy days for me when I went fishing with my dear "King," as I used to call him. Sometimes I tried my hand with a small rod of my own, but generally I preferred to sit on the grass some distance away. Then my reflections became really deep, and, without knowing what meditation meant, my soul was absorbed in prayer. Far-off sounds reached me, the murmuring of the wind, sometimes a few uncertain notes of music from a military band in the town a long way off; all this imparted a touch of melancholy to my thoughts. Earth seemed a place of exile, and I dreamed of Heaven.

The afternoon passed quickly away, and it was soon time to go home, but before packing up I would eat the provisions I had brought in a small basket. Somehow the slices of bread and jam, prepared by my sisters, looked different; they had seemed so tempting, and now they looked stale and uninviting. Even such a trifle as this made the earth seem sadder, and I realised that only in Heaven will there be unclouded joy.

Speaking of clouds, I remember how one day when we were out, the blue sky became overcast and a storm came on, accompanied by vivid lightning. I looked round on every side, so as to lose nothing of the grand sight. A thunderbolt fell in a field close by, and, far from feeling the least bit afraid, I was delighted—it seemed that God was so near. Papa was not so pleased, and put an end to my reverie, for already the tall grass and daisies, taller than I, were sparkling with rain-drops, and we had to cross several fields to reach the road. In spite of his fishing tackle, he carried me in his arms while I looked down in the beautiful jewelled drops, almost sorry that I could not be drenched by them.

I do not think I have told you that in our daily walks at Lisieux, as in Alençon, I often used to give alms to the beggars. One day we came upon a poor old man who dragged himself painfully along on crutches. I went up to give him a penny. He looked sadly at me for a long time, and then, shaking his head with a sorrowful smile, he refused my alms. I cannot tell you what I felt; I had wished to help and comfort him, and instead of that, I had, perhaps, hurt him and caused him pain. He must have guessed my thought, for I saw him turn round and smile at me when we were some way off.

Just then Papa bought me a cake. I wished very much to run after the old man and give it to him, for I thought: "Well, he did not want money, but I am sure he would like to have a cake." I do not know what held me back, and I felt so sad I could hardly keep from crying; then I remembered having heard that one obtains all the favours asked for on one's First Communion Day. This thought consoled me immediately, and though I was only six years old at the time, I said to myself: "I will pray for my poor old man on the day of my First Communion." Five years later I faithfully kept my resolution. I have always thought that my childish prayer for this suffering member of Christ has been blessed and rewarded.

As I grew older my love of God grew more and more. I often offered my heart to Him, using the words my Mother had taught me, and I tried very hard to please Him in all my actions, taking great care never to offend Him. And yet one day I committed a fault which I must tell you here—it gives me a good opportunity of humbling myself, though I believe I have grieved over it with perfect contrition.

It was the month of May, 1878. My sisters decided that I was too small to go to the May devotions every evening, so I stayed at home with the nurse and said my prayers with her before the little altar which I had arranged according to my own taste. Everything was small—candlesticks, vases, and the rest; two wax vestas were quite sufficient to light it up properly. Sometimes Victoire, the maid, gave me some little bits of real candle, but not often.

One evening, when we went to our prayers, I said to her: "Will you begin the *Memorare?* I am going to light the candles." She tried to begin, and then looked at me and burst out laughing. Seeing my precious vestas burning quickly away, I begged her once more to say the *Memorare.* Again there was silence, broken only by bursts of laughter. All my natural good temper deserted me. I got up feeling dreadfully angry, and, stamping my foot furiously, I cried out: "Victoire, you naughty girl!" She stopped laughing at once, and looked at me in utter astonishment, then showed me—too late—the surprise she had in store hidden under her apron—

two pieces of candle. My tears of anger were soon changed into tears of sorrow; I was very much ashamed and grieved, and made a firm resolution never to act in such a way again.

Shortly after this I made my first confession.[3] It is a very sweet memory. Pauline had warned me: "Thérèse, darling, it is not to a man but to God Himself that you are going to tell your sins." I was so persuaded of this that I asked her quite seriously if I should not tell Father Ducellier that I loved him "with my whole heart," as it was really God I was going to speak to in his person.

Well instructed as to what I was to do, I entered the confessional, and turning round to the priest, so as to see him better, I made my confession and received absolution in a spirit of lively faith—my sister having assured me that at this solemn moment the tears of the Holy Child Jesus would purify my soul. I remember well that he exhorted me above all to a tender devotion towards Our Lady, and I promised to redouble my love for her who already filled so large a place in my heart. Then I passed him my Rosary to be blessed, and came out of the Confessional more joyful and lighthearted than I had ever felt before. It was evening, and as soon as I got to a street lamp I stopped and took the newly blessed Rosary out of my pocket, turning it over and over. "What are you looking at, Thérèse, dear?" asked Pauline. "I am seeing what a blessed Rosary looks like." This childish answer amused my sisters very much. I was deeply impressed by the graces I had received, and wished to go to confession again for all the big feasts, for these confessions filled me with joy. The feasts! What precious memories these simple words bring to me. I loved them; and my sisters knew so well how to explain the mysteries hidden in each one. Those days of earth became days of Heaven. Above all I loved the procession of the Blessed Sacrament: what a joy it was to strew flowers in God's path! But before scattering them on the ground I threw them high in the air, and was never so happy as when I saw my rose-leaves touch the sacred Monstrance.

And if the great feasts came but seldom, each week brought one very dear to my heart, and that was Sunday. What a glorious day! The Feast of God! The day of rest! First of all the whole family went to High Mass, and I remember that before the sermon we had to come down from our places, which were some way from the pulpit, and find seats in the nave. This was not always easy, but to little Thérèse and her Father everyone offered a place. My uncle was delighted when he saw us come down; he called me his "Sunbeam," and said that to see the venerable old man leading his little daughter by the hand was a sight which always filled him with joy. I never troubled myself if people looked at me, I was only occupied in listening attentively to the preacher. A sermon on the Passion of our Blessed Lord was the first I understood, and it touched me deeply. I was then five and a half, and after that time I was able to understand and appreciate all instructions. If St. Teresa was mentioned, my Father would bend down and whisper to me: "Listen attentively, little Queen, he is speaking of your holy patroness." I really did listen attentively, but I must own I looked at Papa more than at the preacher, for I read many things in his face. Sometimes his eyes were filled with tears which he strove in vain to keep back; and as he listened to the eternal truths he seemed no longer of this earth, his soul was absorbed in the thought of another world. Alas! Many long and sorrowful years had to pass before Heaven was to be opened to him, and Our Lord with His Own Divine Hand was to wipe away the bitter tears of His faithful servant.

To go back to the description of our Sundays. This happy day which passed so quickly had also its touch of melancholy; my happiness was full till Compline, but after that a feeling of sadness took possession of me. I thought of the morrow when one had to begin again the daily life of work and lessons, and my heart, feeling like an exile on this earth, longed for the repose of Heaven—the never ending Sabbath of our true Home. Every Sunday my aunt invited us in turns to spend the evening with her. I was always glad when mine came, and it was a pleasure to listen to my uncle's conversation. His talk was serious, but it interested me, and he little knew that I paid such attention; but my joy was not unmixed with fear when he took me on his knee and sang "Bluebeard" in his deep voice.

About eight o'clock Papa would come to fetch me. I remember that I used to look up at the stars with inexpressible delight. Orion's belt fascinated me especially, for I saw in it a likeness to the letter "T." "Look, Papa," I would cry, "my name is written in Heaven!" Then, not wishing to see this dull earth any longer, I asked him to lead me, and with my head thrown back, I gazed unweariedly at the starry skies.

I could tell you much about our winter evenings at home. After a game of draughts my sisters read aloud Dom Guéranger's *Liturgical Year,* and then a few pages of some other interesting and instructive book. While this was going on I established myself on Papa's knee, and when the reading was done he used to sing soothing snatches of melody in his beautiful voice, as if to lull me to sleep, and I would lay my head on his breast while he rocked me gently to and fro.

Later on we went upstairs for night prayers, and there again my place was beside my beloved Father, and I had only to look at him to know how the Saints pray. Pauline put me to bed, and I invariably asked her: "Have I been good to-day? Is God pleased with me? Will the Angels watch over me?" The answer was always "Yes," otherwise I should have spent the whole night in tears. After these questions my sisters kissed me, and little Thérèse was left alone in the dark.

I look on it as a real grace that from childhood I was taught to overcome my fears. Sometimes in the evening Pauline would send me to fetch something from a distant room; she would take no refusal, and she was quite right, for otherwise I should have become very nervous, whereas now it is difficult to frighten me. I wonder sometimes how my little Mother was able to bring me up with so much tenderness, and yet without spoiling me, for she did not pass over the least fault. It is true she never scolded me without cause, and I knew well she would never change her mind when once a thing was decided upon.

To this dearly loved sister I confided my most intimate thoughts; she cleared up all my doubts. One day I expressed surprise that God does not give an equal amount of glory to all the elect in Heaven—I was afraid that they would not all be quite happy. She sent me to fetch Papa's big tumbler, and put it beside my tiny thimble, then, filling both with water, she asked me which seemed the fuller. I replied that one was as full as the other—it was impossible to pour more water into either of them, for they could not hold it. In this way Pauline made it clear to me that in Heaven the least of the Blessed does not envy the happiness of the greatest; and so, by bringing the highest mysteries down to the level of my understanding, she gave my soul the food it needed.

Joyfully each year I welcomed the prize day. Though I was the only competitor, justice was none the less strictly observed, and I never received rewards unless they were well merited. My heart used to beat with excitement when I heard the decisions, and in presence of the whole family received prizes from Papa's hands. It was to me like a picture of the Judgment Day!

Seeing Papa so cheerful, no suspicion of the terrible trials which awaited him crossed my mind; but one day God showed me, in an extraordinary vision, a vivid picture of the trouble to come. My Father was away on a journey, and could not return as early as usual. It was about two or three o'clock in the afternoon; the sun was shining brightly, and all the world seemed gay. I was alone at the window, looking on to the kitchen garden, my mind full of cheerful thoughts, when I saw before me, in front of the wash-house, a man dressed exactly like Papa, of the same height and appearance, but more bent and aged. I say *aged,* to describe his general appearance, for I did not see his face as his head was covered with a thick veil. He advanced slowly, with measured step, along my little garden; at that instant a feeling of supernatural fear seized me, and I called out loudly in a trembling voice: "Papa, Papa!" The mysterious person seemed not to hear, he continued his walk without even turning, and went towards a clump of firs which grew in the middle of the garden. I expected to see him reappear at the other side of the big trees, but the prophetic vision had vanished.

It was all over in a moment, but it was a moment which impressed itself so deeply on my memory that even now, after so many years, the remembrance of it is as vivid as the vision itself.

My sisters were all together in an adjoining room. Hearing me call "Papa!" they were frightened themselves, but Marie, hiding her feelings, ran to me and said: "Why are you calling Papa, when he is at Alençon?" I told her what I had seen, and to reassure me they said that Nurse must have covered her head with her apron on purpose to frighten me. Victoire, however, when questioned, declared she had not left the kitchen—besides, the truth was too deeply impressed on my mind: I had seen a man, and that man was exactly like my Father. We all went to look behind the clump of trees, and, finding nothing, my sisters told me to think no more about it. Ah, that was not in my power! Often and often my imagination brought before me this mysterious vision, often and often I tried to raise the veil which hid its true meaning, and deep down in my heart I had a conviction that some day it would be fully revealed to me. And you know all, dear Mother. You know that it was really my Father whom God showed me, bent by age, and bearing on his venerable face and his white head the symbol of his terrible trial.[4]

As the Adorable Face of Jesus was veiled during His Passion, so it was fitting that the face of His humble servant should be veiled during the days of his humiliation, in order that it might shine with greater brilliancy in Heaven. How I admire God's ways! He showed us this precious cross beforehand, as a father shows his children the glorious future he is preparing for them—a future which will bring them an inheritance of priceless treasures.

But a thought comes into my mind: "Why did God give this light to a child who, if she had understood it, would have died of grief?" "Why?" Here is one of those incomprehensible mysteries which we shall only understand in Heaven, where they will be the subject of our eternal admiration. My God, how good Thou art! How well dost Thou suit the trial to our strength!

At that time I had not courage even to think that Papa could die, without being terrified. One day he was standing on a high step-ladder, and as I was close by he called out: "Move away, little Queen; if I fall I shall crush you." Instantly I felt an inward shock, and, going still nearer to the ladder, I thought: "At least if Papa falls I shall not have the pain of seeing him die, for I shall die with him." I could never say how much I loved him. I admired everything he did. When he explained his ideas on serious matters, as if I were a big girl, I answered him naïvely: "It is quite certain, Papa, that if you spoke like that to the great men who govern the country they would take you and make you King. Then France would be happier than it was ever been; but you would be unhappy, because that is the lot of kings; besides you would no longer be my King alone, so I am glad that they do not know you."

When I was six or seven years old I saw the sea for the first time. The sight made a deep impression on me, I could not take my eyes off it. Its majesty, and the roar of the waves, all spoke to my soul of the greatness and power of God. I remember, when we were on the beach, a man and woman looked at me for a long time, then, asking Papa if I was his child, they remarked that I was a very pretty little girl. Papa at once made a sign to them not to flatter me; I was delighted to hear what they said, for I did not think I was pretty. My sisters were most careful never to talk before me in such a way as to spoil my simplicity and childish innocence; and, because I believed so implicitly in them, I attached little importance to the admiration of these people and thought no more about it.

That evening at the hour when the sun seems to sink into the vast ocean, leaving behind it a trail of glory, I sat with Pauline on a bare rock, and gazed for long on this golden furrow which she told me was an image of grace illumining the way of faithful souls here below. Then I pictured my soul as a tiny barque, with a graceful white sail, in the midst of the furrow, and I resolved never to let it withdraw from the sight of Jesus, so that it might sail peacefully and quickly towards the Heavenly Shore.

---

[1] This holy nun had been professed at the Carmel of Poitiers, and was sent from there to make the foundation at Lisieux in 1838. Her memory is held in benediction in both these convents; in the sight of God she constantly practised the most heroic virtue, and on December 5, 1891, crowned a life of good works by a holy death. She was then eighty-six years of age.

[2] This house, an object of deep interest to the clients of Soeur Thérèse, is much frequented by pilgrims to Lisieux. [Ed.]

[3] This first confession was made in the beautiful church of St. Pierre, formerly the cathedral of Lisieux. [Ed.]

[4] It seems advisable, on account of the vague allusions which occur here and elsewhere, to state what happened to M. Louis Martin. At the age of sixty-six, having already had several partial attacks, he was struck with general paralysis, and his mind gave way altogether.

CHAPTER III PAULINE ENTERS THE CARMEL

I was eight and a half when Léonie left school, and I took her place at the Benedictine Abbey in Lisieux. The girls of my class were all older than myself; one of them was fourteen, and, though not clever, she knew how to impose on the little ones. Seeing me so young, nearly always first in class, and a favourite with all the nuns, she was jealous, and used to pay me out in a thousand ways. Naturally timid and sensitive, I did not know how to defend myself, and could only cry in silence. Céline and my elder sisters did not know of my grief, and, not being advanced enough in virtue to rise above these troubles, I suffered considerably.

Every evening I went home, and then my spirits rose. I would climb on to Papa's knee, telling him what marks I had, and his caresses made me forget all my troubles. With what delight I announced the result of my first essay, for I won the maximum number of marks. In reward I received a silver coin which I put in my money box for the poor, and nearly every Thursday I was able to increase the fund.

Indeed, to be spoilt was a real necessity for me. The Little Flower had need to strike its tender roots deeper and deeper into the dearly loved garden of home, for nowhere else could it find the nourishment it required. Thursday was a holiday, but it was not like the holidays I had under Pauline, which I generally spent upstairs with Papa. Not knowing how to play like other children, I felt myself a dull companion. I tried my best to do as the others did, but without success.

After Céline, who was, so to say, indispensable to me, I sought the company of my little cousin Marie, because she left me free to choose the games I liked best. We were already closely united in heart and will, as if God were showing us in advance how one day in the Carmel we should embrace the same religious life.[1]

Very often, at my uncle's house, we used to play at being two austere hermits, with only a poor hut, a little patch of corn, and a garden in which to grow a few vegetables. Our life was to be spent in continual contemplation, one praying while the other engaged in active duties. All was done with religious gravity and decorum. If we went out, the make-believe continued even in the street; the two hermits would say the Rosary, using their fingers to count on, so as not to display their devotion before those who might scoff. One day, however, the hermit Thérèse forgot herself—before eating a cake, given her for lunch, she made a large Sign of the Cross, and some worldly folk did not repress a smile.

We were so bent on always doing the same thing that sometimes we carried it too far. Endeavouring one evening, on our way home from school, to imitate the modest demeanour of the hermits, I said to Marie: "Lead me, I am going to shut my eyes." "So am I," she answered. Being on the pavement we were in no fear of vehicles, and for a short while all went well, and we enjoyed walking with our eyes shut; but presently we both fell over some boxes standing at a shop door and knocked them down. The shopkeeper came out in a rage to replace them, but the would-be blind pair picked themselves up and ran off as fast as they could, with eyes wide open. Then the hermits had to listen to a well-deserved scolding from Jeanne, the maid, who seemed as vexed as the shopkeeper.

I have not yet told you how Céline and I altered when we came to Lisieux. She had now become the little romp, full of mischief, while Thérèse had turned into a very quiet little girl, far too much inclined to tears. I needed a champion, and who can say how courageously my dear little sister played that part. We used to enjoy making each other little presents, for, at that age, the simplicity of our hearts was unspoiled. Like the spring flowers they unfolded, glad to receive the morning dew, while the same soft breezes swayed their petals. Yes, our joys were mutual. I felt this especially on the happy day of Céline's First Communion; I was only seven years old, and had not yet begun school at the Abbey. How sweet is the remembrance of her preparation! Every evening during its last weeks my sisters talked to her of the great event. I listened, eager to prepare myself too, and my heart swelled with grief when I was told to go away because I was still too young. I thought that four years was not too long to spend in making ready to receive Our dear

Lord. One evening I heard someone say to my happy little sister: "From the time of your First Communion you must begin an entirely new life." At once I made a resolution not to wait till the time of my First Communion, but to begin with Céline. During her retreat she remained as a boarder at the Abbey, and it seemed to me she was away a long time; but at last the happy day came. What a delightful impression it has left on my mind — it was like a foretaste of my own First Communion! How many graces I received that day! I look on it as one of the most beautiful of my life.

I have gone back a little in order to recall these happy memories; but now I must tell you of the mournful parting which crushed my heart when Our Lord took from me my little Mother whom I loved so dearly. I told her once that I would like to go away with her to a far-off desert; she replied that it was her wish too, but that she was waiting till I was big enough to set out. This impossible promise I took in earnest, and what was my grief when I heard Pauline talking to Marie about soon entering the Carmel! I did not know the Carmel; but I knew that she was leaving me to enter a convent, and that she would not wait for me.

How can I describe the anguish I suffered! In a flash I saw life spread out before me as it really is, full of sufferings and frequent partings, and I shed bitter tears. At that time I did not know the joy of sacrifice; I was weak—so weak that I look on it as a great grace that I was able to bear such a trial, one seemingly so much beyond my strength—and yet live. I shall never forget how tenderly my little Mother consoled me, while explaining the religious life. Then one evening, when I was thinking over the picture she had drawn, I felt that the Carmel was the desert where God wished me also to hide. I felt this so strongly that I had not the least doubt about it; nor was it a childish dream, but the certainty of a Divine Call. This impression, which I cannot properly describe, left me with a feeling of great inward peace.

Next day I confided my desires to Pauline. They seemed to her as a proof of God's Will, and she promised to take me soon to the Carmel, to see the Mother Prioress and to tell her my secret. This solemn visit was fixed for a certain Sunday, and great was my embarrassment on hearing that my cousin Marie—who was still young enough to be allowed to see the Carmelites—was to come with us.[2]

I had to contrive a means of being alone with the Reverend Mother, and this is what I planned. I told Marie, that, as we were to have the great privilege of seeing her, we must be very good and polite, and tell her our little secrets, and in order to do that, we must go out of the room in turns. Though she did not quite like it, because she had no secrets to confide, Marie took me at my word, and so I was able to be alone with you, dear Mother. You listened to my great disclosure, and believed in my vocation, but you told me that postulants were not received at the age of nine, and that I must wait till I was sixteen. In spite of my ardent desire to enter with Pauline and make my First Communion on her clothing day, I had to be resigned.

At last the 2nd of October came—a day of tears, but also of blessings, when Our Lord gathered the first of His flowers, the chosen flower who, later on, was to become the Mother of her sisters.[3] Whilst Papa, with my uncle and Marie, climbed the mountain of Carmel to offer his first sacrifice, my aunt took me to Mass, with my sisters and cousins. We were bathed in tears, and people gazed at us in astonishment when we entered the church, but that did not stop our crying. I even wondered how the sun could go on shining. Perhaps, dear Mother, you think I exaggerate my grief a little. I confess that this parting ought not to have upset me so much, but my soul was yet far from mature, and I had to pass through many trials before reaching the haven of peace, before tasting the delicious fruits of perfect love and of complete abandonment to God's Will.

In the afternoon of that October day, 1882, behind the grating of the Carmel, I saw my beloved Pauline, now become Sister Agnes of Jesus. Oh, how much I suffered in that parlour! As I am writing the story of my soul, it seems to me that I ought to tell you everything. Well, I acknowledge that I hardly counted the first pains of this parting, in comparison with those which followed. I, who had been accustomed to talk with my little Mother of all that was in my heart, could now scarcely snatch two or three minutes with her at the end of the family visits; even these short minutes were passed in tears, and I went away with my heart torn with grief.

I did not realise that it was impossible to give us each half an hour, and that of course Papa and Marie must have the largest share. I could not understand all this, and I said from the depths of my heart: "Pauline is lost to me."

This suffering so affected me that I soon became seriously ill. The illness was undoubtedly the work of the devil, who, in his fury at this first entry into the Carmel, tried to avenge himself on me for the great harm my family was to do him in the future. However, he little knew that the Queen of Heaven was watching faithfully over her Little Flower, that she was smiling upon it from on high, ready to still the tempest just when the delicate and fragile stalk was in danger of being broken once and for all. At the close of the year 1882 I began to suffer from constant headaches; they were bearable, however, and did not prevent me from continuing my studies. This lasted till the Easter of 1883. Just then Papa went to Paris with my elder sisters, and confided Céline and me to the care of our uncle and aunt. One evening I was alone with my uncle, and he talked so tenderly of my Mother and of bygone days that I was deeply moved and began to cry. My sensitiveness touched him too; he was surprised that one of my age should feel as I did. So he determined to do all he could to divert my mind during the holidays.

But God had decided otherwise. That very evening my headache became acute, and I was seized with a strange shivering which lasted all night. My aunt, like a real mother, never left me for a moment; all through my illness she lavished on me the most tender and devoted care. You may imagine my poor Father's grief when he returned from Paris to find me in this hopeless state; he thought I was going to die, but Our Lord might have said to him: "This sickness is not unto death, but for the glory of God."[4]

Yes, God was glorified by means of this trial, by the wonderful resignation of my Father and sisters. And to Marie especially what suffering it brought, and how grateful I am to this dear sister! She seemed to divine my wants by instinct, for a mother's heart is more knowing than the science of the most skilful doctors.

And now Pauline's clothing day was drawing near; but, fearing to distress me, no one dared mention it in my presence, since it was taken for granted that I should not be well enough to be there. Deep down in my heart, however, I firmly believed that God would give me the consolation of seeing dear Pauline on that day. I was quite sure that this feast would be unclouded; I knew that Our Lord would not try His Spouse by depriving her of my presence, she had already suffered so much on account of my illness. And so it turned out. I was there, able to embrace my dear little Mother, to sit on her knee, and, hiding myself under her veil, to receive her loving caresses. I was able to feast my eyes upon her—she looked so lovely in her veil and mantle of white. Truly it was a day of happiness in the midst of heavy trials; but this day, or rather this hour, passed only too quickly, and soon we were in the carriage which was to take us away from the Carmel. On reaching home I was made to lie down, though I did not feel at all tired; but next day I had a serious relapse, and became so ill that, humanly speaking, there was no hope of any recovery.

I do not know how to describe this extraordinary illness. I said things which I had never thought of; I acted as though I were forced to act in spite of myself; I seemed nearly always to be delirious; and yet I feel certain that I was never, for a minute, deprived of my reason. Sometimes I remained in a state of extreme exhaustion for hours together, unable to make the least movement, and yet, in spite of this extraordinary torpor, hearing the least whisper. I remember it still. And what fears the devil inspired! I was afraid of everything; my bed seemed to be surrounded by frightful precipices; nails in the wall took the terrifying appearance of long fingers, shrivelled and blackened with fire, making me cry out in terror. One day, while Papa stood looking at me in silence, the hat in his hand was suddenly transformed into some horrible shape, and I was so frightened that he went away sobbing.

But if God allowed the devil to approach me in this open way, Angels too were sent to console and strengthen me. Marie never left me, and never showed the least trace of weariness in spite of all the trouble I gave her—for I could not rest when she was away. During meals, when Victoire took care of me, I never ceased calling tearfully "Marie! Marie!" When she wanted to go out, it was only if she were going to Mass or to see Pauline that I kept quiet. As for Léonie and my little Céline, they could not do enough for me. On Sundays they shut themselves up for hours with a poor child who seemed almost to have lost her reason. My own dear sisters, how much I made you suffer! My uncle and aunt were also devoted to me. My aunt came to see me every day, and brought me many little gifts. I could never tell you how my love for these dear ones increased during this illness. I understood better than ever what Papa had so often told us: "Always remember, children, that your uncle and aunt have devoted themselves to you in a way that is quite exceptional." In his old age he experienced this himself, and now he must bless and protect those who lavished upon him such affectionate care.[5]

When my sufferings grew less, my great delight was to weave garlands of daisies and forget-me-nots for Our Lady's statue. We were in the beautiful month of May, when all nature is clothed with the flowers of spring; the Little Flower alone drooped, and seemed as though it had withered for ever. Yet she too had a shining sun, the miraculous statue of the Queen of Heaven. How often did not the Little Flower turn towards this glorious Sun!

One day Papa came into my room in the deepest distress, and I watched him go up to Marie and give her some money, bidding her write to Paris, and have a novena of Masses said at the shrine of Our Lady of Victories,[6] to obtain the cure of his poor little Queen. How touching were his faith and love! How much I longed to get up and tell him I was cured! Alas! my wishes could not work a miracle, and it needed one to restore me to health. Yes, it needed a great miracle, and this was wrought by Our Lady of Victories herself.

One Sunday, during the novena, Marie went into the garden, leaving me with Léonie, who was reading by the window. After a short time I began to call: "Marie! Marie!" very softly. Léonie, accustomed to hear me fret like this, took no notice, so I called louder, until Marie came back to me. I saw her come into the room quite well, but, for the first time, I failed to recognise her. I looked all round and glanced anxiously into the garden, still calling: "Marie! Marie!" Her anguish was perhaps greater than mine, and that was unutterable. At last, after many fruitless efforts to make me recognise her, she whispered a few words to Léonie, and went away pale and trembling. Léonie presently carried me to the window. There I saw the garden, and Marie walking up and down, but still I did not recognise her; she came forward, smiling, and held out her arms to me calling tenderly: "Thérèse, dear little Thérèse!" This last effort failing, she came in again and knelt in tears at the foot of my bed; turning towards the statue of Our Lady, she entreated her with the fervour of a mother who begs the life of her child and will not be refused. Léonie and Céline joined her, and that cry of faith forced the gates of Heaven. I too, finding no help on earth and nearly dead with pain, turned to my Heavenly Mother, begging her from the bottom of my heart to have pity on me. Suddenly the statue seemed to come to life and grow beautiful, with a divine beauty that I shall never find words to describe. The expression of Our Lady's face was ineffably sweet, tender, and compassionate; but what touched me to the very depths of my soul was her gracious smile. Then, all my pain vanished, two big tears started to my eyes and fell silently. . . .

They were indeed tears of unmixed heavenly joy. "Our Blessed Lady has come to me, she has smiled at me. How happy I am, but I shall tell no one, or my happiness will leave me!" Such were my thoughts. Looking around, I recognised Marie; she seemed very much overcome, and looked lovingly at me, as though she guessed that I had just received a great grace.

Indeed her prayers had gained me this unspeakable favour—a smile from the Blessed Virgin! When she saw me with my eyes fixed on the statue, she said to herself: "Thérèse is cured!" And it was true. The Little Flower had come to life again— a bright ray from its glorious Sun had warmed and set it free for ever from its cruel enemy. "The dark winter is past, the rain is over and gone,"[7] and Our Lady's Little Flower gathered such strength that five years later it opened wide its petals on the fertile mountain of Carmel.

As I said before, Marie was convinced that Our Blessed Lady, while restoring my bodily health, had granted me some hidden grace. So, when I was alone with her, I could not resist her tender and pressing inquiries. I was so astonished to find my secret already known, without my having said a word, that I told her everything. Alas! as I had foreseen, my joy was turned into bitterness. For four years the remembrance of this grace was a cause of real pain to me, and it was only in the blessed sanctuary of Our Lady of Victories, at my Mother's feet, that I once again found peace. There it was restored to me in all its fulness, as I will tell you later.

This is how my joy was changed into sadness. When Marie had heard the childish, but perfectly sincere, account of the grace I had received, she begged my leave to tell them at the Carmel, and I did not like to refuse her. My first visit there after my illness was full of joy at seeing Pauline clothed in the habit of Our Lady of Carmel. It was a happy time for us both, we had so much to say, we had both suffered so much. My heart was so full that I could hardly speak.

You were there, dear Mother, and plainly showed your affection for me; I saw several other Sisters too, and you must remember how they questioned me about my cure. Some asked if Our Lady was holding the Infant Jesus in her arms, others if the Angels were with her, and so on. All these questions distressed and grieved me, and I could only make one answer: "Our Lady looked very beautiful; I saw her come towards me and smile." But noticing that the nuns thought something quite different had happened from what I had told them, I began to persuade myself that I had been guilty of an untruth.

If only I had kept my secret I should have kept my happiness also. But Our Lady allowed this trouble to befall me for the good of my soul; perhaps without it vanity would have crept into my heart, whereas now I was humbled, and I looked on myself with feelings of contempt. My God, Thou alone knowest all that I suffered!

---

[1] Marie Guérin entered the Carmel at Lisieux on August 15, 1895, and took the name of Sister Mary of the Eucharist. She died on April 14, 1905, aged thirty-four.

[2] With the Carmelites the grating is only opened for near relatives and very young children. [Ed.]

[3] "Pauline" has several times been Prioress of the Carmel of Lisieux, and in 1909 again succeeded to that office on the death of the young and saintly Mother Mary of St. Angelus of the Child Jesus. [Ed.]

[4] John 11:4.

[5] Mme. Guérin died holily on February 13, 1900, aged fifty-two. During her illness Thérèse assisted her in an extraordinary way, several times making her presence felt. Monsieur Guérin, having for many years used his pen in defence of the Church, and his fortune in the support of good works, died a beautiful death on September 28, 1909, in his sixty-ninth year. [Ed.]

[6] It was in this small church — once deserted and to-day perhaps the most frequented in Paris — that the saintly Abbé Desgenettes was inspired by Our Lady, in 1836, to establish the Confraternity of the Immaculate Heart of Mary for the conversion of sinners. [Ed.]

[7] Cant. 2:11.

CHAPTER IV FIRST COMMUNION AND CONFIRMATION

While describing this visit to the Carmel, my thoughts are carried back to the first one which I paid after Pauline entered. On the morning of that happy day, I wondered what name would be given to me later on. I knew that there was already a Sister Teresa of Jesus; nevertheless, my beautiful name of Thérèse could not be taken from me. Suddenly I thought of the Child Jesus whom I loved so dearly, and I felt how much I should like to be called Teresa of the Child Jesus. I was careful not to tell you of my wish, dear Mother, yet you said to me, in the middle of our conversation: "When you come to us, little one, you will be called 'Teresa of the Child Jesus.'" My joy was great indeed. This happy coincidence of thought seemed a special favour from the Holy Child.

So far I have not said anything about my love for pictures and books, and yet I owe some of the happiest and strongest impressions which have encouraged me in the practice of virtue to the beautiful pictures Pauline used to show me. Everything was forgotten while looking at them. For instance, "The Little Flower of the Divine Prisoner" suggested so many thoughts that I would remain gazing at it in a kind of ecstasy. I offered myself to Our Lord to be His Little Flower; I longed to console Him, to draw as near as possible to the Tabernacle, to be looked on, cared for, and gathered by Him.

As I was of no use at games, I should have preferred to spend all my time in reading. Happily for me, I had visible guardian angels to guide me in this matter; they chose books suitable to my age, which interested me and at the same time provided food for my thoughts and affections. I was only allowed a limited time for this favourite recreation, and it became an occasion of much self-sacrifice, for as soon as the time had elapsed I made it my duty to stop instantly, even in the middle of a most interesting passage.

As to the impressions produced on me by these books, I must frankly own that, in reading certain tales of chivalry, I did not always understand the realities of life. And so, in my admiration of the patriotic deeds of the heroines of France, especially of the Venerable Joan of Arc, I longed to do what they had done. About this time I received what I have looked on as one of the greatest graces of my life, for, at that age, I was not favoured with lights from Heaven, as I am now.

Our Lord made me understand that the only true glory is that which lasts for ever; and that to attain it there is no necessity to do brilliant deeds, but rather to hide from the eyes of others, and even from oneself, so that "the left hand knows not what the right hand does."[1] Then, as I reflected that I was born for great things, and sought the means to attain them, it was made known to me interiorly that my personal glory would never reveal itself before the eyes of men, but that it would consist in becoming a Saint.

This aspiration may very well appear rash, seeing how imperfect I was, and am, even now, after so many years of religious life; yet I still feel the same daring confidence that one day I shall become a great Saint. I am not trusting in my own merits, for I have none; but I trust in Him Who is Virtue and Holiness itself. It is He alone Who, pleased with my feeble efforts, will raise me to Himself, and, by clothing me with His merits, make me a Saint. At that time I did not realise that to become one it is necessary to suffer a great deal; but God soon disclosed this secret to me by means of the trials I have related.

I must now continue my story where I left off. Three months after my cure Papa took me away for a change. It was a very pleasant time, and I began to see something of the world. All around me was joy and gladness; I was petted, made much of, admired — in fact, for a whole fortnight my path was strewn with flowers. The Wise Man is right when he says: "The bewitching of vanity overturneth the innocent mind."[2] At ten years of age the heart is easily fascinated, and I confess that in my case this kind of life had its charms. Alas! the world knows well how to combine its pleasures with the service of God. How little it thinks of death! And yet death has come to many people I knew then, young, rich, and happy. I recall to mind the delightful places where they lived, and ask myself where they are now, and what profit they derive to-day from the beautiful houses and grounds where I saw them enjoying all the good things of this life, and I reflect that "All is vanity besides loving God and serving Him alone." [3]

Perhaps Our Lord wished me to know something of the world before He paid His first visit to my soul, so that I might choose more deliberately the way in which I was to follow Him.

I shall always remember my First Communion Day as one of unclouded happiness. It seems to me that I could not have been better prepared. Do you remember, dear Mother, the charming little book you gave me three months before the great day? I found in it a helpful method which prepared me gradually and thoroughly. It is true I had been thinking about my First Communion for a long time, but, as your precious manuscript told me, I must stir up in my heart fresh transports of love and fill it anew with flowers. So, each day I made a number of little sacrifices and acts of love, which were to be changed into so many flowers: now violets, another time roses, then cornflowers, daisies, or forget-me-nots—in a word, all nature's blossoms were to form in me a cradle for the Holy Child.

I had Marie, too, who took Pauline's place. Every evening I spent a long time with her, listening eagerly to all she said. How delightfully she talked to me! I felt myself set on fire by her noble, generous spirit. As the warriors of old trained their children in the profession of arms, so she trained me for the battle of life, and roused my ardour by pointing to the victor's glorious palm. She spoke, too, of the imperishable riches which are so easy to amass each day, and of the folly of trampling them under foot when one has but to stoop and gather them. When she talked so eloquently, I was sorry that I was the only one to listen to her teaching, for, in my simplicity, it seemed to me that the greatest sinners would be converted if they but heard her, and that, forsaking the perishable riches of this world, they would seek none but the riches of Heaven.

I should have liked at this time to practise mental prayer, but Marie, finding me sufficiently devout, only let me say my vocal prayers. A mistress at the Abbey asked me once what I did on holidays, when I stayed at home. I answered timidly: "I often hide myself in a corner of my room where I can shut myself in with the bed curtains, and then I think." "But what do you think about?" said the good nun, laughing. "I think about the Good God, about the shortness of life, and about eternity: in a word, I *think.*" My mistress did not forget this, and later on she used to remind me of the time when I thought, asking me if I still *thought.* . . . Now, I know that I was really praying, while my Divine Master gently instructed me.

The three months' preparation for First Communion passed quickly by; it was soon time for me to begin my retreat, and, during it, I stayed at the Abbey. Oh, what a blessed retreat it was! I do not think that one can experience such joy except in a religious house; there, with only a few children, it is easy for each one to receive special attention. I write this in a spirit of filial gratitude; our mistresses at the Abbey showed us a true motherly affection. I do not know why, but I saw plainly that they watched over me more carefully than they did over the others.

Every night the first mistress, carrying her little lamp, opened my bed curtains softly, and kissed me tenderly on the forehead. She showed me such affection that, touched by her kindness, I said one night: "Mother, I love you so much that I am going to tell you a great secret." Then I took from under my pillow the precious little book you had given me, and showed it to her, my eyes sparkling with pleasure. She opened it with care, and, looking through it attentively, told me how privileged I was. In fact, several times during the retreat, the truth came home to me that very few motherless children of my age are as lovingly cared for as I was then.

I listened most attentively to the instructions given us by Father
Domin, and wrote careful notes on them, but I did not put down any
of my own thoughts, as I knew I should remember

them quite well.
And so it proved.

How happy I was to attend Divine Office as the nuns did! I was easily distinguished from my companions by a large crucifix, which Léonie had given me, and which, like the missionaries, I carried in my belt. They thought I was trying to imitate my Carmelite sister, and indeed my thoughts did often turn lovingly to her. I knew she was in retreat too, not that Jesus might give Himself to her, but that she might give herself entirely to Jesus, and this on the same day as I made my First Communion. The time of quiet waiting was therefore doubly dear to me.

At last there dawned the most beautiful day of all the days of my life. How perfectly I remember even the smallest details of those sacred hours! the joyful awakening, the reverent and tender embraces of my mistresses and older companions, the room filled with snow-white frocks, where each child was dressed in turn, and, above all, our entrance into the chapel and the melody of the morning hymn: "O Altar of God, where the Angels are hovering."

But I would not and I could not tell you all. Some things lose their fragrance when exposed to the air, and so, too, one's inmost thoughts cannot be translated into earthly words without instantly losing their deep and heavenly meaning. How sweet was the first embrace of Jesus! It was indeed an embrace of love. I felt that I was loved, and I said: "I love Thee, and I give myself to Thee for ever." Jesus asked nothing of me, and claimed no sacrifice; for a long time He and little Thérèse had known and understood one another. That day our meeting was more than simple recognition, it was perfect union. We were no longer two. Thérèse had disappeared like a drop of water lost in the immensity of the ocean; Jesus alone remained—He was the Master, the King! Had not Thérèse asked Him to take away her liberty which frightened her? She felt herself so weak and frail, that she wished to be for ever united to the Divine Strength.

And then my joy became so intense, so deep, that it could not be restrained; tears of happiness welled up and overflowed. My companions were astonished, and asked each other afterwards: "Why did she cry? Had she anything on her conscience? No, it is because neither her Mother nor her dearly loved Carmelite sister is here." And no one understood that all the joy of Heaven had come down into one heart, and that this heart, exiled, weak, and mortal as it was, could not contain it without tears.

How could my Mother's absence grieve me on my First Communion Day? As Heaven itself dwelt in my soul, in receiving a visit from Our Divine Lord I received one from my dear Mother too. Nor was I crying on account of Pauline's absence, for we were even more closely united than before. No, I repeat it—joy alone, a joy too deep for words, overflowed within me.

During the afternoon I read the act of consecration to Our Lady, for myself and my companions. I was chosen probably because I had been deprived of my earthly Mother while still so young. With all my heart I consecrated myself to the Blessed Virgin Mary, and asked her to watch over me. She seemed to look lovingly on her Little Flower and to smile at her again, and I thought of the visible smile which had once cured me, and of all I owed her. Had she not herself, on the morning of that 8th of May, placed in the garden of my soul her Son Jesus—"the Flower of the field and the Lily of the valleys"?[4]

On the evening of this happy day Papa and I went to the Carmel, and I saw Pauline, now become the Spouse of Christ. She wore a white veil like mine and a crown of roses. My joy was unclouded, for I hoped soon to join her, and at her side to wait for Heaven.

I was pleased with the feast prepared for me at home, and was delighted with the beautiful watch given to me by Papa. My happiness was perfect, and nothing troubled the inward peace of my soul. Night came, and so ended that beautiful day. Even the brightest days are followed by darkness; one alone will know no setting, the day of the First and Eternal Communion in our true Home. Somehow the next day seemed sorrowful. The pretty clothes and the presents I had received could not satisfy me. Henceforth Our Lord alone could fill my heart, and all I longed for was the blissful moment when I should receive Him again.

I made my second Communion on Ascension Day, and had the happiness of kneeling at the rails between Papa and Marie. My tears flowed with inexpressible sweetness; I kept repeating those words of St. Paul: "I live now, not I; but Christ liveth in me."[5] After this second visit of Our Lord I longed for nothing else but to receive Him. Alas! the feasts seemed so far apart. . . .

On the eve of these happy days Marie helped me to prepare, as she had done for my First Communion. I remember once she spoke of suffering, and said that in all probability, instead of making me walk by this road, God, in His goodness, would carry me always like a little child. Her words came into my mind next day after my Communion; my heart became inflamed with an ardent desire for suffering, and I felt convinced that many crosses were in store for me. Then my soul was flooded with such consolation as I have never since experienced. Suffering became attractive, and I found in it charms which held me spellbound, though as yet I did not appreciate them to the full.

I had one other great wish; it was to love God only, and to find my joy in Him alone. During my thanksgiving after Holy Communion I often repeated this passage from the *Imitation of Christ*: "O my God, who art unspeakable sweetness, turn for me into bitterness all the consolations of earth."[6] These words rose to my lips quite naturally; I said them like a child, who, without well understanding, repeats what a friend may suggest. Later on I will tell you, dear Mother, how Our Lord has been pleased to fulfill my desire, how He, and He alone, has always been my joy; but if I were to speak of it now I should have to pass on to my girlhood, and there is still much to tell you of my early days.

Soon after my First Communion I went into retreat again, before being confirmed. I prepared myself with the greatest care for the coming of the Holy Ghost; I could not understand anyone not doing so before receiving this Sacrament of Love. As the ceremony could not take place on the day fixed, I had the consolation of remaining somewhat longer in retreat. How happy I felt! Like the Apostles, I looked with joy for the promised Comforter, gladdened by the thought that I should soon be a perfect Christan, and have the holy Cross, the symbol of this wondrous Sacrament, traced upon my forehead for eternity. I did not feel the mighty wind of the first Pentecost, but rather the gentle breeze which the prophet Elias heard on Mount Horeb. On that day I received the gift of fortitude in suffering—a gift I needed sorely, for the martyrdom of my soul was soon to begin.

When these delightful feasts, which can never be forgotten, were over, I had to resume my life as a day scholar, at the Abbey. I made good progress with my lessons, and remembered easily the sense of what I read, but I had the greatest difficulty in learning by heart; only at catechism were my efforts crowned with success. The Chaplain called me his little "Doctor of Theology,"[7] no doubt because of my name, Thérèse.

During recreation I often gave myself up to serious thoughts, while from a distance I watched my companions at play. This was my favourite occupation, but I had another which gave me real pleasure. I would search carefully for any poor little birds that had fallen dead under the big trees, and I then buried them with great ceremony, all in the same cemetery, in a special grass plot. Sometimes I told stories to my companions, and often even the big girls came to listen; but soon our mistress, very rightly, brought my career as an orator to an end, saying she wanted us to exercise our bodies and not our brains. At this time I chose as friends two little girls of my own age; but how shallow are the hearts of creatures! One of them had to stay at home for some months; while she was away I thought about her very often, and on her return I showed how pleased I was. However, all I got was a glance of indifference—my friendship was not appreciated. I felt this very keenly, and I no longer sought an affection which had proved so inconstant. Nevertheless I still love my little school friend, and continue to pray for her, for God has given me a faithful heart, and when once I love, I love for ever.

Observing that some of the girls were very devoted to one or other of the mistresses, I tried to imitate them, but I never succeeded in winning special favour. O happy failure, from how many evils have you saved me! I am most thankful to Our Lord that He let me find only bitterness in earthly friendships. With a heart like mine, I should have been taken captive and had my wings clipped, and how then should I have been able to "fly away and be at rest"?[8]

How can a heart given up to human affections be closely united to God? It seems to me that it is impossible. I have seen so many souls, allured by this false light, fly right into it like poor moths, and burn their wings, and then return, wounded, to Our Lord, the Divine fire which burns and does not consume. I know well Our Lord saw that I was too weak to be exposed to temptation, for, without doubt, had the deceitful light of created love dazzled my eyes, I should have been entirely consumed. Where strong souls find joy and practise detachment faithfully, I only found bitterness. No merit, then, is due to me for not having given up to these frail ties, since I was only preserved from them by the Mercy of God. I fully realised that without Him I should have fallen as low as St. Mary Magdalen, and the Divine Master's words re-echoed sweetly in my soul. Yes, I know that "To whom less is forgiven he loveth less,"[9] but I know too that Our Lord has forgiven me more than St. Mary Magdalen. Here is an example which will, at any rate, show you some of my thoughts.

Let us suppose that the son of a very clever doctor, stumbling over a stone on the road, falls and breaks his leg. His father hastens to him, lifts him lovingly, and binds up the fractured limb, putting forth all his skill. The son, when cured, displays the utmost gratitude, and he has excellent reason for doing so. But let us take another supposition.

The father, aware that a dangerous stone lies in his son's path, is beforehand with the danger and removes it, unseen by anyone. The son, thus tenderly cared for, not knowing of the mishap from which his father's hand has saved him, naturally will not show him any gratitude, and will love him less than if he had cured him of a grievous wound. But suppose he heard the whole truth, would he not in that case love him still more? Well now, I am this child, the object of the foreseeing love of a Father "Who did not send His son to call the just, but sinners."[10] He wishes me to love Him, because He has forgiven me, not much, but everything. Without waiting for me to love Him much, as St. Mary Magdalen did, He has made me understand how He has loved me with an ineffable love and forethought, so that now my love may know no bounds.

I had often heard it said, both in retreats and elsewhere, that He is more deeply loved by repentant souls than by those who have not lost their baptismal innocence. Ah! If I could but give the lie to those words. . . .

But I have wandered so far from my subject that I hardly know where to begin again. It was during the retreat before my second Communion that I was attacked by the terrible disease of scruples. One must have passed through this martyrdom to understand it. It would be quite impossible for me to tell you what I suffered for nearly two years. All my thoughts and actions, even the simplest, were a source of trouble and anguish to me; I had no peace till I had told Marie everything, and this was most painful, since I imagined I was obliged to tell absolutely all my thoughts, even the most extravagant. As soon as I had unburdened myself I felt a momentary peace, but it passed like a flash, and my martyrdom began again. Many an occasion for patience did I provide for my dear sister.

That year we spent a fortnight of our holidays at the sea-side. My aunt, who always showed us such motherly care, treated us to all possible pleasures — donkey rides, shrimping, and the rest. She even spoiled us in the matter of clothes. I remember one day she gave me some pale blue ribbon; although I was twelve and a half, I was still such a child that I quite enjoyed tying it in my hair. But this childish pleasure seemed sinful to me, and I had so many scruples that I had to go to Confession, even at Trouville.

While I was there I had an experience which did me good. My cousin Marie often suffered from sick headaches. On these occasions my aunt used to fondle her and coax her with the most endearing names, but the only response was continual tears and the unceasing cry: "My head aches!" I had a headache nearly every day, though I did not say so; but one evening I thought I would imitate Marie. So I sat down in an armchair in a corner of the room, and set to work to cry. My aunt, as well as my cousin Jeanne, to whom I was very devoted, hastened to me to know what was the matter. I answered like Marie: "My head aches." It would seem that complaining was not in my line; no one would believe that a headache was the reason of my tears. Instead of petting me as usual, my aunt spoke to me seriously. Even Jeanne reproached me, very kindly it is true, and was grieved at my want of simplicity and trust in my aunt. She thought I had a big scruple, and was not giving the real reason of my tears. At last, getting nothing for my pains, I made up my mind not to imitate other people any more. I thought of the fable of the ass and the little dog; I was the ass, who, seeing that the little dog got all the petting, put his clumsy hoof on the table to try and secure his share. If I did not have a beating like the poor beast, at any rate I got what I deserved —a severe lesson, which cured me once for all of the desire to attract attention.

I must go back now to the subject of my scruples. They made me so ill that I was obliged to leave school when I was thirteen. In order to continue my education, Papa took me several times a week to a lady who was an excellent teacher. Her lessons served the double purpose of instructing me and making me associate with other people.

Visitors were often shown into the old-fashioned room where I sat with my books and exercises. As far as possible my teacher's mother carried on the conversation, but still I did not learn much while it lasted. Seemingly absorbed in my book, I could hear many things it would have been better for me not to hear. One lady said I had beautiful hair; another asked, as she left, who was that pretty little girl. Such remarks, the more flattering because I was not meant to hear them, gave me a feeling of pleasure which showed plainly that I was full of self-love.

I am very sorry for souls who lose themselves in this way. It is so easy to go astray in the seductive paths of the world. Without doubt, for a soul somewhat advanced in virtue, the sweetness offered by the world is mingled with bitterness, and the immense void of its desires cannot be filled by the flattery of a moment; but I repeat, if my heart had not been lifted up towards God from the first moment of consciousness, if the world had smiled on me from the beginning of my life, what should I have become? Dearest Mother, with what a grateful heart do I sing "the Mercies of the Lord!" Has He not, according to the words of Holy Wisdom, "taken me away from the world lest wickedness should alter my understanding, or deceit beguile my soul?" [11]

Meanwhile I resolved to consecrate myself in a special way to Our Blessed Lady, and I begged to be enrolled among the Children of Mary.[12] To gain this favour I had to go twice a week to the Convent, and I must confess this cost me something, I was so shy. There was no question of the affection I felt towards my mistresses, but, as I said before, I had no special friend among them, with whom I could have spent many hours like other old pupils. So I worked in silence till the end of the lesson, and then, as no one took any notice of me, I went to the tribune in the Chapel till Papa came to fetch me home. Here, during this silent visit, I found my one consolation—for was not Jesus my only Friend? To Him alone could I open my heart; all conversation with creatures, even on holy subjects, wearied me. It is true that in these periods of loneliness I sometimes felt sad, and I used often to console myself by repeating this line of a beautiful poem Papa had taught me: "Time is thy barque, and not thy dwelling-place."

Young as I was, these words restored my courage, and even now, in spite of having outgrown many pious impressions of childhood, the symbol of a ship always delights me and helps me to bear the exile of this life. Does not the Wise Man tell us —"Life is like a ship that passeth through the waves:

when it is gone by, the trace thereof cannot be found"?[13]

When my thoughts run on in this way, my soul loses itself as it were in the infinite; I seem already to touch the Heavenly Shore and to receive Our Lord's embrace. I fancy I can see Our Blessed Lady coming to meet me, with my Father and Mother, my little brothers and sisters; and I picture myself enjoying true family joys for all eternity.

But before reaching Our Father's Home in Heaven, I had to go through many partings on this earth. The year in which I was made a Child of Mary, Our Lady took from me my sister Marie, the only support of my soul,[14] my oracle and inseparable companion since the departure of Pauline. As soon as I knew of her decision, I made up my mind to take no further pleasure in anything here below. I could not tell you how many tears I shed. But at this time I was much given to crying, not only over big things, but over trifling ones too. For instance: I was very anxious to advance in virtue, but I went about it in a strange way. I was not accustomed to wait on myself; Céline always arranged our room, and I never did any household work. Sometimes, in order to please Our Lord, I used to make my bed, or, if she were out in the evening, to bring in her plants and seedlings. As I said before, it was simply to please Our Lord that I did these things, and so I ought not to have expected any thanks from creatures. But, alas! I did expect them, and, if unfortunately Céline did not seem surprised and grateful for my little services, I was not pleased, and tears rose to my eyes.

Again, if by accident I offended anyone, instead of taking it in the right way, I fretted till I made myself ill, thus making my fault worse, instead of mending it; and when I began to realise my foolishness, I would cry for having cried.

In fact, I made troubles out of everything. Now, things are quite different. God in His goodness has given me grace not to be cast down by any passing difficulty. When I think of what I used to be, my heart overflows with gratitude. The graces I have received have changed me so completely, that I am scarcely the same person.

After Marie entered the Carmel, and I no longer had her to listen to my scruples, I turned towards Heaven and confided them to the four little angels who had already gone before me, for I thought that these innocent souls, who had never known sorrow or fear, ought to have pity on their poor little suffering sister. I talked to them with childish simplicity, telling them that, as I was the youngest of the family, I had always been the most petted and loved by my parents and sisters; that if they had remained on earth they would no doubt have given me the same proofs of their affection. The fact that they had gone to Heaven seemed no reason why they should forget me—on the contrary, as they were able to draw form the treasury of Heaven, they ought to obtain for me the grace of peace, and prove that they still knew how to love me.

The answer was not long in coming; soon my soul was flooded with the sweetest peace. I knew that I was loved, not only on earth but also in Heaven. From that time my devotion for these little brothers and sisters increased; I loved to talk to them and tell them of all the sorrows of this exile, and of my wish to join them soon in our Eternal Home.

---

[1] Cf. Matt. 6:3.

[2] Wisdom 4:12.

[3] *Imit.*, I, ch. i. 3.

[4] Cant. 2:1.

[5] Gal. 2:20.

[6] *Imit.*, III, ch. xxvi. 3.

[7] St. Teresa, who reformed the Carmelite Order, and died in 1582, is sometimes called the Doctor of Mystical Theology, because of her luminous writings on the relations of the soul with God in prayer. [Ed.]

[8] Ps. 54[55]:7.

[9] Luke 7:47.

[10] Luke 5:32.

[11] Cf. Wisdom 4:11.

[12] It was on May 31, 1886, that she became a Sodalist of Our Lady. [Ed.]

[13] Wisdom 5:10.

[14] Marie entered the Carmel of Lisieux on October 15, 1886, taking the name of Sister Mary of the Sacred Heart.

CHAPTER V VOCATION OF THÉRÈSE

I was far from meriting all the graces which Our Lord showered on me. I had a constant and ardent desire to advance in virtue, but often my actions were spoilt by imperfections. My extreme sensitiveness made me almost unbearable. All arguments were useless. I simply could not correct myself of this miserable fault. How, then, could I hope soon to be admitted to the Carmel? A miracle on a small scale was needed to give me strength of character all at once, and God worked this long-desired miracle on Christmas Day, 1886.

On that blessed night the sweet Infant Jesus, scarce an hour old, filled the darkness of my soul with floods of light. By becoming weak and little, for love of me, He made me strong and brave; He put His own weapons into my hands, so that I went from victory to victory, beginning, if I may say so, "to run as a giant."[1] The fountain of my tears was dried up, and from that time they flowed neither easily nor often.

Now I will tell you, dear Mother, how I received this inestimable grace of complete conversion. I knew that when we reached home after Midnight Mass I should find my shoes in the chimney-corner, filled with presents, just as when I was a little child, which proves that my sisters still treated me as a baby. Papa, too, liked to watch my enjoyment and hear my cries of delight at each fresh surprise that came from the magic shoes, and his pleasure added to mine. But the time had come when Our Lord wished to free me from childhood's failings, and even withdraw me from its innocent pleasures. On this occasion, instead of indulging me as he generally did, Papa seemed vexed, and on my way upstairs I heard him say: "Really all this is too babyish for a big girl like Thérèse, and I hope it is the last year it will happen." His words cut me to the quick. Céline, knowing how sensitive I was, whispered: "Don't go downstairs just yet—wait a little, you would cry too much if you looked at your presents before Papa." But Thérèse was no longer the same—Jesus had changed her heart.

Choking back my tears, I ran down to the dining-room, and, though my heart beat fast, I picked up my shoes, and gaily pulled out all the things, looking as happy as a queen. Papa laughed, and did not show any trace of displeasure, and Céline thought she must be dreaming. But happily it was a reality; little Thérèse had regained, once for all, the strength of mind which she had lost at the age of four and a half.

On this night of grace, the third period of my life began—the most beautiful of all, the one most filled with heavenly favours. In an instant Our Lord, satisfied with my good will, accomplished the work I had not been able to do during all these years. Like the Apostle I could say: "Master, we have laboured all night, and have taken nothing."[2]

More merciful to me even than to His beloved disciples, Our Lord Himself took the net, cast it, and drew it out full of fishes. He made me a fisher of men. Love and a spirit of self-forgetfulness took possession of me, and from that time I was perfectly happy.

One Sunday, closing my book at the end of Mass, a picture of Our Lord on the Cross half slipped out, showing only one of His Divine Hands, pierced and bleeding. I felt an indescribable thrill such as I had never felt before. My heart was torn with grief to see that Precious Blood falling to the ground, and no one caring to treasure It as It fell, and I resolved to remain continually in spirit at the foot of the Cross, that I might receive the Divine Dew of Salvation and pour it forth upon souls. From that day the cry of my dying Saviour—"I thirst!"—sounded incessantly in my heart, and kindled therein a burning zeal hitherto unknown to me. My one desire was to give my Beloved to drink; I felt myself consumed with thirst for souls, and I longed at any cost to snatch sinners from the everlasting flames of hell.

In order still further to enkindle my ardour, Our Divine Master soon proved to me how pleasing to him was my desire. Just then I heard much talk of a notorious criminal, Pranzini, who was sentenced to death for several shocking murders, and, as he was quite impenitent, everyone feared he would be eternally lost. How I longed to avert this irreparable calamity! In order to do so I employed all the spiritual means I could think of, and, knowing that my own efforts were unavailing, I offered for his pardon the infinite merits of Our Saviour and the treasures of Holy Church.

Need I say that in the depths of my heart I felt certain my request would be granted? But, that I might gain courage to persevere in the quest for souls, I said in all simplicity: "My God, I am quite sure that Thou wilt pardon this unhappy Pranzini. I should still think so if he did not confess his sins or give any sign of sorrow, because I have such confidence in Thy unbounded Mercy; but this is my first sinner, and therefore I beg for just one sign of repentance to reassure me." My prayer was granted to the letter. My Father never allowed us to read the papers, but I did not think there was any disobedience in looking at the part about Pranzini. The day after his execution I hastily opened the paper, *La Croix,* and what did I see? Tears betrayed my emotion; I was obliged to run out of the room. Pranzini had mounted the scaffold without confessing or receiving absolution, and the executioners were already dragging him towards the fatal block, when all at once, apparently in answer to a sudden inspiration, he turned round, seized the crucifix which the Priest was offering to him, and kissed Our Lord's Sacred Wounds three times. . . . I had obtained the sign I asked for, and to me it was especially sweet. Was it not when I saw the Precious Blood flowing from the Wounds of Jesus that the thirst for souls first took possession of me? I wished to give them to drink of the Blood of the Immaculate Lamb that It might wash away their stains, and the lips of "my first born" had been pressed to these Divine Wounds. What a wonderful answer!

After receiving this grace my desire for the salvation of souls increased day by day. I seemed to hear Our Lord whispering to me, as He did to the Samaritan woman: "Give me to drink!"[3] It was indeed an exchange of love: upon souls I poured forth the Precious Blood of Jesus, and to Jesus I offered these souls refreshed with the Dew of Calvary. In this way I thought to quench His Thirst; but the more I gave Him to drink, so much the more did the thirst of my own poor soul increase, and I accepted it as the most delightful recompense.

In a short time God, in His goodness, had lifted me out of the narrow sphere in which I lived. The great step was taken; but, alas! I had still a long road to travel. Now that I was free from scruples and morbid sensitiveness, my mind developed. I had always loved what was noble and beautiful, and about this time I was seized with a passionate desire for learning. Not content with lessons from my teachers, I took up certain subjects by myself, and learnt more in a few months than I had in my whole school life. Was not this ardour—"vanity and vexation of spirit"?[4] For me, with my impetuous nature, this was one of the most dangerous times of my life, but Our Lord fulfilled in me those words of Ezechiel's prophecy: "Behold thy time was the time of lovers: and I spread my garment over thee. And I swore to thee, and I entered into a covenant with thee, saith the Lord God, and thou becamest Mine. And I washed thee with water, and I anointed thee with oil. I clothed thee with fine garments, and put a chain about thy neck. Thou didst eat fine flour and honey and oil, and wast made exceedingly beautiful, and wast advanced to be a queen."[5]

Yes, Our Lord has done all this for me. I might take each word of that striking passage and show how it has been completely realised in me, but the graces of which I have already told you are sufficient proof. So I will only speak now of the food with which my Divine Master abundantly provided me. For a long time I had nourished my spiritual life with the "fine flour" contained in the *Imitation of Christ*. It was the only book which did me good, for I had not yet found the treasures hidden in the Holy Gospels. I always had it with me, to the amusement of my people at home. My aunt used often to open it, and make me repeat by heart the first chapter she chanced to light upon.

Seeing my great thirst for knowledge, God was pleased, when I was fourteen, to add to the "fine flour," "honey" and "oil" in abundance.

This "honey" and "oil" I found in the conferences of Father Arminjon on *The End of this World and the Mysteries of the World to Come.* While reading this book my soul was flooded with a happiness quite supernatural. I experienced a foretaste of what God has prepared for those who love Him; and, seeing that eternal rewards are so much in excess of the petty sacrifices of this life, I yearned to love Our Lord, to love Him passionately, and to give Him countless proofs of affection while this was still in my power.

Céline had become the most intimate sharer of my thoughts, especially since Christmas. Our Lord, Who wished to make us advance in virtue together, drew us to one another by ties stronger than blood. He made us sisters in spirit as well as in the flesh. The words of our Holy Father, St. John of the Cross, were realised in us:

> Treading within Thy Footsteps
> Young maidens lightly run upon the way.
> From the spark's contact,
> And the spicèd wine,
> They give forth aspirations of a balm divine.

It was lightly indeed that we followed in the footsteps of Our Saviour. The burning sparks which

He cast into our souls, the strong wine which He gave us to drink, made us lose sight of all earthly things, and we breathed forth sighs of love.

Very sweet is the memory of our intercourse. Every evening we went up to our attic window together and gazed at the starry depths of the sky, and I think very precious graces were bestowed on us then. As the *Imitation* says: "God communicates Himself sometimes amid great light, at other times sweetly in signs and figures."[6]

In this way He deigned to manifest Himself to our hearts; but how slight and transparent was the veil! Doubt was no longer possible; already Faith and Hope had given place to Love, which made us find Him whom we sought, even on this earth. When He found us alone—"He gave us His kiss, and now no one may despise us."[7]

These divine impressions could not but bear fruit. The practice of virtue gradually became sweet and natural to me. At first my looks betrayed the effort, but, little by little, self-sacrifice seemed to come more easily and without hesitation. Our Lord has said: "To everyone that hath shall be given, and he shall abound."[8]

Each grace faithfully received brought many others. He gave Himself to me in Holy Communion oftener than I should have dared to hope. I had made it my practice to go to Communion as often as my confessor allowed me, but never to ask for leave to go more frequently. Now, however, I should act differently, for I am convinced that a soul ought to disclose to her director the longing she has to receive her God. He does not come down from Heaven each day in order to remain in a golden ciborium, but to find another Heaven—the Heaven of our souls in which He takes such delight.

Our Lord, Who knew my desire, inspired my confessor to allow me to go to Communion several times a week, and this permission, coming as it did straight from Him, filled me with joy.

In those days I did not dare to speak of my inner feelings; the road which I trod was so direct, so clear, that I did not feel the need of any guide but Jesus. I compared directors to mirrors who faithfully reflect Our Saviour to the souls under their care, and I thought that in my case He did not use an intermediary but acted directly.

When a gardener gives special attention to a fruit which he wishes to ripen early, he does so, not with a view to leaving it on the tree, but in order to place it on a well-spread table. Our Lord lavished His favours on His Little Flower in the same way. He wishes His Mercies to shine forth in me—He Who, while on earth, cried out in a transport of joy: "I bless Thee, O Father, because Thou hast hidden these things from the wise and prudent and hast revealed them to little ones."[9]

And because I was small and frail, He bent down to me and instructed me sweetly in the secrets of His love. As St. John of the Cross says in his "Canticle of the Soul":

> On that happy night
> In secret I went forth, beheld by none,
> And seeing naught;
> Having no light nor guide
> Excepting that which burned within my heart,

> Which lit my way
> More safely than the glare of noon-day sun
> To where, expectant,
> He waited for me Who doth know me well,
> Where none appeared but He.

This place was Carmel, but before I could "sit down under His Shadow Whom I desired,"[10] I had to pass through many trials. And yet the Divine Call was becoming so insistent that, had it been necessary for me to go through fire, I would have thrown myself into it to follow my Divine Master.

Pauline[11] was the only one who encouraged me in my vocation; Marie thought I was too young, and you, dear Mother, no doubt to prove me, tried to restrain my ardour. From the start I encountered nothing but difficulties. Then, too, I dared not speak of it to Céline, and this silence pained me deeply; it was so hard to have a secret she did not share.

However, this dear sister soon found out my intention, and, far from wishing to keep me back, she accepted the sacrifice with wonderful courage. As she also wished to be a nun, she ought to have been given the first opportunity; but, imitating the martyrs of old, who used joyfully to embrace those chosen to go before them into the arena, she allowed me to leave her, and took my troubles as much to heart as if it were a question of her own vocation. From Céline, then, I had nothing to fear, but I did not know how to set about telling Papa. How could his little Queen talk of leaving him when he had already parted with his two eldest daughters? Moreover, this year he had been stricken with a serious attack of paralysis, and though he recovered quickly we were full of anxiety for the future.

What struggles I went through before I could make up my mind to speak! But I had to act decisively; I was now fourteen and a half, and in six months' time the blessed feast of Christmas would be here. I had resolved to enter the Carmel at the same hour at which a year before I had received the grace of conversion.

I chose the feast of Pentecost on which to make my great disclosure. All day I was praying for light from the Holy Ghost, and begging the Apostles to pray for me, to inspire me with the words I ought to use. Were they not the very ones to help a timid child whom God destines to become an apostle of apostles by prayer and sacrifice?

In the afternoon, when Vespers were over, I found the opportunity I wanted. My Father was sitting in the garden, his hands clasped, admiring the wonders of nature. The rays of the setting sun gilded the tops of the tall trees, and the birds chanted their evening prayer.

His beautiful face wore a heavenly expression—I could feel that his soul was full of peace. Without a word, I sat down by his side, my eyes already wet with tears. He looked at me with indescribable tenderness, and, pressing me to his heart, said: "What is it, little Queen? Tell me everything." Then, in order to hide his own emotion, he rose and walked slowly up and down, still holding me close to him.

Through my tears I spoke of the Carmel and of my great wish to enter soon. He, too, wept, but did not say a word to turn me from my vocation; he only told me that I was very young to make such a grave decision, and as I insisted, and fully explained my reasons, my noble and generous Father was soon convinced. We walked about for a long time; my heart was lightened, and Papa no longer shed tears. He spoke to me as Saints speak, and showed me some flowers growing in the low stone wall. Picking one of them, he gave it to me, and explained the loving care with which God had made it spring up and grow till now.

I fancied myself listening to my own story, so close was the resemblance between the little flower and little Thérèse. I received this floweret as a relic, and noticed that in gathering it my Father had pulled it up by the roots without breaking them; it seemed destined to live on, but in other and more fertile soil. Papa had just done the same for me. He allowed me to leave the sweet valley, where I had passed the first years of my life, for the mountain of Carmel. I fastened my little white flower to a picture of Our Lady of Victories—the Blessed Virgin smiles on it, and the Infant Jesus seems to hold it in His Hand. It is there still, but the stalk is broken close to the root. God doubtless wishes me to understand that He will soon break all the earthly ties of His Little Flower and will not leave her to wither on this earth.

Having obtained my Father's consent, I thought I could now fly to the Carmel without hindrance. Far from it! When I told my uncle of my project, he declared that to enter such a severe Order at the age of fifteen seemed to him against all common sense, and that it would be doing a wrong to religion to let a child embrace such a life. He added that he should oppose it in every way possible, and that nothing short of a miracle would make him change his mind.

I could see that all arguments were useless, so I left him, my heart weighed down by profound sadness. My only consolation was prayer. I entreated Our Lord to work this miracle for me because thus only could I respond to His appeal. Some time went by, and my uncle did not seem even to remember our conversation, though I learnt later that it had been constantly in his thoughts.

Before allowing a ray of hope to shine on my soul, Our Lord deigned to send me another most painful trial which lasted for three days. Never had I understood so well the bitter grief of Our Lady and St. Joseph when they were searching the streets of Jerusalem for the Divine Child. I seemed to be in a frightful desert, or rather, my soul was like a frail skiff, without a pilot, at the mercy of the stormy waves. I knew that Jesus was there asleep in my little boat, but how could I see Him while the night was so dark? If the storm had really broken, a flash of lightning would perhaps have pierced the clouds that hung over me: even though it were but a passing ray, it would have enabled me to catch a momentary glimpse of the Beloved of my heart—but this was denied me. Instead, it was night, dark night, utter desolation, death! Like my Divine Master in the Agony in the Garden, I felt that I was alone, and found no comfort on earth or in Heaven.

Nature itself seemed to share my bitter sadness, for during these three days there was not a ray of sunshine and the rain fell in torrents. I have noticed again and again that in all the important events of my life nature has reflected my feelings. When I wept, the skies wept with me; when I rejoiced, no cloud darkened the blue of the heavens. On the fourth day, a Saturday, I went to see my uncle. What was my surprise when I found his attitude towards me entirely changed! He invited me into his study, a privilege I had not asked for; then, after gently reproaching me for being a little constrained with him, he told me that the miracle of which he had spoken was no longer needed. He had prayed

God to guide his heart aright, and his prayer had been heard. I felt as if I hardly knew him, he seemed so different. He embraced me with fatherly affection, saying with much feeling: "Go in peace, my dear child, you are a privileged little flower which Our Lord wishes to gather. I will put no obstacle in the way."

Joyfully I went home. . . . The clouds had quite disappeared from the sky, and in my soul also dark night was over. Jesus had awakened to gladden my heart. I no longer heard the roar of the waves. Instead of the bitter wind of trial, a light breeze swelled my sail, and I fancied myself safe in port. Alas! more than one storm was yet to rise, sometimes even making me fear that I should be driven, without hope of return, from the shore which I longed to reach.

I had obtained my uncle's consent, only to be told by you, dear Mother, that the Superior of the Carmelites would not allow me to enter till I was twenty-one. No one had dreamt of this serious opposition, the hardest of all to overcome. And yet, without losing courage, I went with Papa to lay my request before him. He received me very coldly, and could not be induced to change his mind. We left him at last with a very decided "No." "Of course," he added, "I am only the Bishop's delegate; if he allows you to enter, I shall have nothing more to say."

When we came out of the Presbytery again, it was raining in torrents, and my soul, too, was overcast with heavy clouds. Papa did not know how to console me, but he promised, if I wished, to take me to Bayeux to see the Bishop, and to this I eagerly consented.

Many things happened, however, before we were able to go. To all appearances my life seemed to continue as formerly. I went on studying, and, what is more important, I went on growing in the love of God. Now and then I experienced what were indeed raptures of love.

One evening, not knowing in what words to tell Our Lord how much I loved him, and how much I wished that He was served and honoured everywhere, I thought sorrowfully that from the depths of hell there does not go up to Him one single act of love. Then, from my inmost heart, I cried out that I would gladly be cast into that place of torment and blasphemy so that He might be eternally loved even there. This could not be for His Glory, since He only wishes our happiness, but love feels the need of saying foolish things. If I spoke in this way, it was not that I did not long to go to Heaven, but for me Heaven was nothing else than Love, and in my ardour I felt that nothing could separate me from the Divine Being Who held me captive.

About this time Our Lord gave me the consolation of an intimate knowledge of the souls of children. I gained it in this way. During the illness of a poor woman, I interested myself in her two little girls, the elder of whom was not yet six. It was a real pleasure to see how simply they believed all that I told them. Baptism does indeed plant deeply in our souls the theological virtues, since from early childhood the hope of heavenly reward is strong enough to make us practise self-denial. When I wanted my two little girls to be specially kind to one another, instead of promising them toys and sweets, I talked to them about the eternal recompense the Holy Child Jesus would give to good children. The elder one, who was coming to the use of reason, used to look quite pleased and asked me charming questions about the little Jesus and His beautiful Heaven. She promised me faithfully always to give in to her little sister, adding that all through her life she would never forget what I had taught her. I used to compare these innocent souls to soft wax, ready to receive any impression—evil, alas! as well as good, and I understood the words of Our Lord: "It were better to be thrown into the sea than to scandalise one of these little ones."[12]

How many souls might attain to great sanctity if only they were directed aright from the first! I know God has not need of anyone to help Him in His work of sanctification, but as He allows a clever gardener to cultivate rare and delicate plants, giving him the skill to accomplish it, while reserving to Himself the right of making them grow, so does He wish to be helped in the cultivation of souls. What would happen if an ignorant gardener did not graft his trees in the right way? if he did not understand the nature of each, and wished, for instance, to make roses grow on peach trees?

This reminds me that I used to have among my birds a canary which sang beautifully, and also a little linnet taken from the nest, of which I was very fond. This poor little prisoner, deprived of the teaching it should have received from its parents, and hearing the joyous trills of the canary from morning to night, tried hard to imitate them. A difficult task indeed for a linnet! It was delightful to follow the efforts of the poor little thing; his sweet voice found great difficulty in accommodating itself to the vibrant notes of his master, but he succeeded in time, and, to my great surprise, his song became exactly like the song of the canary.

Oh, dear Mother, you know who taught me to sing from the days of my earliest childhood! You know the voices which drew me on. And now I trust that one day, in spite of my weakness, I may sing for ever the Canticle of Love, the harmonious notes of which I have often heard sweetly sounding here below.

But where am I? These thoughts have carried me too far, and I must resume the history of my vocation.

On October 31, 1887, alone with Papa, I started for Bayeux, my heart full of hope, but also excited at the idea of presenting myself at the Bishop's house. For the first time in my life, I was going to pay a visit without any of my sisters, and this to a Bishop. I, who had never yet had to speak except to answer questions addressed to me, would have to explain and enlarge on my reasons for begging to enter the Carmel, and so give proofs of the genuineness of my vocation.

It cost me a great effort to overcome my shyness sufficiently to do this. But it is true that Love knows no such word as "impossible," for it deems "all things possible, all things allowed." Nothing whatsoever but the love of Jesus could have made me face these difficulties and others which followed, for I had to purchase my happiness by heavy trials. Now, it is true, I think I bought it very cheaply, and I would willingly bear a thousand times more bitter suffering to gain it, if it were not already mine.

When we reached the Bishop's house, the floodgates of Heaven seemed open once more. The Vicar-General, Father Révérony, who had settled the date of our coming, received us very kindly, though he looked a little surprised, and seeing tears in my eyes said: "Those diamonds must not be shown to His Lordship!" We were led through large reception-rooms which made me feel how small I was, and I wondered what I should dare say. The Bishop was walking in a corridor with two Priests. I saw the Vicar-General speak a few words to him, then they came into the room where we were waiting. There were three large armchairs in front of the fireplace, where a bright fire blazed.

As his Lordship entered, my Father and I knelt for his blessing; then he made us sit down. Father Révérony offered me the armchair in the middle. I excused myself politely, but he insisted, telling me to show if I knew how to obey. I did so without any more hesitation, and was mortified to see him take an ordinary chair while I was buried in an enormous seat that would comfortably have held four children like me—more comfortably in fact, for I was far from being at ease. I hoped that Papa was going to do all the talking, but he told me to explain the reason of our visit. I did so as eloquently as I could, though I knew well that one word from the Superior would have carried more weight than all my reasons, while his opposition told strongly against me. The Bishop asked how long I had wanted to enter the Carmel. "A very long time, my Lord!" "Come!" said the Vicar-General, laughing, "it cannot be as long as fifteen years." "That is true," I answered, "but it is not much less, for I have wished to give myself to God from the time I was three." The Bishop, no doubt to please Papa, tried to explain that I ought to remain some time longer with him; but, to his great surprise and edification, my Father took my part, adding respectfully that we were going to Rome with the diocesan pilgrimage, and that I should not hesitate to speak to the Holy Father if I could not obtain permission before then. However, it was decided that, previous to giving an answer, an interview with the Superior was absolutely necessary. This was particularly unpleasant hearing, for I knew his declared and determined opposition; and, in spite of the advice not to allow the Bishop to see any diamonds, I not only showed them but let them fall. He seemed touched, and caressed me fondly. I was afterwards told he had never treated any child so kindly.

"All is not lost, little one," he said, "but I am very glad that you are going to Rome with your good Father; you will thus strengthen your vocation. Instead of weeping, you ought to rejoice. I am going to Lisieux next week, and I will talk to the Superior about you. You shall certainly have my answer when you are in Italy." His Lordship then took us to the garden, and was much interested when Papa told him that, to make myself look older, I had put up my hair for the first time that very morning. This was not forgotten, for I know that even now, whenever the Bishop tells anyone about his "little daughter," he always repeats the story about her hair. I must say I should prefer my little secret to have been kept. As he took us to the door, the Vicar-General remarked that such a thing had never been seen—a father as anxious to give his child to God as the child was to offer herself.

We had to return to Lisieux without a favourable answer. It seemed to me as though my future were shattered for ever; the nearer I drew to the goal, the greater my difficulties became. But all the time I felt deep down in my heart a wondrous peace, because I knew that I was only seeking the Will of my Lord.

---

[1] Cf. Psalm 18[19]:5.

[2] Luke 5:5.

[3] John 4:7.

[4] Eccl. 1:14.

[5] Ezechiel 16:8, 9, 13.

[6] Cf. *Imit.*, III, ch. xliii. 4.

[7] Cf. Cant. 8:1.

[8] Luke 19:26.

[9] Cf. Luke 10:21.

[10] Cant. 2:3.

[11] Sister Agnes of Jesus.

[12] Cf. Matt. 18:6.

CHAPTER VI A PILGRIMAGE TO ROME

Three days after the journey to Bayeux, I started on a much longer one—to the Eternal City. This journey taught me the vanity of all that passes away. Nevertheless I saw splendid monuments; I studied the countless wonders of art and religion; and better than all, I trod the very ground the Holy Apostles had trodden—the ground watered by the blood of martyrs—and my soul grew by contact with these holy things.

I was delighted to go to Rome; but I could quite understand people crediting Papa with the hope that in this way I should be brought to change my mind about the religious life. It might certainly have upset a vocation that was not very strong.

To begin with, Céline and I found ourselves in the company of many distinguished people. In fact, there were scarcely any others in the pilgrimage; but, far from being dazzled thereby, titles seemed to us but a "vapour of smoke,"[1] and I understood the words of the *Imitation:* "Be not solicitous for the shadow of a great name."[2] I understood that true greatness is not found in a name but in the soul. The Prophet Isaias tells us: "The Lord shall call His servants by another name,"[3] and we read in St. John: "To him that overcometh I will give a white counter, and on the counter a new name written which no man knoweth but he that receiveth it."[4] In Heaven, therefore, we shall know our titles of nobility, and "then shall every man have praise from God,"[5] and he who on earth chose to be poorest and least known for love of his Saviour, he will be the first, the noblest, and the richest.

The second thing I learnt had to do with Priests. Up to this time I had not understood the chief aim of the Carmelite Reform. To pray for sinners delighted me; to pray for Priests, whose souls seemed pure as crystal, that indeed astonished me. But in Italy I realised my vocation, and even so long a journey was a small price to pay for such valuable knowledge. During that month I met with many holy Priests, and yet I saw that even though the sublime dignity of Priesthood raises them higher than the Angels, they are still but weak and imperfect men. And so if holy Priests, whom Our

Lord in the Gospel calls the salt of the earth, have need of our prayers, what must we think of the lukewarm? Has not Our Lord said: "If the salt lose its savour wherewith shall it be salted?"[6] Oh, dear Mother, how beautiful is our vocation! We Carmelites are called to preserve "the salt of the earth." We offer our prayers and sacrifices for the apostles of the Lord; we ourselves ought to be their apostles, while they, by word and example, are preaching the Gospel to our brethren. Have we not a glorious mission to fulfill? But I must say no more, for I feel that on this subject my pen would run on for ever.

Now let me describe my journey in some detail. At three o'clock in the morning of November 4, we passed through the silent streets. Lisieux still lay shrouded in the darkness of night. I felt that I was going out into the unknown, and that great things were awaiting me in Rome. When we reached Paris, Papa took us to see all the sights. For me there was but one—Our Lady of Victories. I can never tell you what I felt at her shrine; the graces Our Lady granted me were like those of my First Communion Day. I was filled with peace and happiness. In this holy spot the Blessed Virgin, my Mother, told me plainly that it was really she who had smiled on me and cured me. With intense fervour I entreated her to keep me always, and to realise my heart's desire by hiding me under her spotless mantle, and I also asked her to remove from me every occasion of sin.

I was well aware that during this journey I should come across things that might disturb me; knowing nothing of evil, I feared I might discover it. As yet I had not experienced that "to the pure all things are pure,"[7] that a simple and upright soul does not see evil in anything, because evil only exists in impure hearts and not in inanimate objects. I prayed specially to St. Joseph to watch over me; from my childhood, devotion to him has been interwoven with my love for our Blessed Lady. Every day I said the prayer beginning: "St. Joseph, Father and Protector of Virgins" . . . so I felt I was well protected and quite safe from danger.

We left Paris on November 7, after our solemn Consecration to the Sacred Heart in the Basilica of Montmartre.[8] Each compartment of the train was named after a Saint, and the selection was made in honour of some Priest occupying it—his own patron or that of his parish being chosen. But in the presence of all the pilgrims our compartment was named after St. Martin! My Father, deeply touched by this compliment, went at once to thank Mgr.

Legoux, Vicar-General of Coutances and director of the pilgrimage. From this onwards he was often called "Monsieur Saint Martin."

Father Révérony watched my behaviour closely. I could tell that he was doing so; at table, if I were not opposite to him, he would lean forward to look at me and listen to what I was saying. I think he must have been satisfied with his investigations, for, towards the end of the journey, he seemed more favourably disposed. I say towards the end, for in Rome he was far from being my advocate, as I will tell you presently. Still I would not have it thought he deceived me in any way by falling short of the good will he had shown at Bayeux. On the contrary, I am sure that he always felt kindly towards me, and that if he opposed my wishes it was only to put me to the test.

On our way into Italy we passed through Switzerland, with its high mountains, their snowy peaks lost in the clouds, its rushing torrents, and its deep valleys filled with giant ferns and purple heather. Great good was wrought in my soul by these beauties of nature so abundantly scattered abroad. They lifted it to Him Who had been pleased to lavish such masterpieces upon this transient earth.

Sometimes we were high up the mountain side, while at our feet an unfathomable abyss seemed ready to engulf us. A little later we were passing through a charming village with its cottages and graceful belfry, above which light fleecy clouds floated lazily. Farther on a great lake with its blue waters, so calm and clear, would blend with the glowing splendour of the setting sun. I cannot tell you how deeply I was impressed with this scenery so full of poetry and grandeur. It was a foretaste of the wonders of Heaven. Then the thought of religious life would come before me, as it really is, with its constraints and its little daily sacrifices made in secret. I understood how easily one might become wrapped in self and forget the sublime end of one's vocation, and I thought: "Later on, when the time of trial comes, when I am enclosed in the Carmel and shall only be able to see a little bit of sky, I will remember this day and it will encourage me. I will make light of my own small interests by thinking of the greatness and majesty of God; I will love Him alone, and will not be so foolish as to attach myself to the fleeting trifles of this world, now that my heart has had a glimpse of what is reserved for those who love Him."

After having contemplated the works of God, I turned next to admire those of His creatures. Milan was the first Italian town we visited, and we carefully studied its Cathedral of white marble, adorned with countless statues. Céline and I left the timid ones, who hid their faces in fear after climbing to the first stage, and, following the bolder pilgrims, we reached the top, from whence we viewed the city below. When we came down we started on the first of our expeditions; these lasted the whole month of the pilgrimage, and quite cured me of a desire to be always lazily riding in a carriage.

The "Campo Santo"[9] charmed us. The whole vast enclosure is covered with marble statues, so exquisitely carved as to be life-like, and placed with an apparent negligence that only enhances their charm. You feel almost tempted to console the imaginary personages that surround you, their expression so exactly portrays a calm and Christian sorrow. And what works of art! Here is a child putting flowers on its father's grave—one forgets how solid is marble—the delicate petals appear to slip through its fingers. Sometimes the light veils of the widows, and the ribbons of the young girls, seem floating on the breeze.

We could not find words to express our admiration, but an old gentleman who followed us everywhere—regretting no doubt his inability to share our sentiments—said in a tone of ill-temper: "Oh, what enthusiasts these French people are!" and yet he also was French. I think the poor man would have done better to stay at home. Instead of enjoying the journey he was always grumbling: nothing pleased him, neither cities, hotels, people, nor anything else. My Father, whose disposition was the exact opposite, was quite content, no matter what happened, and tried to cheer our friend, offering him his place in the carriage or elsewhere, and with his wonted goodness encouraging him to look on the bright side of things. But nothing could cheer him. How many different kinds of people we saw and how interesting it is to study the world when one is just about to leave it!

In Venice the scene changed completely. Instead of the bustle of a large city, silence reigned, broken only by the lapping of the waters and the cries of the gondoliers as they plied their oars; it is a city full of charm but full of sadness. Even the Palace of the Doges, splendid though it be, is sad; we walked through halls whose vaulted roofs have long since ceased to re-echo the voices of the governors in their sentences of life and death. Its dark dungeons are no longer a living tomb for unfortunate prisoners to pine within.

While visiting these dreadful prisons I fancied myself in the times of the martyrs, and gladly would I have chosen this sombre abode for my dwelling if there had been any question of confessing my faith. Presently the guide's voice roused me from my reverie, and I crossed the "Bridge of Sighs," so called because of the sighs uttered by the wretched prisoners as they passed from their dungeons to sentence and to death. After leaving Venice we visited Padua and there venerated the relic of St. Anthony's tongue; then Bologna, where St. Catherine's body rests. Her face still bears the impress of the kiss bestowed on her by the Infant Jesus.

I was indeed happy when on the way to Loreto. Our Lady had chosen an ideal spot in which to place her Holy House. Everything is poor, simple, and primitive; the women still wear the graceful dress of the country and have not, as in the large towns, adopted the modern Paris fashions. I found Loreto enchanting. And what shall I say of the Holy House? I was overwhelmed with emotion when I realised that I was under the very roof that had sheltered the Holy Family. I gazed on the same walls Our Lord had looked on. I trod the ground once moistened with the sweat of St. Joseph's toil, and saw the little chamber of the Annunciation, where the Blessed Virgin Mary held Jesus in her arms after she had borne Him there in her virginal womb. I even put my Rosary into the little porringer used by the Divine Child. How sweet those memories!

But our greatest joy was to receive Jesus in His own House, and thus become His living temple in the very place which He had honoured by His Divine Presence. According to Roman custom the Blessed Sacrament is reserved at one Altar in each Church, and there only is it given to the faithful. At Loreto this Altar was in the Basilica—which is built round the Holy House, enclosing it as a precious stone might be enclosed in a casket of white marble. The exterior mattered little to us, it was in the *diamond* itself that we wished to receive the Bread of Angels. My Father, with his habitual gentleness, followed the other pilgrims, but his daughters, less easily satisfied, went towards the Holy House.

God favoured us, for a Priest was on the point of celebrating Mass; we told him of our great wish, and he immediately asked for two hosts, which he placed on the paten. You may picture, dear Mother, the ecstatic happiness of that Communion; no words can describe it. What will be our joy when we communicate eternally in the dwelling of the King of Heaven? It will be undimmed by the grief of parting, and will know no end. His House will be ours for all eternity, and there will be no need to covet fragments from the walls hallowed by the Divine Presence. He will not give us His earthly Home—He only shows it to us to make us love poverty and the hidden life. What He has in store for us is the Palace of His Glory, where we shall no longer see Him veiled under the form of a child or the appearance of bread, but as He is, in the brightness of His Infinite Beauty.

Now I am going to tell you about Rome—Rome, where I thought to find comfort and where I found the cross. It was night when we arrived. I was asleep, and was awakened by the porters calling: "Roma!" The pilgrims caught up the cry and repeated: "Roma, Roma!" Then I knew that it was not a dream, I was really in Rome!

Our first day, and perhaps the most enjoyable, was spent outside the walls. There, everything retains its stamp of antiquity, whilst in Rome, with its hotels and shops, one might fancy oneself in

Paris. This drive in the Roman Campagna has left a specially delightful impression on my mind.

How shall I describe the feelings which thrilled me when I gazed on the Coliseum? At last I saw the arena where so many Martyrs had shed their blood for Christ. My first impulse was to kiss the ground sanctified by their glorious combats. But what a disappointment! The soil has been raised, and the real arena is now buried at the depth of about twenty-six feet.

As the result of excavations the centre is nothing but a mass of rubbish, and an insurmountable barrier guards the entrance; in any case no one dare penetrate into the midst of these dangerous ruins. But was it possible to be in Rome and not go down to the real Coliseum? No, indeed! And I no longer listened to the guide's explanations: one thought only filled my mind—I must reach the arena.

We are told in the Gospel that St. Mary Magdalen remained close to the Sepulchre and stooped down constantly to look in; she was rewarded by seeing two Angels. So, like her, I kept stooping down and I saw, not two Angels, but what I was in search of. I uttered a cry of joy and called out to my sister: "Come, follow me, we shall be able to get through."

We hurried on at once, scrambling over the ruins which crumbled under our feet. Papa, aghast at our boldness, called out to us, but we did not hear.

As the warriors of old felt their courage grow in face of peril, so our joy increased in proportion to the fatigue and danger we had to face to attain the object of our desires. Céline, more foreseeing than I, had listened to the guide. She remembered that he had pointed out a particular stone marked with a cross, and had told us it was the place where the Martyrs had fought the good fight. She set to work to find it, and having done so we threw ourselves on our knees on this sacred ground. Our souls united in one and the same prayer. My heart beat violently when I pressed my lips to the dust reddened with the blood of the early Christians. I begged for the grace to be a martyr for Jesus, and I felt in the depths of my heart that my prayer was heard. All this took but a short time. After collecting some stones we approached the walls once more to face the danger. We were so happy that Papa had not the heart to scold us, and I could see that he was proud of our courage.

From the Coliseum we went to the Catacombs, and there Céline and I laid ourselves down in what had once been the tomb of St. Cecilia, and took some of the earth sanctified by her holy remains. Before our journey to Rome I had not felt any special devotion to St. Cecilia, but on visiting the house where she was martyred, and hearing her proclaimed "Queen of harmony"—because of the sweet song she sang in her heart to her Divine Spouse—I felt more than devotion towards her, it was real love as for a friend. She became my chosen patroness, and the keeper of all my secrets; her abandonment to God and her boundless confidence delighted me beyond measure. They were so great that they enabled her to make souls pure which had never till then desired aught but earthly pleasures.

St. Cecilia is like the Spouse in the Canticles. I find in her the Scriptural "choir in an armed camp." [10] Her life was one melodious song in the midst of the greatest trials; and this is not strange, because we read that "the Book of the Holy Gospels lay ever on her heart,"[11] while in her heart reposed the Spouse of Virgins.

Our visit to the Church of St. Agnes was also very delightful. I tried, but without success, to obtain a relic to take back to my little Mother, Sister Agnes of Jesus. Men refused me, but God Himself came to my aid: a little bit of red marble, from an ancient mosaic dating back to the time of the sweet martyr, fell as my feet. Was this not touching? St. Agnes herself gave me a keepsake from her house.

We spent six days in visiting the great wonders in Rome, and on the seventh saw the greatest of all—Leo XIII. I longed for, yet dreaded, that day, for on it depended my vocation. I had received no answer from the Bishop of Bayeux, and so the Holy Father's permission was my one and only hope. But in order to obtain this permission I had first to ask it. The mere thought made me tremble, for I must dare speak to the Pope, and that, in presence of many Cardinals, Archbishops, and Bishops!

On Sunday morning, November 20, we went to the Vatican, and were taken to the Pope's private chapel. At eight o'clock we assisted at his Mass, during which his fervent piety, worthy of the Vicar of Christ, gave evidence that he was in truth the "Holy Father."

The Gospel for that day contained these touching words: "Fear not, little flock, for it hath pleased your Father to give you a Kingdom."[12] My heart was filled with perfect confidence. No, I would not fear, I would trust that the Kingdom of the Carmel would soon be mine. I did not think of those other words of Our Lord: "I dispose to you, as my Father hath disposed to Me, a Kingdom."[13] That is to say, I will give you crosses and trials, and thus will you become worthy to possess My Kingdom. *If you desire to sit on His right hand you must drink the chalice which He has drunk Himself.*[14] "Ought not Christ to have suffered these things, and so to enter into His glory?"[15]

A Mass of thanksgiving followed, and then the audience began. Leo XIII, whose cassock and cape were of white, was seated on a raised chair, and round him were grouped various dignitaries of the church. According to custom each visitor knelt in turn and kissed, first the foot and next the hand of the venerable Pontiff, and finally received his blessing; then two of the Noble Guard signed to the pilgrim that he must rise and pass on to the adjoining room to make way for those who followed.

No one uttered a word, but I was firmly determined to speak, when suddenly the Vicar-General of Bayeux, Father Révérony, who was standing at the Pope's right hand, told us in a loud voice that he absolutely forbade anyone to address the Holy Father. My heart beat fast. I turned to Céline, mutely inquiring what I should do. "Speak!" she said.

The next moment I found myself on my knees before the Holy Father. I kissed his foot and he held out his hand; then raising my eyes, which were filled with tears, I said entreatingly: "Holy Father, I have a great favour to ask you." At once he bent towards me till his face almost touched mine, and his piercing black eyes seemed to read my very soul. "Holy Father," I repeated, "in honour of your jubilee, will you allow me to enter the Carmel when I am fifteen?"

The Vicar-General, surprised and displeased, said quickly: "Holy Father, this is a child who desires to become a Carmelite, but the Superiors of the Carmel are looking into the matter." "Well, my child," said His Holiness, "do whatever the Superiors decide." Clasping my hands and resting them on his knee, I made a final effort: "Holy Father, if only you say 'yes,' everyone else would agree."

He looked at me fixedly and said clearly and emphatically: "Well, well! You will enter if it is God's Will." I was going to speak again, when the Noble Guards motioned to me. As I paid little attention they came forward, the Vicar-General with them, for I was still kneeling before the Pope with my hands resting on his knee. Just as I was forced to rise, the dear Holy Father gently placed his hand on my lips, then lifted it to bless me, letting his eyes follow me for quite a long time.

My Father was much distressed to find me coming from the audience in tears; he had passed out before me, and so did not know anything about my request. The Vicar-General had shown him unusual kindness, presenting him to Leo XIII as the father of two Carmelites. The Sovereign Pontiff, as a special sign of benevolence, had placed his hand on his head, thus appearing in the name of Christ Himself to mark him with a mysterious seal. But now that this father of *four* Carmelites is in Heaven, it is no longer the hand of Christ's Vicar which rests on his brow, prophesying his martyrdom: it is the hand of the Spouse of Virgins, of the King of Heaven; and this Divine Hand will never be taken away from the head which it has blessed.

This trial was indeed a heavy one, but I must admit that in spite of my tears I felt a deep inward peace, for I had made every effort in my power to respond to the appeal of my Divine Master. This peace, however, dwelt in the depths of my soul—on the surface all was bitterness; and Jesus was silent—absent it would seem, for nothing revealed that He was there.

On that day, too, the sun dared not shine, and the beautiful blue sky of Italy, hidden by dark clouds, mingled its tears with mine. All was at an end. My journey had no further charm for me since it had failed in its object. It is true the Holy Father's words: "You will enter if it is God's Will," should have consoled me, they were indeed a prophecy. In spite of all these obstacles, what God in His goodness willed, has come to pass. He has not allowed His creatures to do what they will but only what He wills. Sometime before this took place I had offered myself to the Child Jesus to be His little plaything. I told Him not to treat me like one of those precious toys which children only look at and dare not touch, but to treat me like a little ball of no value, that could be thrown on the ground, kicked about, pierced, left in a corner, or pressed to His Heart just as it might please Him. In a word I wished to amuse the Holy child and to let Him play with me as He fancied. Here indeed He was answering my prayer. In Rome Jesus pierced His little plaything. He wanted to see what was inside . . . and when satisfied, He let it drop and went to sleep. What was He doing during His sweet slumber, and what became of the ball thus cast on one side? He dreamed that He was still at play, that He took it up or threw it down, that He rolled it far away, but at last He pressed it to His Heart, nor did He allow it again to slip from His tiny Hand. Dear Mother, you can imagine the sadness of the little ball lying neglected on the ground! And yet it continued to hope against hope.

After our audience my Father went to call on Brother Simeon—the founder and director of St. Joseph's College—and there he met Father Révérony. He reproached him gently for not having helped me in my difficult task, and told the whole story to Brother Simeon. The good old man listened with much interest and even made notes, saying with evident feeling: "This kind of thing is not seen in Italy."

The next day we started for Naples and Pompeii. Vesuvius did us the honour of emitting from its crater a thick volume of smoke, accompanied by numerous loud reports. The traces of the devastation of Pompeii are terrifying. They show forth the power of God: "He looketh upon the earth, and maketh it tremble; He toucheth the mountains and they smoke."

I should like to have wandered alone among its ruins, meditating on the instability of human things, but such solitude was not to be thought of.

At Naples we made an expedition to the monastery of San Martino; it crowns a high hill overlooking the whole city. On the way back the horses took the bit in their teeth, and it is solely to our Guardian Angels that I attribute our safe return to the splendid hotel. This word "splendid" is not too strong to describe it; in fact during the whole journey we stayed only at the most expensive hotels. I had never been surrounded by such luxury, but it is indeed a true saying that riches do not make happiness. I should have been a thousand times more contented under a thatched room, with the hope of entering the Carmel, than I was amid marble staircases, gilded ceilings, and silken hangings, with my heart full of sorrow.

I realised thoroughly that joy is not found in the things which surround us, but lives only in the soul. One could possess it as well in an obscure prison as in the palace of a king. And so now I am happier at the Carmel, in the midst of trials within and without, than I was in the world where I had everything I wanted, and, above all, the joys of a happy home.

Although I felt heavy of heart, outwardly I was as usual, for I thought no one had any knowledge of my petition to the Pope. I was mistaken. One day, when the other pilgrims had gone to the refreshment-room and Céline and I were alone, Mgr. Legoux came to the door of the carriage. He looked at me attentively and smiling said: "Well, and how is our little Carmelite?" This showed me that my secret was known to all the pilgrims, and I gathered it, too, from their kindly looks; but happily no one spoke to me on the subject.

At Assisi I had a little adventure. While visiting the places sanctified by the virtues of St. Francis and St. Clare I lost the buckle of my belt in the monastery. It took me some time to find and put it back in place, and when I reached the door all the carriages had started except one; that belonged to the Vicar-General of Bayeux! Should I run after those which were no longer in sight and so perhaps miss the train, or should I beg for a seat in the carriage of Father Révérony? I decided that this was the wiser plan.

I tried to hide my extreme embarrassment and explained things. He was placed in a difficulty himself, for all the seats were occupied, but one of the party promptly gave me his place and sat by the driver. I felt like a squirrel caught in a snare. I was ill at ease in the midst of these great people, and I had to sit face to face with the most formidable of all. He was exceedingly kind, however, and now and then interrupted his conversation to talk to me about the Carmel and promise that he would do all in his power to realise my desire of entering at fifteen. This meeting was like balm to my wounds, though it did not prevent me from suffering. I had now lost all trust in creatures and could only lean on God Himself.

And yet my distress did not hinder me from taking a deep interest in the holy places we visited. In Florence we saw the shrine of St. Mary Magdalen of Pazzi, in the choir of the Carmelite Church. All the pilgrims wanted to touch the Saint's tomb with their Rosaries, but my hand was the only one small enough to pass through the grating. So I was deputed for this important and lengthy task, and I did it with pride.

It was not the first time I had obtained special favours. One day, at *Santa Croce,* in Rome, we venerated the relics of the True Cross, together with two of the Thorns, and one of the Sacred Nails. I wanted to examine them closely, so I remained behind, and when the monk in charge was going to replace them on the Altar, I asked if I might touch the precious treasures. He said I might do so, but was doubtful if I should succeed; however, I put my little finger into one of the openings of the reliquary and was able to touch the Sacred Nail once hallowed by the Blood of Our Saviour. You see I behaved towards Him like a child who thinks it may do as it pleases and looks on its Father's treasures as its own.

Having passed through Pisa and Genoa we came back to France by one of the loveliest routes. At times we were close to the sea, and one day during a storm it seemed as though the waves would reach the train. Farther on we travelled through plains covered with orange trees, olives, and feathery palms, while at night the numerous seaports twinkled with lights, and stars came out in the deep blue sky. But I watched the fairy picture fade away from my eyes without any regret—my heart was set elsewhere.

My Father proposed to take me to Jerusalem, but in spite of the natural wish I had to visit the places sanctified by Our Lord's Footsteps, I was weary of earthly pilgrimages and only longed for the beauties of Heaven. In order to win these beauties for souls I wanted to become a prisoner as quickly as possible. I felt that I must suffer and struggle still more before the gates of my blessed prison would open; yet my trust in God did not grow less, and I still hoped to enter at Christmas.

We had hardly reached home when I paid a visit to the Carmel. You must remember well that interview, dear Mother. I left myself entirely in your hands, for I had exhausted all my resources. You told me to write to the Bishop and remind him of his promise. I obeyed at once, and as soon as my letter was posted I felt I should obtain the coveted permission without any delay. Alas! each day brought fresh disappointments. The beautiful feast of Christmas dawned; still Jesus slept. He left His little ball on the ground without even glancing that way.

This was indeed a sore trial, but Our Lord, Whose Heart is always watching, taught me that He granted miracles to those whose faith is small as a grain of mustard seed, in the hope of strengthening this slender faith; whilst for His intimate friends, for His Mother, He did not work miracles till He had proved their faith. Did He not permit Lazarus to die even though Mary and Martha had sent word that he was sick? And at the marriage feast of Cana, when Our Lady asked her Divine Son to aid the master of the house, did He not answer that His hour had not yet come? But after the trial what a reward! Water is changed into wine, and Lazarus rises from the dead. In this way did my Beloved act with His little Thérèse; after He had tried her for a long time He granted all her desires.

For my New Year's gift of 1888, Jesus again gave me His Cross. You told me, dear Mother, that you had had the Bishop's answer since December 28, the feast of Holy Innocents; that he authorised my immediate entry into the Carmel, but that nevertheless you had decided not to open its doors till after Lent. I could not restrain my tears at the thought of such a long delay. This trial affected me in a special manner, for I felt my earthly ties were severed, and yet the Ark in its turn refused to admit the poor little dove.

How did these three months pass? They were fruitful in sufferings and still more so in other graces. At first the thought came into my mind that I would not put any extra restraint on myself, I would lead a life somewhat less strictly ordered than was my custom. But Our Lord made me understand the benefit I might derive from this time He had granted me, and I then resolved to give myself up to a more serious and mortified life. When I say mortified, I do not mean that I imitated the penances of the Saints; far from resembling those beautiful souls who have practised all sorts of mortifications from their infancy, I made mine consist in simply checking my inclinations, keeping back an impatient answer, doing little services to those around me without setting store thereby, and a hundred other things of the kind. By practising these trifles I prepared myself to become the Spouse of Jesus, and I can never tell you, Mother, how much the added delay helped me to grow in abandonment, in humility, and in other virtues.

---

[1] Joel 2:19.

[2] *Imitation of Christ*, III, xxiv. 2.

[3] Isa. 65:15.

[4] Apoc. 2:17.

[5] 1 Cor. 4:5.

[6] Matt. 5:13.

[7] Tit. 1:15.

[8] Montmartre—the "Mount of Martyrs"—is the hill whereon St. Denis, apostle and bishop of Paris, was martyred with his two companions in the third

century. It was a famous place of pilgrimage in medieval times, and here St. Ignatius and the first Jesuits took their vows. Under the presidency of Marshal MacMahon, the erection of the well-known Basilica was voted in 1873 by the French Chamber of Deputies as a national act of reparation to the Sacred Heart. [Ed.]

[9] Cemetery.

[10] Cf. Cant. 7:1.

[11] Office of St. Cecilia.

[12] Luke 12:32.

[13] Luke 22:29.

[14] Cf. Matt. 20:22.

[15] Luke 24:26.

CHAPTER VII THE LITTLE FLOWER ENTERS THE CARMEL

Monday, April 9, 1888, being the Feast of the Annunciation, transferred from Passiontide, was the day chosen for me to enter the Carmel. On the evening before, we were gathered around the table where I was to take my place for the last time. These farewells are in themselves heartrending, and just when I would have liked to be forgotten I received the tenderest expressions of affection, as if to increase the pain of parting.

The next morning, after a last look at the happy home of my childhood, I set out for the Carmel, where we all heard Mass. At the moment of Communion, when Jesus had entered our hearts, I heard sobs on all sides. I did not shed a tear, but as I led the way to the cloister door my heart beat so violently that I wondered if I were going to die. Oh, the agony of that moment! One must have experienced it in order to understand. I embraced all my dear ones and knelt for my Father's blessing. He, too, knelt down and blessed me through his tears. It was a sight to gladden the Angels, this old man giving his child to God while she was yet in the springtime of life. At length the doors of the Carmel closed upon me. . . . I found a welcome in your arms, dear Mother, and received the embraces of another family, whose devotedness and love is not dreamt of by the outside world.

At last my desires were realised, and I cannot describe the deep sweet peace which filled my soul. This peace has remained with me during the eight and a half years of my life here, and has never left me even amid the greatest trials.

Everything in the Convent delighted me, especially our little cell.[1] I fancied myself transported to the desert. I repeat that my happiness was calm and peaceful—not even the lightest breeze ruffled the tranquil waters on which my little barque sailed; no cloud darkened the blue sky. I felt fully recompensed for all I had gone through, and I kept saying: "Now I am here for ever." Mine was no passing joy, it did not fade like first illusions. From illusions God in His Mercy has ever preserved me. I found the religious life just what I expected, and sacrifice was never a matter of surprise. Yet you know well that from the beginning my ways was strewn with thorns rather than with roses.

In the first place, my soul had for its daily food the bread of spiritual dryness. Then, too, dear Mother, Our Lord allowed you, unconsciously, to treat me very severely. You found fault with me whenever you met me. I remember once I had left a cobweb in the cloister, and you said to me before the whole community: "It is easy to see that our cloisters are swept by a child of fifteen. It is disgraceful! Go and sweep away that cobweb, and be more careful in future."

On the rare occasions when I spent an hour with you for spiritual direction, you seemed to be scolding me nearly all the time, and what pained me most of all was that I did not see how to correct my faults: for instance, my slow ways and want of thoroughness in my duties, faults which you were careful to point out.

One day it occurred to me that you would certainly prefer me to spend my free time in work instead of in prayer, as was my custom; so I plied my needle industriously without even raising my eyes. No one ever knew of this, as I wished to be faithful to Our Lord and do things solely for Him to see.

When I was a postulant our Mistress used to send me every afternoon at half-past four to weed the garden. This was a real penance, the more so, dear Mother, because I was almost sure to meet you on the way, and once you remarked: "Really, this child does absolutely nothing. What are we to think of a novice who must have a walk every day?" And yet, dear Mother, how grateful I am to you for giving me such a sound and valuable training. It was an inestimable grace. What should I have become, if, as the world outside believed, I had been but the pet of the Community? Perhaps, instead of seeing Our Lord in the person of my superiors, I should only have considered the creature, and my heart, which had been so carefully guarded in the world, would have been ensnared by human affection in the cloister. Happily, your motherly prudence saved me from such a disaster.

And not only in this matter, but in other and more bitter trials, I can truly say that Suffering opened her arms to me from the first, and I took her to my heart. In the solemn examination before my profession I declared—as was customary—the reason of my entry into the Carmel: "I have come to save souls, and especially to pray for Priests." One cannot attain the end without adopting the means, and as Our Lord made me understand that it was by the Cross He would give me souls, the more crosses I met with, the stronger grew my attraction to suffering. For five years this way was mine, but I alone knew it; this was precisely the flower I wished to offer to Jesus, a hidden flower which keeps its perfume only for Heaven.

Two months after my entry Father Pichon was surprised at the workings of grace in my soul; he thought my piety childlike and my path an easy one. My conversation with this good Father would have brought me great comfort, had it not been for the extreme difficulty I found in opening my heart. Nevertheless I made a general confession, and after it he said to me: "Before God, the Blessed Virgin, and Angels, and all the Saints, I declare that you have never committed a mortal sin. Thank God for the favours He has so freely bestowed on you without any merit on your part."

Without any merit on my part! That was not difficult to believe. Fully conscious of my weakness and imperfection, my heart overflowed with gratitude. I had distressed myself, fearing I might have stained my baptismal robe, and this assurance, coming as it did from the lips of a director, a man of wisdom and holiness, such as our Mother St. Teresa desired, seemed to come from God Himself. Father Pichon added: "May Our Lord always be your Superior and your Novice Master!" And indeed He ever was, and likewise my Director. In saying this I do not mean to imply that I was not communicative with my superiors; far from being reserved, I always tried to be as an open book.

Our Mistress was a true saint, the perfect type of the first Carmelites, and I seldom left her side, for she had to teach me how to work. Her kindness was beyond words, I loved and appreciated her, and yet my soul did not expand. I could not explain myself, words failed me, and so the time of spiritual direction became a veritable martyrdom.

One of the older nuns seemed to understand what I felt, for she once said to me during recreation: "I should think, child, you have not much to tell your superiors." "Why do you think that, dear Mother?" I asked. "Because your soul is very simple; but when you are perfect you will become more simple still. The nearer one approaches God, the simpler one becomes."

This good Mother was right. Nevertheless the great difficulty I found in opening my heart, though it came from simplicity, was a genuine trial. Now, however, without having lost my simplicity, I am able to express my thoughts with the greatest ease.

I have already said that Our Lord Himself had acted as my Spiritual Guide. Hardly had Father Pichon become my director when his Superiors sent him to Canada. I was only able to hear from him once in the year, so now the Little Flower which had been transplanted to the mountain of Carmel quickly turned to the Director of Directors, and unfolded itself under the shadow of His Cross, having for refreshing dew His Tears, His Precious Blood, and for radiant sun His Adorable Face.

Until then I had not appreciated the beauties of the Holy Face; it was my dear Mother, Agnes of Jesus, who unveiled them to me. As she had been the first of her sisters to enter the Carmel, so she was the first to penetrate the mysteries of love hidden in the Face of Our Divine Spouse. Then she showed them to me and I understood better than ever, in what true glory consists. He whose "Kingdom is not of this world"[2] taught me that the only royalty to be coveted lies in being "unknown and esteemed as naught,"[3] and in the joy of self-abasement. And I wished that my face, like the Face of Jesus, "should be, as it were, hidden and despised,"[4] so that no one on earth should esteem me. I thirsted to suffer and to be forgotten.

Most merciful has been the way by which the Divine Master has ever led me. He has never inspired me with any desire and left it unsatisfied, and that is why I have always found His bitter chalice full of sweetness.

At the end of May, Marie, our eldest, was professed, and Thérèse, the Benjamin, had the privilege of crowning her with roses on the day of her mystical espousals. After this happy feast trials again came upon us. Ever since his first attack of paralysis we realised that my Father was very easily tired. During our journey to Rome I often noticed that he seemed exhausted and in pain. But, above all, I remarked his progress in the path of holiness; he had succeeded in obtaining a complete mastery over the impetuosity of his natural disposition, and earthly things were unable to ruffle his calm. Let me give you an instance.

During our pilgrimage we were in the train for days and nights together, and to wile away the time our companions played cards, and occasionally grew very noisy. One day they asked us to join them, but we refused, saying we knew little about the game; we did not find the time long—only too short, indeed, to enjoy the beautiful views which opened before us. Presently their annoyance became evident, and then dear Papa began quietly to defend us, pointing out that as we were on pilgrimage, more of our time might be given to prayer.

One of the players, forgetting the respect due to age, called out thoughtlessly: "Thank God, Pharisees are rare!" My Father did not answer a word, he even seemed pleased; and later on he found an opportunity of shaking hands with this man, and of speaking so pleasantly that the latter must have thought his rude words had either not been heard, or at least were forgotten.

His habit of forgiveness did not date from this day; my Mother and all who knew him bore witness that no uncharitable word ever passed his lips.

His faith and generosity were likewise equal to any trial. This is how he announced my departure to one of his friends: "Thérèse, my little Queen, entered the Carmel yesterday. God alone could ask such a sacrifice; but He helps me so mightily that even in the midst of tears my heart is overflowing with joy."

This faithful servant must needs receive a reward worthy of his virtues, and he himself claimed that reward. You remember the interview when he said to us: "Children, I have just come back from Alençon, and there, in the Church of Notre Dame, I received such graces and consolations that I made this prayer: 'My God, it is too much, yes, I am too happy; I shall not get to Heaven like this, I wish to suffer something for Thee—and I offered myself as a'"—the word *victim* died on his lips. He dared not pronounce it before us, but we understood. You know, dear Mother, the story of our trial; I need not recall its sorrowful details.

And now my clothing day drew near. Contrary to all expectations, my Father had recovered from a second attack, and the Bishop fixed the ceremony for January 10. The time of waiting had been long indeed, but now what a beautiful feast! Nothing was wanting, not even snow.

Do you remember my telling you, dear Mother, how fond I am of snow? While I was still quite small, its whiteness entranced me. Why had I such a fancy for snow? Perhaps it was because, being a little winter flower, my eyes first saw the earth clad in its beautiful white mantle. So, on my clothing day, I wished to see it decked, like myself, in spotless white. The weather was so mild that it might have been spring, and I no longer dared hope for snow. The morning of the feast brought no change and I gave up my childish desire, as impossible to be realised. My Father came to meet me at the enclosure door, his eyes full of tears, and pressing me to his heart exclaimed: "Ah! Here is my little Queen!" Then, giving me his arm, we made our solemn entry into the public Chapel. This was his day of triumph, his last feast on earth; now his sacrifice was complete, and his children belonged to God.[5] Céline had already confided to him that later on she also wished to leave the world for the Carmel. On hearing this he was beside himself with joy: "Let us go before the Blessed Sacrament," he said, "and thank God for all the graces He has granted us and the honour He has paid me in choosing His Spouses from my household. God has indeed done me great honour in asking for my children. If I possessed anything better I would hasten to offer it to Him." That something better was himself, "and God received him as a victim of holocaust; He tried him as gold in the furnace, and found him worthy of Himself."[6]

After the ceremony in the Chapel I re-entered the Convent and the Bishop intoned the *Te Deum*. One of the Priests observed to him that this hymn of thanksgiving was only sung at professions, but, once begun, it was continued to the end. Was it not right that this feast should be complete, since in it all other joyful days were reunited?

The instant I set foot in the enclosure again my eyes fell on the statue of the Child Jesus smiling on me amid the flowers and lights; then, turning towards the quadrangle, I saw that, in spite of the mildness of the weather, it was covered with snow. What a delicate attention on the part of Jesus! Gratifying the least wish of His little Spouse, He even sent her this. Where is the creature so mighty that he can make one flake of it fall to please his beloved?

Everyone was amazed, and since then many people, hearing of my desire, have described this event as "the little miracle" of my clothing day, and thought it strange I should be so fond of snow. So much the better, it shows still more the wonderful condescension of the Spouse of Virgins—of Him Who loves lilies white as the snow. After the ceremony the Bishop entered. He gave me many proofs of his fatherly tenderness, and, in presence of all the Priests, spoke of my visit to Bayeux and the journey to Rome; nor did he forget to tell them how I had put up my hair before visiting him. Then, laying his hand on my head, he blessed me affectionately. My mind dwelt with ineffable sweetness on the caresses Our Lord will soon lavish upon me before all the Saints, and this consoling thought was a foretaste of Heaven. I have just said that January 10 was a day of triumph for my dear

Father. I liken it to the feast of the entry of Christ into Jerusalem, on Palm Sunday. As in the case of Our Divine Master, his day of triumph was followed by long days of sorrow; and, even as the agony of Jesus pierced the heart of His divine Mother, so our hearts were deeply wounded by the humiliations and sufferings of him, whom we loved best on earth. . . . I remember that in the month of June 1888, when we were fearing another stroke of paralysis, I surprised our Novice Mistress by saying: "I am suffering a great deal, Mother, yet I feel I can suffer still more." I did not then foresee the trial awaiting us. I did not know that on February 12, one month after my clothing day, our beloved Father would drink so deeply of such a bitter chalice. I no longer said I could suffer more, words cannot express our grief; nor shall I attempt to describe it here.

In Heaven, we shall enjoy dwelling on these dark days of exile. Yet the three years of my Father's martyrdom seem to me the sweetest and most fruitful of our lives. I would not exchange them for the most sublime ecstasies, and my heart cries out in gratitude for such a priceless treasure: "We have rejoiced for the days wherein Thou hast afflicted us."[7] Precious and sweet was this bitter cross, and our hearts only breathed out sighs of grateful love. We no longer walked—we ran, we flew along the path of perfection.

Léonie and Céline, though living in the world, were no longer of the world. The letters they wrote were full of the most edifying resignation. And what talks I had with Céline! Far from separating us, the grating of the Carmel united us more closely: the same thoughts, the same desires, the same love for Our Lord and for souls, made our very life. Not a word concerning things of earth entered into our conversation; but, just as in former days we lifted longing eyes to Heaven, so now our hearts strained after the joys beyond time and space, and, for the sake of an eternal happiness, we chose to suffer and be despised here below.

Though my suffering seemed to have reached its height, yet my attraction thereto did not grow less, and soon my soul shared in the trials my heart had to bear. My spiritual aridity increased, and I found no comfort either in Heaven or on earth; yet, amid these waters of tribulation that I had so thirsted for, I was the happiest of mortals.

Thus passed the time of my betrothal, too long a time for me. At the end of the year you told me, dear Mother, that I must not yet think of my profession, as our Ecclesiastical Superior expressly forbade it. I had therefore to wait for eight months more. At first I found it very difficult to be resigned to such a sacrifice, but divine light penetrated my soul before long.

At this time I was using for my meditations Surin's *Foundations of the Spiritual life*. One day during prayer, it was brought home to me that my too eager desire to take my vows was mingled with much self-love; as I belonged to Our Lord and was His little plaything to console and please Him, it was for me to do His Will, not for Him to do mine. I also understood that a bride would not be pleasing to the bridegroom on her wedding day were she not magnificently attired. But, what had I made ready? So I said to Our Lord: "I do not ask Thee to hasten the day of my profession, I will wait as long as Thou pleasest, only I cannot bear that through any fault of mine my union with Thee should be delayed; I will set to work and carefully prepare a wedding-dress enriched with diamonds and precious stones, and, when Thou findest it sufficiently rich, I am sure that nothing will keep Thee from accepting me as Thy Spouse."

I took up the task with renewed zest. Since my clothing day I had received abundant lights on religious perfection, chiefly concerning the vow of poverty. Whilst I was a postulant I liked to have nice things to use and to find everything needful ready to hand. Jesus bore with me patiently, for He gives His light little by little. At the beginning of my spiritual life, about the age of fourteen, I used to ask myself how, in days to come, I should more clearly understand the true meaning of perfection. I imagined I then understood it completely, but I soon came to realise that the more one advances along this path the farther one seems from the goal, and now I am resigned to be always imperfect, and I even find joy therein.

To return to the lessons which Our Lord taught me. One evening after Compline I searched in vain for our lamp on the shelves where they are kept, and, as it was the time of the "Great Silence," I could not recover it. I guessed rightly that a Sister, believing it to be her own, had taken it; but just on that evening I had counted much on doing some work, and was I to spend a whole hour in the dark on account of this mistake? Without the interior light of grace I should undoubtedly have pitied myself, but, with that light, I felt happy instead of aggrieved, and reflected that poverty consists in being deprived not only of what is convenient, but of what is necessary. And, in this exterior darkness, I found my soul illumined by a brightness that was divine.

At this time I was seized with a craving for whatever was ugly and inconvenient; and was thus quite pleased when a pretty little jug was taken from our cell and a large chipped one put in its place. I also tried hard not to make excuses, but I found this very difficult, especially with our Mistress; from her I did not like to hide anything.

My first victory was not a great one, but it cost me a good deal. A small jar, left behind a window, was found broken. No one knew who had put it there, but our Mistress was displeased, and, thinking I was to blame in leaving it about, told me I was very untidy and must be more careful in future. Without answering, I kissed the ground and promised to be more observant. I was so little advanced in virtue that these small sacrifices cost me dear, and I had to console myself with the thought that at the day of Judgment all would be known.

Above all I endeavoured to practise little hidden acts of virtue; thus I took pleasure in folding the mantles forgotten by the Sisters, and I sought for every possible occasion of helping them. One of God's gifts was a great attraction towards penance, but I was not permitted to satisfy it; the only mortification allowed me consisted in mortifying my self-love, and this did me far more good than bodily penance would have done.

However, Our Lady helped me with my wedding-dress, and, as soon as it was finished, every obstacle vanished and my profession was fixed for September 8, 1890.

All that I have set down in these few words would take many pages to relate; but those pages will never be read on earth. . . .

---

[1] Nuns, in the spirit of poverty, avoid using the word *my*, as denoting private possessions; so, later on, "our lamp," "our handkerchief," will occur. [Ed.]

[2] John 18:36.

[3] *Imit.*, I, ii. 3.

[4] Is. 53:3.

[5] Léonie, having entered an order too severe for her delicate health, had been obliged to return home to her Father. Later she became a Visitation nun at Caen, and took the name of Sister Frances Teresa.

[6] Cf. Wisdom 3:5,6.

[7] Ps. 89[90]:15.

CHAPTER VIII PROFESSION OF SOEUR THÉRÈSE

Need I tell you, dear Mother, about the retreat before my profession? Far from receiving consolation, I went through it in a state of utter dryness and as if abandoned by God. Jesus, as was His wont, slept in my little barque. How rarely do souls suffer Him to sleep in peace! This Good Master is so wearied with continually making fresh advances that He eagerly avails Himself of the repose I offer Him, and, no doubt, He will sleep on until my great and everlasting retreat; but, instead of being grieved at this, I am glad.

In truth I am no Saint, as this frame of mind well shows. I ought not to rejoice in my dryness of soul, but rather attribute it to my want of fervour and fidelity. That I fall asleep so often during meditation, and thanksgiving after Communion, should distress me. Well, I am not distressed. I reflect that little children are equally dear to their parents whether they are asleep or awake; that, in order to perform operations, doctors put their patients to sleep; and finally that "The Lord knoweth our frame, He remembereth that we are but dust."[1] Yet, apparently barren as was my retreat—and those which followed have been no less so—I unconsciously received many interior lights on the best means of pleasing God, and practising virtue. I have often observed that Our Lord will not give me any store of provisions, but nourishes me each moment with food that is ever new; I find it within me without knowing how it has come there. I simply believe that it is Jesus Himself hidden in my poor heart, who is secretly at work, inspiring me with what He wishes me to do as each occasion arises.

Shortly before my profession I received the Holy Father's blessing, through the hands of Brother Simeon; and this precious Blessing undoubtedly helped me through the most terrible storm of my whole life.

On the eve of the great day, instead of being filled with the customary sweetness, my vocation suddenly seemed to me as unreal as a dream. The devil—for it was he—made me feel sure that I was wholly unsuited for life in the Carmel, and that I was deceiving my superiors by entering on a way to which I was not called. The darkness was so bewildering that I understood but one thing—I had no religious vocation, and must return to the world. I cannot describe the agony I endured. What was I to do in such a difficulty? I chose the right course, deciding to tell my Novice Mistress of the temptation without delay. I sent for her to come out of choir, and though full of confusion, I confessed the state of my soul. Fortunately she saw more clearly than I did, and reassured me completely by laughing frankly at my story. The devil was put to instant flight by my humble avowal; what he wanted was to keep me from speaking, and thus draw me into his snares. But it was my turn now to ensnare him, for, to make my humiliation more complete, I also told you everything, dear Mother, and your consoling words dispelled my last fears.

On the morning of September 8, a wave of peace flooded my soul, and, in "that peace which surpasseth all understanding,"[2] I pronounced my holy vows.

Many were the graces I asked. I felt myself truly a queen and took advantage of my title to obtain every favour from the King for His ungrateful subjects. No one was forgotten. I wished that every sinner on earth might be converted; that on that day Purgatory should set its captives free; and I bore upon my heart this letter containing what I desired for myself:

"O Jesus, my Divine Spouse, grant that my baptismal robe may never be sullied. Take me from this world rather than let me stain my soul by committing the least wilful fault. May I never seek or find aught but Thee alone! May all creatures be nothing to me and I nothing to them! May no earthly thing disturb my peace!

"O Jesus, I ask but Peace. . . . Peace, and above all, Love. . . .
Love—without limit. Jesus, I ask that for Thy sake I may die a
Martyr; give me martyrdom of soul or body. Or rather give me both
the one and the other.

"Grant that I may fulfill my engagements in all their perfection; that no one may think of me; that I may be trodden under foot, forgotten, as a little grain of sand. I offer myself to Thee, O my Beloved, that Thou mayest ever perfectly accomplish in me Thy Holy Will, without let or hindrance from creatures."

When at the close of this glorious day I laid my crown of roses, according to custom, at Our Lady's feet, it was without regret. I felt that time would never lessen my happiness.

It was the Nativity of Mary. What a beautiful feast on which to become the Spouse of Jesus! It was the *little* new-born Holy Virgin who presented her *little* Flower to the *little* Jesus. That day everything was little except the graces I received—except my peace and joy in gazing upon the beautiful star-lit sky at night, and in thinking that soon I should fly away to Heaven and be united to my Divine Spouse amid eternal bliss.

On September 24 took place the ceremony of my receiving the veil. This feast was indeed *veiled* in tears. Papa was too ill to come and bless his little Queen; at the last minute Mgr. Hugonin, who should have presided, was unable to do so, and, for other reasons also, the day was a painful one. And yet amid it all, my soul was profoundly at peace. That day it pleased Our Lord that I should not be able to restrain my tears, and those tears were not understood. It is true I had borne far harder trials without shedding a tear; but then I had been helped by special graces, whilst on this day Jesus left me to myself, and I soon showed my weakness.

Eight days after I had taken the veil my cousin, Jeanne Guérin, was married to Dr. La Néele. When she came to see us afterwards and I heard of all the little attentions she lavished on her husband, my heart thrilled and I thought: "It shall never be said that a woman in the world does more for her husband than I do for Jesus, my Beloved." And, filled with fresh ardour, I set myself more earnestly than ever to please my Heavenly Spouse, the King of Kings, Who had deigned to honour me by a divine alliance.

Having seen the letter announcing the marriage, I amused myself by composing the following invitation, which I read to the novices in order to bring home to them what had struck me so forcibly — that the glory of all earthly unions is as nothing compared to the titles of a Spouse of Our Divine Lord.

"God Almighty, Creator of Heaven and Earth, Sovereign Ruler of the Universe, and the Glorious Virgin Mary, Queen of the Heavenly Court, announce to you the Spiritual Espousals of their August Son, Jesus, King of Kings and Lord of Lords, with little Thérèse Martin, now Princess and Lady of His Kingdoms of the Holy Childhood and the Passion, assigned to her as a dowry, by her Divine Spouse, from which Kingdoms she holds her titles of nobility—*of the Child Jesus and of the Holy Face*. It was not possible to invite you to the Wedding Feast which took place on the Mountain of Carmel, September 8, 1890—the Heavenly Court was alone admitted—but you are requested to be present at the Wedding Feast which will take place tomorrow, the day of Eternity, when Jesus, the Son of God, will come in the clouds of Heaven, in the splendour of His Majesty, to judge the living and the dead.

"The hour being still uncertain, you are asked to hold yourselves in readiness and watch."[3]

And now, Mother, what more shall I say? It was through your hands that I gave myself to Our Lord, and you have known me from childhood—need I write my secrets? Forgive me if I cut short the story of my religious life.

During the general retreat following my profession I received great graces. As a rule I find preached retreats most trying, but this one was quite an exception. I anticipated so much suffering that I prepared myself by a fervent novena. It was said that the good Priest understood better how to convert sinners than to direct the souls of nuns. Well then, I must be a great sinner, for God made use of this holy religious to bring me much consolation. At that time I had all kinds of interior trials which I found it impossible to explain to anyone; suddenly, I was able to lay open my whole soul. The Father understood me in a marvellous way; he seemed to divine my state, and launched me full sail upon that ocean of confidence and love in which I had longed to advance, but so far had not dared. He told me that my faults did not pain the Good God, and added: "At this moment I hold His place, and I assure you from Him that He is well pleased with your soul." How happy these consoling words made me! I had never been told before that it was possible for faults not to pain the Sacred Heart; this assurance filled me with joy and helped me to bear with patience the exile of this life. It was also the echo of my inmost thoughts. In truth I had long known that the Lord is more tender than a mother, and I have sounded the depths of more than one mother's heart. I know that a mother is ever ready to forgive her child's small thoughtless faults. How often have I not had this sweet experience! No reproach could have touched me more than one single kiss from my Mother. My nature is such that fear makes me shrink, while, under love's sweet rule, I not only advance—I fly.

Two months after this happy retreat our Venerable Foundress, Mother Genevieve of St. Teresa, quitted our little convent to enter the Heavenly Carmel. Before speaking of my impressions at the time of her death, I should like to tell you what a joy it was to have lived for some years with a soul whose holiness was not inimitable, but lay in the practice of simple and hidden virtues. More than once she was to me a source of great consolation.

One Sunday I went to the infirmary to pay her a visit, but, as two of the older nuns were there, I was retiring quietly, when she called me and said, with something of inspiration in her manner: "Wait, my child, I have just a word for you; you are always asking me for a spiritual bouquet, well, to-day I give you this one: Serve the Lord in peace and in joy. Remember that Our God is the God of peace."

I thanked her quite simply and went out of the room. I was moved almost to tears, and was convinced that God had revealed to her the state of my soul. That day I had been sorely tried, almost to sadness. Such was the darkness that I no longer knew if I were beloved of God, and so, dear Mother, you can understand what light and consolation succeeded this gloom.

The following Sunday I asked her whether she had received any revelation about me, but she assured me that she had not, and this only made me admire her the more, for it showed how intimately Jesus lived in her soul and directed her words and actions. Such holiness seems to me the most true, the most holy; it is the holiness I desire, for it is free from all illusion.

On the day when this revered Mother ended her exile, I received a very special grace. It was the first time I had assisted at a death-bed, yet though the sight enchanted me by its beauty, my two hours of watching had made me very drowsy. I was grieved at this, but, at the moment her soul took its flight to Heaven, my feelings were completely changed. In an instant I was filled with an indescribable joy and fervour, as if the soul of our blessed Foundress made me share in the happiness she already enjoyed—for I am quite convinced she went straight to Heaven. I had said to her some time previously: "You will not go to Purgatory, dear Mother." "I hope not," she answered sweetly. Certainly God would not disappoint a hope so full of humility; and the proof that He did not, lies in the many favours we have received.

The Sisters hastened to claim something belonging to our beloved Mother, and you know what a precious relic is mine. During her agony I had noticed a tear glistening like a beautiful diamond. That tear, the last she shed on this earth, did not fall, I still saw it shining when her body was exposed in the choir. When evening came, I made bold to approach unseen, with a little piece of linen, and I now have the happiness of possessing the last tear of a Saint.

I attach no importance to my dreams, and indeed, they seldom have any special meaning, though I do often wonder how it is that, as I think of God all the day, my mind does not dwell on Him more in my sleep. Generally I dream of the woods and the flowers, the brooks and the sea, and nearly always of pretty children; or I chase birds and butterflies such as I have never seen. But, if my dreams are sometimes poetical, they are never mystical.

However, one night after Mother Genevieve's death, I had a more consoling one. I thought I saw her giving to each of us something that had belonged to herself. When my turn came, her hands were empty, and I was afraid I was not to receive anything; but she looked at me lovingly, and said three times: "To you I leave my heart."

About a month after that seraphic death, towards the close of the year 1891, an epidemic of influenza raged in the Community; I only had it slightly and was able to be about with two other Sisters. It is impossible to imagine the heartrending state of our Carmel throughout those days of sorrow. The worst sufferers were nursed by those who could hardly drag themselves about; death was all around us, and, when a Sister had breathed her last, we had to leave her instantly.

My nineteenth birthday was saddened by the death of Mother Sub-Prioress; I assisted with the infirmarian during her agony, and two more deaths quickly followed. I now had to do the Sacristy work single-handed, and I wonder sometimes how I was equal to it all.

One morning, when it was time to rise, I had a presentiment that Sister Magdalen was no more. The dormitory was quite in darkness, no one was leaving her cell. I decided, however, to go in to Sister Magdalen, and I found her dressed, but lying dead on her bed. I was not in the least afraid, and running to the Sacristy I quickly brought a blessed candle, and placed on her head a wreath of roses. Amid all this desolation I felt the Hand of God and knew that His Heart was watching over us. Our dear Sisters left this life for a happier one without any struggle; an expression of heavenly joy shone on their faces, and they seemed only to be enjoying a pleasant sleep. During all these long and trying weeks I had the unspeakable consolation of receiving Holy Communion every day. How sweet it was! For a long time Jesus treated me as a spoilt child, for a longer time than His more faithful Spouses. He came to me daily for several months after the influenza had ceased, a privilege not granted to the Community. I had not asked this favour, but I was unspeakably happy to be united day after day to my Beloved.

Great was my joy in being allowed to touch the Sacred Vessels and prepare the Altar linen on which Our Lord was to be laid. I felt that I must increase in fervour, and I often recalled those words addressed to deacons at their ordination: "Be you holy, you who carry the Vessels of the Lord."

What can I tell you, dear Mother, about my thanksgivings after Communion? There is no time when I taste less consolation. But this is what I should expect. I desire to receive Our Lord, not for my own satisfaction, but simply to give Him pleasure.

I picture my soul as a piece of waste ground and beg Our Blessed Lady to take away my imperfections—which are as heaps of rubbish—and to build upon it a splendid tabernacle worthy of Heaven, and adorn it with her own adornments. Then I invite all the Angels and Saints to come and sing canticles of love, and it seems to me that Jesus is well pleased to see Himself received so grandly, and I share in His joy. But all this does not prevent distractions and drowsiness from troubling me, and not unfrequently I resolve to continue my thanksgiving throughout the day, since I made it so badly in choir.

You see, dear Mother, that my way is not the way of fear; I can always make myself happy, and profit by my imperfections, and Our Lord Himself encourages me in this path. Once, contrary to my usual custom, I felt troubled when I approached the Holy Table. For several days there had not been a sufficient number of Hosts, and I had only received a small part of one; this morning I foolishly thought: "If the same thing happens to-day, I shall imagine that Jesus does not care to come into my heart." I approached the rails. What a joy awaited me! The Priest hesitated a moment, then gave me two entire Hosts. Was this not a sweet response?

I have much to be thankful for. I will tell you quite openly what the Lord has done for me. He has shown unto me the same mercy as unto King Solomon. All my desires have been satisfied; not only my desires of perfection, but even those of which I understood the vanity, in theory, if not in practice. I had always looked on Sister Agnes of Jesus as my model, and I wished to be like her in everything. She used to paint exquisite miniatures and write beautiful poems, and this inspired me with a desire to learn to paint,[4] and express my thoughts in verse, that I might do some good to those around me. But I would not ask for these natural gifts, and my desire remained hidden in my heart.

Jesus, too, had hidden Himself in this poor little heart, and He was pleased to show me once more the vanity of all that passes. To the great astonishment of the Community, I succeeded in painting several pictures and in writing poems which have been a help to certain souls. And just as Solomon, "turning to all the works which his hand had wrought, and to the labours wherein he had laboured in vain, saw in all things vanity and vexation of mind,"[5] so experience showed me that the sole happiness of earth consists in lying hidden, and remaining in total ignorance of created things. I understood that without love even the most brilliant deeds count for nothing. These gifts, which Our Lord lavished upon me, far from doing me any harm, drew me towards Him; I saw that He alone is unchangeable, He alone can fill the vast abyss of my desires.

Talking of my desires, I must tell you about others of quite a different kind, which the Divine Master has also been pleased to grant: childish desires, like the wish for snow on my clothing day. You know, dear Mother, how fond I am of flowers. When I made myself a prisoner at the age of fifteen, I gave up for ever the delights of rambling through meadows bright with the treasures of spring. Well, I never possessed so many flowers as I have had since entering the Carmel. In the world young men present their betrothed with beautiful bouquets, and Jesus did not forget me. For His Altar I received, in abundance, all the flowers I loved best: cornflowers, poppies, marguerites — one little friend only was missing, the purple vetch. I longed to see it again, and at last it came to gladden me and show that, in the least as in the greatest, God gives a hundred-fold, even in this life, to those who have left all for His Love.

But one desire, the dearest of all, and for many reasons the most difficult, remained unfulfilled. It was to see Céline enter the Carmel of Lisieux. However, I had made a sacrifice of my longing, and committed to God alone the future of my loved sister. I was willing she should be sent to far distant lands if it must be so; but I wanted above all things to see her like myself, the Spouse of Jesus. I suffered deeply, aware that she was exposed in the world to dangers I had never even known. My affection for her was maternal rather than sisterly, and I was filled with solicitude for the welfare of her soul.

She was to go one evening with my aunt and cousins to a dance. I know not why, but I felt more anxious than usual, and I shed many tears, imploring Our Lord to hinder her dancing. And this was just what happened; for He did not suffer His little Spouse to dance that evening, although as a rule she did so most gracefully. And, to the astonishment of everyone, her partner, too, found that he was only able to walk gravely up and down with Mademoiselle. The poor young man slipped away in confusion, and did not dare appear again that evening. This unique occurrence increased my confidence in Our Lord, and showed me clearly that He had already set His seal on my sister's brow.

On July 29, 1894, God called my saintly and much-tried Father to Himself. For the last two years of his life he was completely paralysed; so my uncle took him into his house and surrounded him with the tenderest care. He became quite helpless and was only able to visit us once during the whole course of his illness. It was a sad interview. At the moment of parting, as we said good-bye, he raised his eyes, and pointing upwards said in a voice full of tears: "In Heaven!"

Now that he was with God, the last ties which kept his consoling Angel in the world were broken. Angels do not remain on this earth; when they have accomplished their mission, they return instantly to Heaven. That is why they have wings. Céline tried therefore to fly to the Carmel; but the obstacles seemed insurmountable. One day, when matters were going from bad to worse, I said to Our Lord after Holy Communion: "Thou knowest, dear Jesus, how earnestly I have desired that the trials my Father endured should serve as his purgatory. I long to know if my wish is granted. I do not ask

Thee to speak to me, I only want a sign. Thou knowest how much opposed is Sister N. to Céline's entering; if she withdraw her opposition, I shall regard it as an answer from Thee, and in this way I shall know that my Father went straight to Heaven."

God, Who holds in His Hand the hearts of His creatures, and inclines them as He will, deigned in His infinite mercy and ineffable condescension to change that Sister's mind. She was the first person I met after my thanksgiving, and, with tears in her eyes, she spoke of Céline's entrance, which she now ardently desired. Shortly afterwards the Bishop set every obstacle aside, and then you were able, dear Mother, without any hesitation, to open our doors to the poor little exile.[6]

Now I have no desire left, unless it be to love Jesus even unto folly! It is Love alone that draws me. I no longer wish either for suffering or death, yet both are precious to me. Long did I call upon them as the messengers of joy. I have suffered much, and I have thought my barque near indeed to the Everlasting Shore. From earliest childhood I have imagined that the Little Flower would be gathered in its springtime; now, the spirit of self-abandonment alone is my guide. I have no other compass, and know not how to ask anything with eagerness, save the perfect accomplishment of God's designs upon my soul. I can say these words of the Canticle of our Father, St. John of the Cross:

"I drank deep in the cellar of my Friend, And, coming forth again,
Knew naught of all this plain, And lost the flock I erst was wont
to tend. My soul and all its wealth I gave to be His Own; No more
I tend my flock, all other work is done, And all my exercise is
Love alone."[7]

Or rather:

"Love hath so wrought in me Since I have known its sway, That all within me, whether good or ill, It makes subservient to the end it seeks, And soon transforms my soul into itself."[8]

Full sweet is the way of Love. It is true one may fall and be unfaithful to grace; but Love, knowing how to profit by everything, quickly consumes whatever is displeasing to Jesus, leaving in the heart only a deep and humble peace. I have obtained many spiritual lights through the works of St. John of the Cross. When I was seventeen and eighteen they were my only food; but, later on, and even now, all spiritual authors leave me cold and dry. However beautiful and touching a book may be, my heart does not respond, and I read without understanding, or, if I understand, I cannot meditate. In my helplessness the Holy Scriptures and the *Imitation* are of the greatest assistance; in them I find a hidden manna, genuine and pure. But it is from the Gospels that I find most help in the time of prayer; from them I draw all that I need for my poor soul. I am always discovering in them new lights and hidden mysterious meanings. I know and I have experienced that "the Kingdom of God is within us."[9] Our Lord has no need of books or teachers to instruct our souls. He, the Teacher of Teachers, instructs us without any noise of words. I have never heard Him speak, yet I know He is within me. He is there, always guiding and inspiring me; and just when I need them, lights, hitherto unseen, break in. This is not as a rule during my prayers, but in the midst of my daily duties. Sometimes, however, as this evening, at the close of a meditation spent in utter dryness, a word of comfort is given to me: "Here is the Master I give thee, He will teach thee all that thou shouldst do. I wish thee to read in the Book of Life in which is contained the science of love. . . ."[10]

The Science of Love! How sweetly do these words echo in my soul! That science alone do I desire. Having given all my substance for it, like the Spouse in the Canticles, "I think that I have given nothing."[11] After so many graces, may I not sing with the Psalmist that "the Lord is good, that His Mercy endureth for ever"?[12]

It seems to me that if everyone were to receive such favours God would be feared by none, but loved to excess; that no one would ever commit the least wilful fault—and this through love, not fear.

Yet all souls cannot be alike. It is necessary that they should differ from one another in order that each Divine Perfection may receive its special honour. To me, He has given His Infinite Mercy, and it is in this ineffable mirror that I contemplate his other attributes. Therein all appear to me radiant with Love. His Justice, even more perhaps than the rest, seems to me to be clothed with Love. What joy to think that Our Lord is just, that is to say, that He takes our weakness into account, that He knows perfectly the frailty of our nature! Of what, then, need I be afraid?

Will not the God of Infinite Justice, Who deigns so lovingly to pardon the sins of the Prodigal Son, be also just to me "who am always with Him"?[13]

In the year 1895 I received the grace to understand, more than ever, how much Jesus desires to be loved. Thinking one day of those who offer themselves as victims to the Justice of God, in order to turn aside the punishment reserved for sinners by taking it upon themselves, I felt this offering to be noble and generous, but was very far from feeling myself drawn to make it. "O my Divine Master," I cried from the bottom of my heart, "shall Thy Justice alone receive victims of holocaust? Has not Thy Merciful Love also need thereof? On all sides it is ignored, rejected . . . the hearts on which Thou wouldst lavish it turn to creatures, there to seek their happiness in the miserable satisfaction of a moment, instead of casting themselves into Thine Arms, into the unfathomable furnace of Thine Infinite Love.

"O my God! must Thy Love which is disdained lie hidden in Thy Heart? Methinks, if Thou shouldst find souls offering themselves as victims of holocaust to Thy Love, Thou wouldst consume them rapidly; Thou wouldst be well pleased to suffer the flames of infinite tenderness to escape that are imprisoned in Thy Heart.

"If Thy Justice—which is of earth—must needs be satisfied, how much more must Thy Merciful Love desire to inflame souls, since "*Thy mercy reacheth even to the Heavens*"?[14] O Jesus! Let me be that happy victim—consume Thy holocaust with the Fire of Divine Love!"

Dear Mother, you know the love, or rather the oceans of grace which flooded my soul immediately after I made that Act of Oblation on June 9, 1895. From that day I have been penetrated and surrounded with love. Every moment this Merciful Love renews me and purifies me, leaving in my soul no trace of sin. I cannot fear Purgatory; I know I do not merit to enter, even, into that place of expiation with the Holy Souls, but I also know that the fire of Love is more sanctifying than the fire of Purgatory. I know that Jesus could not wish useless suffering for us, and He would not inspire me with the desires I feel, were He not willing to fulfill them.

---

[1] Psalm 102[103]:14.

[2] Phil. 4:7.

[3] This letter, the style of which may seem strange to English ears, is modelled closely on the formal and quaint letters whereby French parents of the better class announce to their friends the marriage of their children. Such letters of "*faire-part*" are issued in the name of relatives to the third or fourth degree. [Ed.]

[4] Thérèse had kept this wish hidden in her heart from the days of her childhood, and later in life she made the following confidence: "I was ten the day Papa told Céline that she was to begin painting lessons. I felt quite envious. Then he turned to me and said: 'Well, little Queen, would you like to learn painting too?' I was going to say: 'Yes, indeed I should,' when Marie remarked that I had not the same taste for it as Céline. She carried her point, and I said nothing, thinking it was a splendid opportunity to make a big sacrifice for Our Lord; I was so anxious to learn, that even now I wonder how I was able to keep silence."

[5] Eccl. 2:11.

[6] Céline entered the Convent on September 14, 1894, and took the name of Sister Genevieve of St. Teresa.

[7] Spiritual Canticle: Stanzas 18 and 20.

[8] Hymn to the Deity.

[9] Luke 17:21.

[10] Revelation of Our Lord to Bd. Margaret Mary.

[11] Cant. 8:7.

[12] Psalm 103[104]:1.

[13] Luke 15:31.

[14] Cf. Psalm 35[36]:6.

CHAPTER IX THE NIGHT OF THE SOUL

Dear Mother, I thought I had written enough, and now you wish for more details of my religious life. I will not argue, but I cannot help smiling when I have to tell you things that you know quite as well as I do. Nevertheless, I will obey. I do not ask what use this manuscript can be to any one, I assure you that even were you to burn it before my eyes, without having read it, I should not mind in the least.

The opinion is not uncommon in the Community that you have always indulged me, ever since I entered the Convent; however, "Man seeth those things that appear, but the Lord beholdeth the heart."[1] Dear Mother, once again I thank you for not having spared me. Jesus knew well that His Little Flower needed the life-giving water of humiliation—it was too weak to take root otherwise, and to you it owes so great a blessing. But for some months, the Divine Master has entirely changed His method of cultivating His Little Flower. Finding no doubt that it has been sufficiently watered, He now allows it to expand under the warm rays of a brilliant sun. He smiles on it, and this favour also comes through you, dear Mother, but far from doing it harm, those smiles make the Little Flower grow in a wondrous way. Deep down in its heart it treasures those precious drops of dew—the mortifications of other days—and they remind it that it is small and frail. Even were all creatures to draw near to admire and flatter it, that would not add a shade of idle satisfaction to the true joy which thrills it, on realising that in

God's Eyes it is but a poor, worthless thing, and nothing more.

When I say that I am indifferent to praise, I am not speaking, dear Mother, of the love and confidence you show me; on the contrary I am deeply touched thereby, but I feel that I have now nothing to fear, and I can listen to those praises unperturbed, attributing to God all that is good in me. If it please Him to make me appear better than I am, it is nothing to me, He can act as He will. My God, how many ways dost Thou lead souls! We read of Saints who left absolutely nothing at their death, not the least thing by which to remember them, not even a single line of writing; and there are others like our holy Mother, St. Teresa, who have enriched the Church with their sublime teaching, and have not hesitated to reveal "the secrets of the King,"[2] that He may be better known and better loved.

Which of these two ways is more pleasing to Our Lord? It seems to me that they are equally so.

All those beloved by God have followed the inspiration of the Holy Ghost, who commanded the prophets to write: "Tell the just man that all is well."[3] Yes, all is well when one seeks only the Master's

Will, and so I, poor Little Flower, obey my Jesus when I try to please you, who represent him here on earth.

You know it has ever been my desire to become a Saint, but I have always felt, in comparing myself with the Saints, that I am as far removed from them as the grain of sand, which the passer-by tramples underfoot, is remote from the mountain whose summit is lost in the clouds.

Instead of being discouraged, I concluded that God would not inspire desires which could not be realised, and that I may aspire to sanctity in spite of my littleness. For me to become great is impossible. I must bear with myself and my many imperfections; but I will seek out a means of getting to Heaven by a little way—very short and very straight, a little way that is wholly new. We live in an age of inventions; nowadays the rich need not trouble to climb the stairs, they have lifts instead. Well, I mean to try and find a lift by which I may be raised unto God, for I am too tiny to climb the steep stairway of perfection. I have sought to find in Holy Scripture some suggestion as to what this lift might be which I so much desired, and I read these words uttered by the Eternal Wisdom Itself: "Whosoever is a little one, let him come to Me."[4] Then I drew near to God, feeling sure that I had discovered what I sought; but wishing to know further what He would do to the little one, I continued my search and this is what I found: "You shall be carried at the breasts and upon the knees; as one whom the mother caresseth, so will I comfort you."[5]

Never have I been consoled by words more tender and sweet. Thine Arms, then, O Jesus, are the lift which must raise me up even unto Heaven. To get there I need not grow; on the contrary, I must remain little, I must become still less. O my God, thou hast gone beyond my expectation, and I . . . "I will sing Thy mercies! Thou hast taught me, O Lord, from my youth and till now I have declared Thy wonderful works, and thus unto old age and grey hairs."[6]

What will this old age be for me? It seems to me that it could as well be now as later: two thousand years are no more in the Eyes of the Lord than twenty years . . . than a single day! But do not think, dear Mother, that your child is anxious to leave you, and deems it a greater grace to die in the morning rather than in the evening of life; to please Jesus is what [s]he really values and desires above all things. Now that He seems to come near and draw her to His Heavenly Home, she is glad; she has understood that God has need of no one to do good upon earth, still less of her than of others. Meantime I know your will, dear Mother. You wish me to carry out, at your side, a work which is both sweet and easy,[7] and this work I shall complete in Heaven. You have said to me, as Our Lord said to St. Peter: "Feed my lambs." I am amazed, for I feel that I am so little. I have entreated you to feed your little lambs yourself and to keep me among them. You have complied in part with my reasonable wish, and have called me their companion, rather than their mistress, telling me nevertheless to lead them through fertile and shady pastures, to point out where the grass is sweetest and best, and warn them against the brilliant but poisonous flowers, which they must never touch except to crush under foot.

How is it, dear Mother, that my youth and inexperience have not frightened you? Are you not afraid that I shall let your lambs stray afar? In acting as you have done, perhaps you remembered that Our Lord is often pleased to give wisdom to little ones.

On this earth it is rare indeed to find souls who do not measure God's Omnipotence by their own narrow thoughts. The world is always ready to admit exceptions everywhere here below. God alone is denied this liberty. It has long been the custom among men to reckon experience by age, for in his youth the holy King David sang to His Lord: "I am young and despised,"[8] but in the same Psalm he does not fear to say: "I have had understanding above old men, because I have sought Thy commandments, Thy word is a lamp to my feet, and a light to my paths; I have sworn, and I am determined, to keep the judgments of Thy Justice."[9]

And you did not even consider it imprudent to assure me one day, that the Divine Master had enlightened my soul and given me the experience of years. I am too little now to be guilty of vanity; I am likewise too little to endeavour to prove my humility by fine-sounding words. I prefer to own in all simplicity that "He that is mighty hath done great things to me" — [10] and the greatest is that He has shown me my littleness and how incapable I am of anything good.

My soul has known trials of many kinds. I have suffered much on this earth. In my childhood I suffered with sadness, but now I find sweetness in all things. Anyone but you, dear Mother, who know me thoroughly, would smile at reading these pages, for has ever a soul seemed less tried than mine? But if the martyrdom which I have endured for the past year were made known, how astonished everyone would be! Since it is your wish I will try to describe it, but there are no words really to explain these things. The words will always fall short of the reality.

During Lent last year I felt much better than ever and continued so until Holy Week, in spite of the fast which I observed in all its rigour. But in the early hours of Good Friday, Jesus gave me to hope that I should soon join Him in His beautiful Home. How sweet is this memory!

I could not obtain permission to remain watching at the Altar of Repose throughout the Thursday night, and I returned to our cell at midnight. Scarcely was my head laid on the pillow when I felt a hot stream rise to my lips. I thought I was going to die, and my heart nearly broke with joy. But as I had already put out our lamp, I mortified my curiosity until the morning and slept in peace. At five o'clock, when it was time to get up, I remembered at once that I had some good news to learn, and going to the window I found, as I had expected, that our handkerchief was soaked with blood. Dearest Mother, what hope was mine! I was firmly convinced that on this anniversary of His Death, my Beloved had allowed me to hear His first call, like a sweet, distant murmur, heralding His joyful approach.

I assisted at Prime and Chapter most fervently, and then I hastened to cast myself at my Mother's knees and confide to her my happiness. I did not feel the least pain, so I easily obtained permission to finish Lent as I had begun, and on this Good Friday I shared in all the austerities of the Carmel without any relaxation. Never had these austerities seemed sweeter to me; the hope of soon entering Heaven transported me with joy.

Still full of joy, I returned to our cell on the evening of that happy day, and was quietly falling asleep, when my sweet Jesus gave me the same sign as on the previous night, of my speedy entrance to Eternal Life. I felt such a clear and lively Faith that the thought of Heaven was my sole delight. I could not believe it possible for men to be utterly devoid of Faith, and I was convinced that those who deny the existence of another world really lie in their hearts.

But during the Paschal days, so full of light, our Lord made me understand that there really are in truth souls bereft of Faith and Hope, who, through abuse of grace, lose these precious treasures, the only source of pure and lasting joy. He allowed my soul to be overwhelmed with darkness, and the thought of Heaven, which had consoled me from my earliest childhood, now became a subject of conflict and torture. This trial did not last merely for days or weeks; I have been suffering for months, and I still await deliverance. I wish I could express what I feel, but it is beyond me. One must have passed through this dark tunnel to understand its blackness. However, I will try to explain it by means of a comparison.

Let me suppose that I had been born in a land of thick fogs, and had never seen the beauties of nature, or a single ray of sunshine, although I had heard of these wonders from my early youth, and knew that the country wherein I dwelt was not my real home—there was another land, unto which I should always look forward. Now this is not a fable, invented by an inhabitant of the land of fogs, it is the solemn truth, for the King of that sunlit country dwelt for three and thirty years in the land of darkness, and alas!—the darkness did not understand that He was the Light of the World._[11]

But, dear Lord, Thy child has understood Thou art the Light Divine; she asks Thy pardon for her unbelieving brethren, and is willing to eat the bread of sorrow as long as Thou mayest wish. For love of Thee she will sit at that table of bitterness where these poor sinners take their food, and she will not stir from it until Thou givest the sign. But may she not say in her own name, and the name of her guilty brethren: "O God, be merciful to us sinners!"[12] Send us away justified. May all those on whom Faith does not shine see the light at last! O my God, if that table which they profane can be purified by one that loves Thee, I am willing to remain there alone to eat the bread of tears, until it shall please Thee to bring me to Thy Kingdom of Light: the only favour I ask is, that I may never give Thee cause for offence.

From the time of my childhood I felt that one day I should be set free from this land of darkness. I believed it, not only because I had been told so by others, but my heart's most secret and deepest longings assured me that there was in store for me another and more beautiful country — an abiding dwelling-place. I was like Christopher Columbus, whose genius anticipated the discovery of the New World. And suddenly the mists about me have penetrated my very soul and have enveloped me so completely that I cannot even picture to myself this promised country . . . all has faded away. When my heart, weary of the surrounding darkness, tries to find some rest in the thought of a life to come, my anguish increases. It seems to me that out of the darkness I hear the mocking voice of the unbeliever: "You dream of a land of light and fragrance, you dream that the Creator of these wonders will be yours for ever, you think one day to escape from these mists where you now languish. Nay, rejoice in death, which will give you, not what you hope for, but a night darker still, the night of utter nothingness!" . . .

Dear Mother, this description of what I suffer is as far removed from reality as the first rough outline is from the model, but I fear that to write more were to blaspheme . . . even now I may have said too much. May God forgive me! He knows that I try to live by Faith, though it does not afford me the least consolation. I have made more acts of Faith in this last year than during all the rest of my life.

Each time that my enemy would provoke me to combat, I behave as a gallant soldier. I know that a duel is an act of cowardice, and so, without once looking him in the face, I turn my back on the foe, then I hasten to my Saviour, and vow that I am ready to shed my blood in witness of my belief in Heaven. I tell him, if only He will deign to open it to poor unbelievers, I am content to sacrifice all pleasure in the thought of it as long as I live. And in spite of this trial, which robs me of all comfort, I still can say: "Thou hast given me, O Lord, delight in all Thou dost."[13] For what joy can be greater than to suffer for Thy Love? The more the suffering is and the less it appears before men, the more is it to Thy Honour and Glory. Even if—but I know it to be impossible—Thou shouldst not deign to heed my sufferings, I should still be happy to bear them, in the hope that by my tears I might perhaps prevent or atone for one sin against Faith.

No doubt, dear Mother, you will think I exaggerate somewhat *the night of my soul*. If you judge by the poems I have composed this year, it must seem as though I have been flooded with consolations, like a child for whom the veil of Faith is almost rent asunder. And yet it is not a veil—it is a wall which rises to the very heavens and shuts out the starry sky.

When I sing of the happiness of Heaven and the eternal possession of God, I do not feel any joy therein, for I sing only of what I wish to believe.

Sometimes, I confess, a little ray of sunshine illumines my dark night, and I enjoy peace for an instant, but later, the remembrance of this ray of light, instead of consoling me, makes the blackness thicker still.

And yet never have I felt so deeply how sweet and merciful is the Lord. He did not send me this heavy cross when it might have discouraged me, but at a time when I was able to bear it. Now it simply takes from me all natural satisfaction I might feel in my longing for Heaven.

Dear Mother, it seems to me that at present there is nothing to impede my upward flight, for I have no longer any desire save to love Him till I die. I am free; I fear nothing now, not even what I dreaded more than anything else, a long illness which would make me a burden to the Community. Should it please the Good God, I am quite content to have my bodily and mental sufferings prolonged for years. I do not fear a long life; I do not shrink from the struggle. The Lord is the rock upon which I stand —"Who teacheth my hands to fight, and my fingers to war. He is my Protector and I have hoped in Him."[14] I have never asked God to let me die young, It is true I have always thought I should do so, but it is a favour I have not tried to obtain.

Our Lord is often content with the wish to do something for His Glory, and you know the immensity of my desires. You know also that Jesus has offered me more than one bitter chalice through my dearly loved sisters. The holy King David was right when he sang: "Behold how good and how pleasant it is for brethren to dwell together in unity."[15] But such unity can only exist upon earth in the midst of sacrifice. It was not in order to be with my sisters that I came to this holy Carmel; on the contrary, I knew well that in curbing my natural affection I should have much to suffer.

How can it be said that it is more perfect to separate oneself from home and friends? Has anyone ever reproached brothers who fight side by side, or together win the martyr's palm? It is true, no doubt, they encourage each other; but it is also true that the martyrdom of each is a martyrdom to them all.

And so it is in the religious life; theologians call it a martyrdom. A heart given to God loses nothing of its natural affection — on the contrary, this affection grows stronger by becoming purer and more spiritual. It is with this love, dear Mother, that I love you and my sisters. I am glad to fight beside you for the glory of the King of Heaven, but I am ready to go to another battlefield, did the Divine Commander but express a wish. An order would not be necessary: a simple look, a sign, would suffice.

Ever since I came to the Carmel I have thought that if Our Lord did not take me quickly to Heaven, my lot would be that of Noe's dove, and that one day he would open the window of the Ark and bid me fly to heathen lands, bearing the olive branch. This thought has helped me to soar above all created things.

Knowing that even in the Carmel there must be partings, I tried to make my abode in Heaven; and I accepted not only exile in the midst of an unknown people, but what was far more bitter, I accepted exile for my sisters. And indeed, two of them were asked for by the Carmel of Saïgon, our own foundation. For a time there was serious question of their being sent, and I would not say a word to hold them back, though my heart ached at the thought of the trials awaiting them. Now all that is at an end; the superiors were absolutely opposed to their departure, and I only touched the cup with my lips long enough to taste of its bitterness.

Let me tell you, dear Mother, why, if Our Lady cures me, I wish to respond to the call from our Mothers of Hanoï. It appears that to live in foreign Carmels, a very special vocation is needed, and many souls think they are called without being so in reality. You have told me that I have this vocation, and that my health alone stands in the way. But if I am destined one day to leave this Carmel, it will not be without a pang. My heart is naturally sensitive, and because this is a cause of much suffering, I wish to offer Jesus whatsoever it can bear. Here, I am loved by you and all the Sisters, and this love is very sweet to me, and I dream of a convent where I should be unknown, where I should taste the bitterness of exile. I know only too well how useless I am, and so it is not for the sake of the services I might render to the Carmel of Hanoï that I would leave all that is dearest to me—my sole reason would be to do God's Will, and sacrifice myself for Him.

And I should not suffer any disappointment, for when we expect nothing but suffering, then the least joy is a surprise; and later on suffering itself becomes the greatest of all joys, when we seek it as a precious treasure.

But I know I shall never recover from this sickness, and yet I am at peace. For years I have not belonged to myself, I have surrendered myself wholly to Jesus, and He is free to do with me whatsoever He pleases. He has spoken to me of exile, and has asked me if I would consent to drink of that chalice. At once I essayed to grasp it, but He, withdrawing His Hand, showed me that my consent was all He desired.

O my God! from how much disquiet do we free ourselves by the vow of obedience! Happy is the simple religious. Her one guide being the will of her superiors, she is ever sure of following the right path, and has no fear of being mistaken, even when it seems that her superiors are making a mistake. But if she ceases to consult the unerring compass, then at once her soul goes astray in barren wastes, where the waters of grace quickly fail. Dear Mother, you are the compass Jesus has given me to direct me safely to the Eternal Shore. I find it most sweet to fix my eyes upon you, and then do the Will of my Lord. By allowing me to suffer these temptations against Faith, He has greatly increased the spirit of Faith, which makes me see Him living in your soul, and through you communicating His holy commands.

I am well aware that you lighten the burden of obedience for me, but deep in my heart I feel that my attitude would not change, nor would my filial affection grow less, were you to treat me with severity: and this because I should still see the Will of God manifesting itself in another way for the greater good of my soul.

Among the numberless graces that I have received this year, not the least is an understanding of how far-reaching is the precept of charity. I had never before fathomed these words of Our Lord: "The second commandment is like to the first: Thou shalt love thy neighbour as thyself."[16] I had set myself above all to love God, and it was in loving Him that I discovered the hidden meaning of these other words: "It is not those who say, Lord, Lord! who enter into the Kingdom of Heaven, but he who does the Will of My Father."[17]

Jesus revealed me this Will when at the Last Supper He gave His New Commandment in telling His Apostles to *love one another as He had loved them.* [18] I set myself to find out how He had loved His Apostles; and I saw that it was not for their natural qualities, for they were ignorant men, full of earthly ideas. And yet He calls them His Friends, His Brethren; He desires to see them near Him in the

Kingdom of His Father, and in order to admit them to this Kingdom He wills to die on the Cross, saying: "Greater love than this no man hath, that a man lay down his life for his friends."[19]

As I meditated on these Divine words, I saw how imperfect was the love I bore my Sisters in religion. I understood that I did not love them as Our Lord loves them. I know now that true charity consists in bearing all our neighbours' defects—not being surprised at their weakness, but edified at their smallest virtues. Above all I know that charity must not remain shut up in the heart, for "No man lighteth a candle, and putteth it in a hidden place, nor under a bushel; but upon a candlestick, that they who come in may see the light."[20]

It seems to me, dear Mother, this candle represents that charity which enlightens and gladdens, not only those who are dear to us, but all *those who are of the household.*

In the Old Law, when God told His people to love their neighbour as themselves, He had not yet come down upon earth; and knowing full well how man loves himself, He could not ask anything greater. But when Our Lord gave His Apostles a New Commandment—"His own commandment"[21]—

He was not content with saying: "Thou shalt love thy neighbour as thyself," but would have them love even as He had loved, and as He will love till the end of time.

O my Jesus! Thou does never ask what is impossible; Thou knowest better than I, how frail and imperfect I am, and Thou knowest that I shall never love my Sisters as Thou hast loved them, unless within me Thou lovest them, dear Lord! It is because Thou dost desire to grant me this grace that Thou hast given a New Commandment. Oh how I love it, since I am assured thereby that it is Thy Will to love in me all those Thou dost bid me love!

Yes, I know when I show charity to others, it is simply Jesus acting in me, and the more closely I am united to Him, the more dearly I love my Sisters. If I wish to increase this love in my heart, and the devil tries to bring before me the defects of a Sister, I hasten to look for her virtues, her good motives; I call to mind that though I may have seen her fall once, no doubt she has gained many victories over herself, which in her humility she conceals. It is even possible that what seems to me a fault, may very likely, on account of her good intention, be an act of virtue. I have no difficulty in persuading myself of this, because I have had the same experience. One day, during recreation, the portress came to ask for a Sister to help her. I had a childish longing to do this work, and it happened the choice fell upon me. I therefore began to fold up our needlework, but so slowly that my neighbour, who I knew would like to take my place, was ready before me. The Sister who had asked for help, seeing how deliberate I was, said laughingly: "I thought you would not add this pearl to your crown, you are so extremely slow," and all the Community thought I had yielded to natural reluctance. I cannot tell you what profit I derived from this incident, and it made me indulgent towards others. It still checks any feelings of vanity, when I am praised, for I reflect that since my small acts of virtue can be mistaken for imperfections, why should not my imperfections be mistaken for virtue? And I say with St. Paul: "To me it is a very small thing to be judged by you, or by man's day. But neither do I judge myself. He that judgeth me is the Lord."[22]

And it is the Lord, it is Jesus, Who is my judge. Therefore I will try always to think leniently of others, that He may judge me leniently, or rather not at all, since He says: "Judge not, and ye shall not be judged."[23]

But returning to the Holy Gospel where Our Lord explains to me clearly in what His New Commandment consists, I read in St. Matthew: "You have heard that it hath been said, Thou shalt love thy neighbour, and hate thy enemy: but I say unto you, Love your enemies, and pray for them that persecute you."[24]

There are, of course, no enemies in the Carmel; but, after all, we have our natural likes and dislikes. We may feel drawn towards one Sister, and may be tempted to go a long way round to avoid meeting another. Well, Our Lord tells me that this is the Sister to love and pray for, even though her behaviour may make me imagine she does not care for me. "If you love them that love you, what thanks are to you? For sinners also love those that love them."[25] And it is not enough to love, we must prove our love; naturally one likes to please a friend, but that is not charity, for sinners do the same.

Our Lord also taught me: "Give to everyone that asketh thee; and of him that taketh away thy goods, ask them not again."[26] To give to everyone who asks is not so pleasant as to give of one's own accord. If we are asked pleasantly, it is easy to give; but if we are asked discourteously, then, unless we are perfect in charity, there is an inward rebellion, and we find no end of excuses for refusing. Perhaps, after first pointing out the rudeness of the request, we make such a favour of consenting thereto, that the slight service takes far less time to perform than was lost in arguing the point. And if it is difficult to give to whosoever asks, it is far more difficult to let what belongs to us be taken without asking it again. Dear Mother, I say this is hard, but I should rather say that it seems hard, for "The yoke of the Lord is sweet and His burden light."[27] And when we submit to that yoke, we at once feel its sweetness.

I have said Jesus does not wish me to ask again for what is my own. This ought to seem quite easy, for, in reality, nothing is mine. I ought, then, to be glad when an occasion arises which brings home to me the poverty to which I am vowed. I used to think myself completely detached, but since Our Lord's words have become clear, I see that I am indeed very imperfect.

For instance: when starting to paint, if I find the brushes in disorder, and a ruler or penknife gone, I feel inclined to lose patience, and have to keep a firm hold over myself not to betray my feelings. Of course I may ask for these needful things, and if I do so humbly I am not disobeying Our Lord's command. I am then like the poor who hold out their hands for the necessaries of life, and, if refused, are not surprised, since no one owes them anything. Deep peace inundates the soul when it soars above mere natural sentiments. There is no joy equal to that which is shared by the truly poor in spirit. If they ask with detachment for something necessary, and not only is it refused, but an attempt is made to take away what they already possess, they are following the Master's advice: "If any man will take away thy coat, let him have thy cloak also." [28] To give up one's cloak is, it seems to me, to renounce every right, and to regard oneself as the servant, the slave, of all. Without a cloak it is easier to walk or run, and so the Master adds: "And whosoever shall force thee to go one mile, go with him other two."[29]

It is therefore not enough for me to give to whoever asks—I ought to anticipate the wish, and show myself glad to be of service; but if anything of mine be taken away, I should show myself glad to be rid of it. I cannot always carry out to the letter the words of the Gospel, for there are occasions when I am compelled to refuse some request. Yet when charity is deeply rooted in the soul it lets itself be outwardly seen, and there is a way of refusing so graciously what one is unable to give, that the refusal affords as much pleasure as the gift would have done. It is true that people do not hesitate to ask from those who readily oblige, nevertheless I ought not to avoid importunate Sisters on the pretext that I shall be forced to refuse. The Divine Master has said: "From him that would borrow of thee turn not away."[30] Nor should I be kind in order to appear so, or in the hope that the Sister will return the service, for once more it is written: "If you lend to them of whom you hope to receive, what thanks are to you? For sinners also lend to sinners for to receive as much. But you do good and lend, hoping for nothing thereby, and your reward shall be great."[31]

Verily, the reward is great even on earth. In this path it is only the first step which costs. To lend without hope of being repaid seems hard; one would rather give outright, for what you give is no longer yours. When a Sister says confidently: "I want your help for some hours—I have our Mother's leave, and be assured I will do as much for you later," one may know well that these hours *lent* will not be repaid, and be sorely tempted to say: "I prefer to *give* them." But that would gratify self-love, besides letting the Sister feel that you do not rely much on her promise. The Divine precepts run contrary to our natural inclinations, and without the help of grace it would be impossible to understand them, far less to put them in practice.

Dear Mother, I feel that I have expressed myself with more than usual confusion, and I do not know what you can find to interest you in these rambling pages, but I am not aiming at a literary masterpiece, and if I weary you by this discourse on charity, it will at least prove your child's good will. I must confess I am far from living up to my ideal, and yet the very desire to do so gives me a feeling of peace. If I fall into some fault, I arise again at once—and for some months now I have not even had to struggle. I have been able to say with our holy Father, St. John of the Cross: "My house is entirely at peace," and I attribute this interior peace to a victory I gained over myself. Since that victory, the hosts of Heaven have hastened to my aid, for they will not allow me to be wounded, now that I have fought so valiantly.

A holy nun of our community annoyed me in all that she did; the devil must have had something to do with it, and he it was undoubtedly who made me see in her so many disagreeable points. I did not want to yield to my natural antipathy, for I remembered that charity ought to betray itself in deeds, and not exist merely in the feelings, so I set myself to do for this sister all I should do for the one I loved most. Every time I met her I prayed for her, and offered to God her virtues and merits. I felt that this was very pleasing to Our Lord, for there is no artist who is not gratified when his works are praised, and the Divine Artist of souls is pleased when we do not stop at the exterior, but, penetrating to the inner sanctuary He has chosen, admire its beauty.

I did not rest satisfied with praying for this Sister, who gave me such occasions for self-mastery, I tried to render her as many services as I could, and when tempted to answer her sharply, I made haste to smile and change the subject, for the *Imitation* says: "It is more profitable to leave everyone to his way of thinking than to give way to contentious discourses." And sometimes when the temptation was very severe, I would run like a deserter from the battlefield if I could do so without letting the Sister guess my inward struggle.

One day she said to me with a beaming face: "My dear Soeur Thérèse, tell me what attraction you find in me, for whenever we meet, you greet me with such a sweet smile." Ah! What attracted me was

Jesus hidden in the depths of her soul—Jesus who maketh sweet even that which is most bitter.

I spoke just now, dear Mother, of the flight that is my last resource to escape defeat. It is not honourable, I confess, but during my noviciate, whenever I had recourse to this means, it invariably succeeded. I will give you a striking example, which will, I am sure, amuse you. You had been ill with bronchitis for several days, and we were all uneasy about you. One morning, in my duty as sacristan, I came to put back the keys of the Communion-grating. This was my work, and I was very pleased to have an opportunity of seeing you, though I took good care not to show it. One of the Sisters, full of solicitude, feared I should awake you, and tried to take the keys from me. I told her as politely as I could, that I was quite as anxious as she was there should be no noise, and added that it was my right to return them. I see now that it would have been more perfect simply to yield, but I did not see it then, and so I followed her into the room. Very soon what she feared came to pass: the noise did awaken you. All the blame fell upon me; the Sister I had argued with began a long discourse, of which the point was: Soeur Thérèse made all the noise. I was burning to defend myself, but a happy inspiration of grace came to me. I thought that if I began to justify myself I should certainly lose my peace of mind, and as I had too little virtue to let myself be unjustly accused without answering, my last chance of safety lay in flight. No sooner thought than done. I hurried away, but my heart beat so violently, I could not go far, and I was obliged to sit down on the stairs to enjoy in quiet the fruit of my victory. This is an odd kind of courage, undoubtedly, but I think it is best not to expose oneself in the face of certain defeat.

When I recall these days of my noviciate I understand how far I was from perfection, and the memory of certain things makes me laugh. How good God has been, to have trained my soul and given it wings All the snares of the hunter can no longer frighten me, for "A net is spread in vain before the eyes of them that have wings."[32]

It may be that some day my present state will appear to me full of defects, but nothing now surprises me, and I do not even distress myself because I am so weak. On the contrary I glory therein, and expect each day to find fresh imperfections. Nay, I must confess, these lights on my own nothingness are of more good to my soul than lights on matters of Faith. Remembering that

"Charity covereth a multitude of sins,"[33] I draw from this rich mine, which Our Saviour has opened to us in the Gospels. I search the depths of His adorable words, and cry out with David: "I have run in the way of Thy commandments since Thou hast enlarged my heart."[34] And charity alone can make wide the heart. O Jesus! Since its sweet flame consumes my heart, I run with delight in the way of Thy New Commandment, and I desire to run therein until that blessed day when, with Thy company of Virgins, I shall follow Thee through Thy boundless Realm, singing Thy New Canticle—The Canticle of Love.

---

[1] 1 Kings 16:7.

[2] Tobias 12:7.

[3] Cf. Isaias 3:10.

[4] Prov. 9:4.

[5] Isa. 66:12, 13.

[6] Cf. Ps. 70[71]:17, 18.

[7] Soeur Thérèse had charge of the novices without being given the title of Novice Mistress.

[8] Ps. 118[119]:141.

[9] Ps. 118[119]:100, 105, 106.

[10] Luke 1:49.

[11] Cf. John 1:5.

[12] Cf. Luke 18:13.

[13] Ps. 91[92]:5.

[14] Ps. 143[144]:1, 2.

[15] Ps. 132[133]:1.

[16] Matt. 22:39.

[17] Cf. Matt. 7:21.

[18] Cf. John 13:34.

[19] John 15:12.

[20] Luke 11:33.

[21] John 15:12.

[22] 1 Cor. 4:3,4.

[23] Luke 6:37.

[24] Matt. 5:43, 44.

[25] Luke 6:32.

[26] Luke 6:30.

[27] Matt. 11:30.

[28] Matt. 5:40.

[29] Matt. 5:41.

[30] Matt. 5:42.

[31] Luke 6:34, 35.

[32] Prov. 1:27.

[33] Prov. 10:12.

[34] Ps. 118[119]:32.

CHAPTER X THE NEW COMMANDMENT

Dear Mother, God in His infinite goodness has given me a clear insight into the deep mysteries of Charity. If I could but express what I know, you would hear a heavenly music; but alas! I can only stammer like a child, and if God's own words were not my support, I should be tempted to beg leave to hold my peace. When the Divine Master tells me to give to whosoever asks of me, and to let what is mine be taken without asking it again, it seems to me that He speaks not only of the goods of earth, but also of the goods of Heaven. Besides, neither one nor the other are really mine; I renounced the former by the vow of poverty, and the latter gifts are simply lent. If God withdraw them, I have no right to complain.

But our very own ideas, the fruit of our mind and heart, form a treasury on which none dare lay hands. For instance, if I reveal to a Sister some light given me in prayer, and she repeats it later on as though it were her own, it seems as though she appropriates what is mine. Or, if during recreation someone makes an apt and witty remark, which her neighbour repeats to the Community, without acknowledging whence it came, it is a sort of theft; and the person who originated the remark is naturally inclined to seize the first opportunity of delicately insinuating that her thoughts have been borrowed.

I could not so well explain all these weaknesses of human nature had I not experienced them. I should have preferred to indulge in the illusion that I was the only one who suffered thus, had you not bidden me advise the novices in their difficulties. I have learnt much in the discharge of this duty, and especially I feel bound to put in practice what I teach.

I can say with truth that by God's grace I am no more attached to the gifts of the intellect than to material things. If it happens that a thought of mine should please my Sisters, I find it quite easy to let them regard it as their own. My thoughts belong to the Holy Ghost. They are not mine. St. Paul assures us that *without the Spirit of Love, we cannot call God our Father.*[1]

And besides, though far from depreciating those beautiful thoughts which bring us nearer to God, I have long been of opinion that we must be careful not to over-estimate their worth. The highest inspirations are of no value without good works. It is true that others may derive much profit therefrom, if they are duly grateful to our Lord for allowing them to share in the abundance of one of His privileged souls; but should this privileged soul take pride in spiritual wealth, and imitate the Pharisee, she becomes like to a hostess dying of starvation at a well-spread table, while her guests enjoy the richest fare, and perhaps cast envious glances at the possessor of so many treasures.

Verily it is true that God alone can sound the heart. How short-sighted are His creatures! When they see a soul whose lights surpass their own, they conclude that the Divine Master loves them less. Since when has He lost the right to make use of one of His children, in order to supply the others with the nourishment they need? That right was not lost in the days of Pharaoh, for God said unto him: "And therefore have I raised thee, that I may show My power in thee, and My name may be spoken of throughout all the earth."[2]

Generations have passed away since the Most High spoke these words, and His ways have not changed. He has ever chosen human instruments for the accomplishment of His work.

If an artist's canvas could but think and speak, surely it would never complain of being touched and re-touched by the brush, nor would it feel envious thereof, knowing that all its beauty is due to the artist alone. So, too, the brush itself could not boast of the masterpiece it had helped to produce, for it must know that an artist is never at a loss; that difficulties do but stimulate him; and that at times it pleases him to make use of instruments the most unlikely and defective.

Dear Mother, I am the little brush that Jesus has chosen to paint His likeness in the souls you have confided to my care. Now an artist has several brushes—two at the least: the first, which is more useful, gives the ground tints and rapidly covers the whole canvas; the other, and smaller one, puts in the lesser touches. Mother, you represent the big brush which our Lord holds lovingly in His Hand when He wishes to do some great work in the souls of your children; and I am the little one He deigns to use afterwards, to fill in the minor details.

The first time the Divine Master took up His little brush was about December 8, 1892. I shall always remember that time as one of special grace.

When I entered the Carmel, I found in the noviciate a companion about eight years older than I was. In spite of this difference of age, we became the closest friends, and to encourage an affection which gave promise of fostering virtue we were allowed to converse together on spiritual subjects. My companion charmed me by her innocence and by her open and frank disposition, though I was surprised to find how her love for you differed from mine; and besides, I regretted many things in her behaviour. But God had already given me to understand that there are souls for whom in His Mercy He waits unweariedly, and to whom He gives His light by degrees; so I was very careful not to forestall Him.

One day when I was thinking over the permission we had to talk together, so that we might—as our holy constitutions tells us—incite ourselves more ardently to the love of our Divine Spouse, it came home to me sadly that our conversations did not attain the desired end; and I understood that either I must no longer fear to speak out, or else I must put an end to what was degenerating into mere worldly talk. I begged our Lord to inspire me with words, kind and convincing; or better still, to speak Himself for me. He heard my prayer, for those *who look upon Him shall be enlightened,*[3] and "to the upright a light is risen in the darkness."[4] The first of these texts I apply to myself, the other to my companion, who was truly upright in heart.

The next time we met, the poor little Sister saw at once that my manner had changed, and, blushing deeply, she sat down beside me. I pressed her to my heart, and told her gently what was in my mind; then I pointed out to her in what true love consists, and proved that in loving her Prioress with such natural affection she was in reality loving herself. I confided to her the sacrifices of this kind which I had been obliged to make at the beginning of my religious life, and before long her tears were mingled with mine. She admitted very humbly that she was in the wrong and that I was right, and, begging me as a favour always to point out her faults, she promised to begin a new life. From this time our love for one another became truly spiritual; in us were fulfilled these words of the Holy Ghost: "A brother that is helped by his brother is like a strong city."[5]

Dear Mother, you know very well that it was not my wish to turn my companion away from you, I only wanted her to grasp that true love feeds on sacrifice, and that in proportion as our souls renounce natural enjoyments our affections become stronger and more detached.

I remember that when I was a postulant I was sometimes so violently tempted to seek my own satisfaction by having a word with you, that I was obliged to hurry past your cell and hold on to the banisters to keep myself from turning back. Numerous permissions I wanted to ask, and a hundred pretexts for yielding to my desires suggested themselves, but now I am truly glad that I did not listen. I already enjoy the reward promised to those who fight bravely. I no longer feel the need of refusing myself these consolations, for my heart is fixed on God. Because it has loved Him only, it has grown, little by little, and now it can give to those who are dear to Him a far deeper and truer love than if it were centred in a barren and selfish affection.

I have told you of the first piece of work which you accomplished together with Our Lord by means of the little brush, but that was only the prelude to the masterpiece which was afterwards to be painted. From the moment I entered the sanctuary of souls, I saw at a glance that the task was beyond my strength. Throwing myself without delay into Our Lord's Arms, I imitated those tiny children, who, when they are frightened, hide their faces on their father's shoulder, and I said:

"Dear Lord, Thou seest that I am too small to feed these little ones, but if through me Thou wilt give to each what is suitable, then fill my hands, and without leaving the shelter of Thine Arms, or even turning away, I will distribute Thy treasures to the souls who come to me asking for food. Should they find it to their taste, I shall know that this is due not to me, but to Thee; and if, on the contrary, they find fault with its bitterness, I shall not be cast down, but try to persuade them that it cometh from Thee, while taking good care to make no change in it."

The knowledge that it was impossible to do anything of myself rendered my task easier. My one interior occupation was to unite myself more and more closely to God, knowing that the rest would be given to me over and above. And indeed my hope has never been deceived; I have always found my hands filled when sustenance was needed for the souls of my Sisters. But had I done otherwise, and relied on my own strength, I should very soon have been forced to abandon my task.

From afar it seems so easy to do good to souls, to teach them to love God more, and to model them according to one's own ideas. But, when we draw nearer, we quickly feel that without God's help this is quite as impossible as to bring back the sun when once it has set. We must forget ourselves, and put aside our tastes and ideas, and guide souls not by our own way, but along the path which Our Lord points out. Even this is not the most difficult part; what costs me more than all is having to observe their faults, their slightest imperfections, and wage war against them.

Unhappily for me—I was going to say, but that would be cowardly, so I will say—happily for my Sisters, ever since I placed myself in the Arms of

Jesus I have been like a watchman on the look-out for the enemy from the highest turret of a fortified castle. Nothing escapes my vigilance; indeed, I am sometimes surprised at my own clear-sightedness, and I think it was quite excusable in the prophet Jonas to fly before the face of the Lord, that he might not have to announce the ruin of Ninive. Rather than make one single reproach, I would prefer to receive a thousand, yet I feel it is necessary that the task should cause me pain, for if I spoke only through natural impulse, then the soul in fault would not understand its defects and would simply think: "This Sister is displeased, and her displeasure falls on me although I am full of the best intentions."

But in this, as in all else, I must practise sacrifice and self-denial. Even in the matter of writing a letter, I feel that it will produce no fruit, unless I am disinclined to write, and only do so from obedience.

When conversing with a novice I am on the watch to mortify myself, and I avoid asking questions which would satisfy my curiosity. If she begins to speak on an interesting subject, and, leaving it unfinished, passes on to another that wearies me, I take care not to remind her of the interruption, for it seems to me that no good can come of self-seeking.

I know, dear Mother, that your little lambs find me severe; if they were to read these lines, they would say that, so far as they can see, it does not distress me to run after them, and show them how they have soiled their beautiful white fleece, or torn it in the brambles. Well, the little lambs may say what they like—in their hearts they know I love them dearly; there is no fear of my imitating "the hireling . . . who seeth the wolf coming and leaveth the sheep, and flieth."[6]

I am ready to lay down my life for them, and my affection is so disinterested that I would not have my novices know this. By God's help, I have never tried to draw their hearts to myself, for I have always understood that my mission was to lead them to Him and to you, dear Mother, who on this earth hold His place in their regard, and whom, therefore, they must love and respect.

I said before, that I have learnt much by guiding others. In the first place I see that all souls have more or less the same battles to fight, and on the other hand, that one soul differs widely from another, so each must be dealt with differently. With some I must humble myself, and not shrink from acknowledging my own struggles and defeats; then they confess more readily the faults into which they fall, and are pleased that I know by experience what they suffer. With others, my only means of success is to be firm, and never go back on what I have once said; self-abasement would be taken for weakness.

Our Lord has granted me the grace never to fear the conflict; at all costs I must do my duty. I have more than once been told: "If you want me to obey, you must be gentle and not severe, otherwise you will gain nothing." But no one is a good judge in his own case. During a painful operation a child will be sure to cry out and say that the remedy is worse than the disease; but if after a few days he is cured, then he is greatly delighted that he can run about and play. And it is the same with souls: they soon recognise that a little bitter is better than too much sweet, and they are not afraid to make the acknowledgment. Sometimes the change which takes place from one day to another seems almost magical.

A novice will say to me: "You did well to be severe yesterday; at first I was indignant, but when I thought it all over, I saw that you were quite right. I left your cell thinking: 'This ends it. I will tell Our Mother that I shall never go to Soeur Thérèse again'; but I knew this was the devil's suggestion, and then

I felt you were praying for me, and I grew calm. I began to see things more clearly, and now I come to you for further guidance."

I am only too happy to follow the dictates of my heart and hasten to console with a little sweetness, but I see that one must not press forward too quickly—a word might undo the work that cost so many tears. If I say the least thing which seems to tone down the hard truths of the previous day, I see my little Sister trying to take advantage of the opening thus given her. At once I have recourse to prayer, I turn to Our Blessed Lady, and Jesus always triumphs. Verily in prayer and sacrifice lies all my strength, they are my invincible arms; experience has taught me that they touch hearts far more easily than words.

Two years ago, during Lent, a novice came to me smiling, and said: "You would never imagine what I dreamt last night—I thought I was with my sister, who is so worldly, and I wanted to withdraw her from all vain things; to this end I explained the words of your hymn:

'They richly lose who love Thee, dearest Lord;
Thine are my perfumes, Thine for evermore.'

I felt that my words sank deep into her soul, and I was overjoyed. This morning it seems to me that perhaps Our Lord would like me to gain Him this soul. How would it do if I wrote at Easter and described my dream, telling her that Jesus desires to have her for His Spouse?" I answered that she might certainly ask permission.

As Lent was not nearly over, you were surprised, dear Mother, at such a premature request, and, evidently guided by God, you replied that Carmelites should save souls by prayer rather than by letters. When I heard your decision I said to the little Sister: "We must set to work and pray hard; if our prayers are answered at the end of Lent, what a joy it will be!" O Infinite Mercy of our Lord! At the close of Lent, one soul more had given herself to God. It was a real miracle of grace—a miracle obtained through the fervour of a humble novice.

How wonderful is the power of prayer! It is like unto a queen, who, having free access to the king, obtains whatsoever she asks. In order to secure a hearing there is no need to recite set prayers composed for the occasion—were it so, I ought indeed to be pitied!

Apart from the Divine Office, which in spite of my unworthiness is a daily joy, I have not the courage to look through books for beautiful prayers. I only get a headache because of their number, and besides, one is more lovely than another. Unable therefore to say them all, and lost in choice, I do as children who have not learnt to read—I simply tell Our Lord all that I want, and He always understands.

With me prayer is an uplifting of the heart; a glance towards heaven; a cry of gratitude and love, uttered equally in sorrow and in joy. In a word, it is something noble, supernatural, which expands my soul and unites it to God. Sometimes when I am in such a state of spiritual dryness that not a single good thought occurs to me, I say very slowly the "Our Father" or the "Hail Mary," and these prayers suffice to take me out of myself, and wonderfully refresh me.

But what was I speaking of? Again I am lost in a maze of reflections. Forgive me, dear Mother, for wandering thus. My story is like a tangled skein, but I fear I can do no better. I write my thoughts as they come; I fish at random in the stream of my heart, and offer you all that I catch.

I was telling you about the novices. They often say: "You have an answer for everything. This time I thought I should puzzle you. Where do you find all that you teach us?" Some are even simple enough to think I can read their souls, because at times it happens I discover to them—without revelation—the subject of their thoughts. The senior novice had determined to hide from me a great sorrow. She spent the night in anguish, keeping back her tears lest her eyes might betray her. Yet she came to me with a smile next day, seeming even more cheerful than usual, and when I said: "You are in trouble, I am sure," she looked at me in inexpressible amazement. Her surprise was so great that it reacted on me, and imparted a sense of the supernatural. I felt that God was close to us. Unwittingly—for I have not the gift of reading souls—I had spoken as one inspired, and was able to console her completely.

And now, dear Mother, I will tell you wherein I gain most with the novices. You know they are allowed without restriction to say anything to me, agreeable or the reverse; this is all the easier since they do not owe me the respect due to a Novice-Mistress. I cannot say that Our Lord makes me walk in the way of exterior humiliation; He is satisfied with humbling me in my inmost soul. In the eyes of creatures all is success, and I walk in the dangerous path of honour—if a religious may so speak. I understand God's way and that of my superiors in this respect; for if the Community thought me incapable, unintelligent, and wanting in judgment, I could be of no possible use to you, dear Mother. This is why the Divine Master has thrown a veil over all my shortcomings, both interior and exterior. Because of this veil I receive many compliments from the novices—compliments without flattery, for they really mean what they say; and they do not inspire me with vanity, for the remembrance of my weakness is ever before me. At times my soul tires of this over-sweet food, and I long to hear something other than praise; then Our Lord serves me with a nice little salad, well spiced, with plenty of vinegar—oil alone is wanting, and this it is which makes it more to my taste. And the salad is offered to me by the novices at the moment I least expect. God lifts the veil that hides my faults, and my dear little Sisters, beholding me as I really am, do not find me altogether agreeable. With charming simplicity, they tell me how I try them and what they dislike in me; in fact, they are as frank as though they were speaking of someone else, for they are aware that I am pleased when they act in this way.

I am more than pleased—I am transported with delight by this splendid banquet set before me. How can anything so contrary to our natural inclinations afford such extraordinary pleasure? Had I not experienced it, I could not have believed it possible.

One day, when I was ardently longing for some humiliation, a young postulant came to me and sated my desire so completely, that I was reminded of the occasion when Semei cursed David, and I repeated to myself the words of the holy King: "Yea, it is the Lord who hath bidden him say all these things."[7] In this way God takes care of me. He cannot always provide that strength-giving bread, exterior humiliation, but from time to time He allows me to eat of "the crumbs from the table of the children."[8] How magnificent are His Mercies!

Dear Mother, since that Infinite Mercy is the subject of this my earthly song, I ought also to discover to you one real advantage, reaped with many others in the discharge of my task. Formerly, if I saw a Sister acting in a way that displeased me, and was seemingly contrary to rule, I would think:

"Ah, how glad I should be if only I could warn her and point out where she is wrong." Since, however, this burden has been laid upon me my ideas have changed, and when I happen to see something not quite right, I say with a sigh of relief: "Thank God! It is not a novice, and I am not obliged to correct"; and at once I try to find excuses, and credit the doer with the good intentions she no doubt possesses.

Your devotedness, dear Mother, now that I am ill, has also taught me many a lesson of charity. No remedy is too costly, and if one does not succeed, you unhesitatingly try something new. When I am present at recreation, how careful you are to shield me from draughts. I feel that I ought to be as compassionate for the spiritual infirmities of my Sisters as you are for my bodily ills.

I have noticed that it is the holiest nuns who are most deeply loved; everyone is anxious to seek their company, and do them service, without even being asked. These very souls who are well able to bear with want of affection and little attentions are always surrounded by an atmosphere of love. Our Father, St. John of the Cross, says with great truth: "All good things have come unto me, since I no longer sought them for myself."

Imperfect souls, on the contrary, are left alone. They are treated, it is true, with the measure of politeness which religious life demands; yet their company is avoided, lest a word might be said which would hurt their feelings. When I say imperfect souls, I am not referring to souls with spiritual imperfections only, for the holiest souls will not be perfect till they are in heaven. I mean those who are also afflicted with want of tact and refinement, as well as ultra-sensitive souls. I know such defects are incurable, but I also know how patient you would be, in nursing and striving to relieve me, were my illness to last for many years.

From all this I draw the conclusion: — I ought to seek the companionship of those Sisters towards whom I feel a natural aversion, and try to be their good Samaritan. A word or a smile is often enough to put fresh life in a despondent soul. And yet it is not merely in the hope of giving consolation that I try to be kind. If it were, I know that I should soon be discouraged, for well-intentioned words are often totally misunderstood. Consequently, not to lose my time or labour, I try to act solely to please Our Lord, and follow this precept of the Gospel: "When thou makest a dinner or a supper, call not thy friends or thy brethren, lest perhaps they also invite thee again and a recompense be made to thee. But when thou makest a feast, call the poor, the maimed, the blind, and the lame, and thou shalt be blessed, because they have naught wherewith to make thee recompense, and thy Father Who seeth in secret will repay thee."[9]

What feast can I offer my Sisters but a spiritual one of sweet and joyful charity! I know none other, and I wish to imitate St. Paul, who rejoiced with those who rejoiced. It is true that he wept with those who wept, and at my feast, too, the tears must sometimes fall, still I shall always try to change them into smiles, for "God loveth a cheerful giver." [10]

I remember an act of charity with which God inspired me while I was still a novice, and this act, though seemingly small, has been rewarded even in this life by Our Heavenly Father, "Who seeth in secret."

Shortly before Sister St. Peter became quite bedridden, it was necessary every evening, at ten minutes to six, for someone to leave meditation and take her to the refectory. It cost me a good deal to offer my services, for I knew the difficulty, or I should say the impossibility, of pleasing the poor invalid. But I did not want to lose such a good opportunity, for I recalled Our Lord's words: "As long as you did it to one of these my least brethren, you did it to Me."[11] I therefore humbly offered my aid. It was not without difficulty I induced her to accept it, but after considerable persuasion I succeeded. Every evening, when I saw her shake her sand-glass, I understood that she meant: "Let us go!" Summoning up all my courage I rose, and the ceremony began. First of all, her stool had to be moved and carried in a particular way, and on no account must there be any hurry. The solemn procession ensued. I had to follow the good Sister, supporting her by her girdle; I did it as gently as possible, but if by some mischance she stumbled, she imagined I had not a firm hold, and that she was going to fall. "You are going too fast," she would say, "I shall fall and hurt myself!" Then when I tried to lead her more quietly: "Come quicker . . . I cannot feel you . . . you are letting me go! I was right when I said you were too young to take care of me."

When we reached the refectory without further mishap, more troubles were in store. I had to settle my poor invalid in her place, taking great pains not to hurt her. Then I had to turn back her sleeves, always according to her own special rubric, and after that I was allowed to go.

But I soon noticed that she found it very difficult to cut her bread, so I did not leave her till I had performed this last service. She was much touched by this attention on my part, for she had not expressed any wish on the subject; it was by this unsought-for kindness that I gained her entire confidence, and chiefly because—as I learnt later—at the end of my humble task I bestowed upon her my sweetest smile.

Dear Mother, it is long since all this happened, but Our Lord allows the memory of it to linger with me like a perfume from Heaven. One cold winter evening, I was occupied in the lowly work of which I have just spoken, when suddenly I heard in the distance the harmonious strains of music outside the convent walls. I pictured a drawing-room, brilliantly lighted and decorated, and richly furnished. Young ladies, elegantly dressed, exchanged a thousand compliments, as is the way of the world. Then I looked on the poor invalid I was tending. Instead of sweet music I heard her complaints, instead of rich gilding I saw the brick walls of our bare cloister, scarcely visible in the dim light. The contrast was very moving. Our Lord so illuminated my soul with the rays of truth, before which the pleasures of the world are but as darkness, that for a thousand years of such worldly delights, I would not have bartered even the ten minutes spent in my act of charity.

If even now, in days of pain and amid the smoke of battle, the thought that God has withdrawn us from the world is so entrancing, what will it be when, in eternal glory and everlasting repose, we realise the favour beyond compare He has done us here, by singling us out to dwell in His Carmel, the very portal of Heaven?

I have not always felt these transports of joy in performing acts of charity, but at the beginning of my religious life Jesus wished to make me feel how sweet to Him is charity, when found in the hearts of his Spouses. Thus when I led Sister St. Peter, it was with so much love that I could not have shown more were I guiding Our Divine Lord Himself.

The practice of charity has not always been so pleasant as I have just pointed out, dear Mother, and to prove it I will recount some of my many struggles.

For a long time my place at meditation was near a Sister who fidgeted continually, either with her Rosary, or something else; possibly, as I am very quick of hearing, I alone heard her, but I cannot tell you how much it tried me. I should have liked to turn round, and by looking at the offender, make her stop the noise; but in my heart I knew that I ought to bear it tranquilly, both for the love of God and to avoid giving pain. So I kept quiet, but the effort cost me so much that sometimes I was bathed in perspiration, and my meditation consisted merely in suffering with patience. After a time I tried to endure it in peace and joy, at least deep down in my soul, and I strove to take actual pleasure in the disagreeable little noise. Instead of trying not to hear it, which was impossible, I set myself to listen, as though it had been some delightful music, and my meditation—which was not the "prayer of quiet"—was passed in offering this music to Our Lord.

Another time I was working in the laundry, and the Sister opposite, while washing handkerchiefs, repeatedly splashed me with dirty water. My first impulse was to draw back and wipe my face, to show the offender I should be glad if she would behave more quietly; but the next minute I thought how foolish it was to refuse the treasures God offered me so generously, and I refrained from betraying my annoyance. On the contrary, I made such efforts to welcome the shower of dirty water, that at the end of half an hour I had taken quite a fancy to this novel kind of aspersion, and I resolved to come as often as I could to the happy spot where such treasures were freely bestowed.

Dear Mother, you see that I am a very little soul, who can only offer very little things to Our Lord. It still happens that I frequently let slip the occasion of these slender sacrifices, which bring so much peace, but this does not discourage me; I bear the loss of a little peace, and I try to be more watchful for the future.

How happy does Our Lord make me, and how sweet and easy is His service on this earth! He has always given me what I desired, or rather He has made me desire what He wishes to give. A short time before my terrible temptation against Faith, I had reflected how few exterior trials, worthy of mention, had fallen to my lot, and that if I were to have interior trials, God must change my path; and this I did not think He would do. Yet I could not always live at ease. Of what means, then, would He make use?

I had not long to wait for an answer, and it showed me that He whom I love is never at a loss, for without changing my way, He sent me this great trial; and thus mingled a healing bitterness with all the sweet. _____

[1] Cf. Rom. 8:15.

[2] Exod. 9:16.

[3] Cf. Ps. 33[34]:6.

[4] Ps. 111[112]:4.

[5] Prov. 18:19.

[6] John 10:12.

[7] Cf. 2 Kings 16:10.

[8] Mark 7:28.

[9] Cf. Luke 14:12, 13, 14.

[10] 2 Cor. 9:7.

[11] Matt. 25:40.

CHAPTER XI A CANTICLE OF LOVE

It is not only when He is about to send me some trial that Our Lord gives me warning and awakens my desire for it. For years I had cherished a longing which seemed impossible of realisation—to have a brother a Priest. I often used to think that if my little brothers had not gone to Heaven, I should have had the happiness of seeing them at the Altar. I greatly regretted being deprived of this joy. Yet God went beyond my dream; I only asked for one brother who would remember me each day at the Holy Altar, and He has united me in the bonds of spiritual friendship with two of His apostles. I should like to tell you, dear Mother, how Our Divine Master fulfilled my desire.

In 1895 our holy Mother, St. Teresa, sent my first brother as a gift for my feast. It was washing day, and I was busy at my work, when Mother Agnes of Jesus, then Prioress, called me aside and read me a letter from a young Seminarist, in which he said he had been inspired by St. Teresa to ask for a sister who would devote herself specially to his salvation, and to the salvation of his future flock. He promised always to remember this spiritual sister when saying Mass, and the choice fell upon me. Dear Mother, I cannot tell you how happy this made me.

Such unlooked-for fulfillment of my desire awoke in my heart the joy of a child; it carried me back to those early days, when pleasures were so keen, that my heart seemed too small to contain them. Years had passed since I had tasted a like happiness, so fresh, so unfamiliar, as if forgotten chords had been stirred within me.

Fully aware of my obligations, I set to work, and strove to redouble my fervour. Now and again I wrote to my new brother. Undoubtedly, it is by prayer and sacrifice that we can help our missionaries, but sometimes, when it pleases Our Lord to unite two souls for His Glory, He permits them to communicate their thoughts, and thus inspire each other to love God more. Of course an express command from those in authority is needed for this, otherwise, it seems to me, that such a correspondence would do more harm than good, if not to the missionary, at least to the Carmelite, whose manner of life tends to continual introversion. This exchange of letters, though rare, would occupy her mind uselessly; instead of uniting her to God, she would perhaps fancy she was doing wonders, when in reality, under cover of zeal, she was doing nothing but producing needless distraction. — And here am I, launched, not upon a distraction, but upon a dissertation equally superfluous. I shall never be able to correct myself of these lengthy digressions which must be so wearisome to you, dear Mother. Forgive me, should I offend again.

Last year, at the end of May, it was your turn to give me my second brother, and when I represented that, having given all my merits to one future apostle, I feared they could not be given to another, you told me that obedience would double their value. In the depths of my heart I thought the same thing, and, since the zeal of a Carmelite ought to embrace the whole world, I hope, with God's help, to be of use to even more than two missionaries. I pray for all, not forgetting our Priests at home, whose ministry is quite as difficult as that of the missionary preaching to the heathen. . . . In a word, I wish to be a true daughter of the Church, like our holy Mother St. Teresa, and pray for all the intentions of Christ's Vicar. That is the one great aim of my life. But just as I should have had a special interest in my little brothers had they lived, and that, without neglecting the general interests of the Church, so now, I unite myself in a special way to the new brothers whom Jesus has given me. All that I possess is theirs also. God is too good to give by halves; He is so rich that He gives me all I ask for, even though I do not lose myself in lengthy enumerations. As I have two brothers and my little sisters, the novices, the days would be too short were I to ask in detail for the needs of each soul, and I fear I might forget something important. Simple souls cannot understand complicated methods, and, as I am one of their number, Our Lord has inspired me with a very simple way of fulfilling my obligations. One day, after Holy Communion, He made me understand these words of the Canticles: "Draw me: we will run after Thee to the odour of Thy ointments."[1] O my Jesus, there is no need to say: "In drawing me, draw also the souls that I love": these words, "Draw me," suffice. When a soul has let herself be taken captive by the inebriating odour of Thy perfumes, she cannot run alone; as a natural consequence of her attraction towards Thee, the souls of all those she loves are drawn in her train.

Just as a torrent carries into the depths of the sea all that it meets on its way, so, my Jesus, does the soul who plunges into the shoreless ocean of Thy Love bring with it all its treasures. My treasures are the souls it has pleased thee to unite with mine; Thou hast confided them to me, and therefore I do not fear to use Thy own words, uttered by Thee on the last night that saw Thee still a traveller on this earth. Jesus, my Beloved! I know not when my exile will have an end. Many a night I may yet sing Thy Mercies here below, but for me also will come the last night, and then I shall be able to say:

"I have glorified Thee upon earth: I have finished the work which Thou gavest me to do. I have manifested Thy name to the men whom Thou hast given me out of the world. Thine they were, and to me Thou gavest them; and they have kept Thy word. Now they have known that all things which Thou hast given me are from Thee: because the words which Thou gavest me I have given to them; and they have received them, and have known for certain that I came forth from Thee, and they have believed that Thou didst send me. I pray for them: I pray not for the world, but for them whom Thou hast given me, because they are Thine. And all mine are Thine, and Thine are mine; and I am glorified in them. And now I am no more in the world, and these are in the world, and I come to Thee. Holy Father, keep them in Thy name, whom Thou hast given me, that they may be one, as we also are one. And now I come to Thee, and these things I speak in the world, that they may have my joy filled in themselves. I do not ask that Thou take them away out of the world, but that Thou preserve them from evil. They are not of the world, as I also am not of the world. And not for them only do I pray, but for those also who through their word shall believe in me. Father, I will that where I am they also whom Thou hast given me may be with me, that they may see my glory which Thou hast given me, because Thou hast loved me before the foundation of the world. And I have made known Thy name unto them, and will make it known, that the love wherewith Thou hast loved me may be in them and I in them."[2]

Yea, Lord, thus would I repeat Thy words, before losing myself in Thy loving embrace. Perhaps it is daring, but, for a long time, hast thou not allowed me to be daring with Thee? Thou hast said to me, as the Prodigal's father to his elder son: "All I have is thine."[3] And therefore I may use thy very own words to draw down favours from Our Heavenly Father on all who are dear to me.

My God, Thou knowest that I have ever desired to love Thee alone. It has been my only ambition. Thy love has gone before me, even from the days of my childhood. It has grown with my growth, and now it is an abyss whose depths I cannot fathom.

Love attracts love; mine darts towards Thee, and would fain make the abyss brim over, but alas! it is not even as a dewdrop in the ocean. To love Thee as Thou lovest me, I must make Thy Love mine own. Thus alone can I find rest. O my Jesus, it seems to me that Thou couldst not have overwhelmed a soul with more love than Thou hast poured out on mine, and that is why I dare ask Thee to love those Thou hast given me, even as Thou lovest me.

If, in Heaven, I find that thou lovest them more than Thou lovest me, I shall rejoice, for I acknowledge that their deserts are greater than mine, but now, I can conceive no love more vast than that with which Thou hast favoured me, without any merit on my part.

. . . .

Dear Mother, what I have just written amazes me. I had no intention of writing it. When I said: "The words which Thou gavest me I have given unto them," I was thinking only of my little sisters in the noviciate. I am not able to teach missionaries, and the words I wrote for them were from the prayer of Our Lord: "I do not ask that Thou shouldst take them out of the world; I pray also for them who through their word shall believe in Thee."

How could I forget those souls they are to win by their sufferings and exhortations?

But I have not told you all my thoughts on this passage of the Sacred Canticles: "Draw me—we will run!" Our Lord has said: "No man can come to Me except the Father Who hath sent Me, draw him,"[4] and later He tells us that *whosoever seeks shall find, whosoever asks shall receive, that unto him that knocks it shall be opened,* and He adds that whatever we ask the Father in His Name shall be given us. It was no doubt for this reason that, long before the birth of Our Lord, the Holy Spirit dictated these prophetic words: "Draw me—we will run!" By asking to be drawn, we desire an intimate union with the object of our love. If iron and fire were endowed with reason, and the iron could say: "Draw me!" would not that prove its desire to be identified with the fire to the point of sharing its substance? Well, this is precisely my prayer. I asked Jesus to draw me into the Fire of His love, and to unite me so closely to Himself that He may live and act in me. I feel that the more the fire of love consumes my heart, so much the more shall I say: "Draw me!" and the more also will souls who draw near me *run swiftly in the sweet odour of the Beloved.*

Yes, they will run—we shall all run together, for souls that are on fire can never be at rest. They may indeed, like St. Mary Magdalen, sit at the feet of Jesus, listening to His sweet and burning words, but, though they seem to give Him nothing, they give much more than Martha, who busied herself about many things. It is not Martha's work that Our Lord blames, but her over-solicitude; His Blessed Mother humbly occupied herself in the same kind of work when she prepared the meals for the Holy Family. All the Saints have understood this, especially those who have illumined the earth with the light of Christ's teaching. Was it not from prayer that St. Paul, St. Augustine, St. Thomas Aquinas, St. John of the Cross, St. Teresa, and so many other friends of God drew that wonderful science which has enthralled the loftiest minds? "Give me a lever and a fulcrum on which to lean it," said Archimedes, "and I will lift the world."

What he could not obtain because his request had only a material end, without reference to God, the Saints have obtained in all its fulness. They lean on God Almighty's power itself and their lever is the prayer that inflames with love's fire. With this lever they have raised the world—with this lever the

Saints of the Church Militant still raise it, and will raise it to the end of time.

Dear Mother, I have still to tell you what I understand by the *sweet odour of the Beloved.* As Our Lord is now in Heaven, I can only follow Him by the footprints He has left—footprints full of life, full of fragrance. I have only to open the Holy Gospels and at once I breathe the perfume of Jesus, and then I know which way to run; and it is not to the first place, but to the last, that I hasten. I leave the Pharisee to go up, and full of confidence I repeat the humble prayer of the Publican. Above all I follow Magdalen, for the amazing, rather I should say, the loving audacity, that delights the Heart of Jesus, has cast its spell upon mine. It is not because I have been preserved from mortal sin that I lift up my heart to God in trust and love. I feel that even had I on my conscience every crime one could commit, I should lose nothing of my confidence: my heart broken with sorrow, I would throw myself into the Arms of my Saviour. I know that He loves the Prodigal Son, I have heard His words to St. Mary Magdalen, to the woman taken in adultery, and to the woman of Samaria. No one could frighten me, for I know what to believe concerning His Mercy and His Love. And I know that all that multitude of sins would disappear in an instant, even as a drop of water cast into a flaming furnace.

It is told in the Lives of the Fathers of the Desert how one of them converted a public sinner, whose evil deeds were the scandal of the whole country. This wicked woman, touched by grace, followed the Saint into the desert, there to perform rigorous penance. But on the first night of the journey, before even reaching the place of her retirement, the bonds that bound her to earth were broken by the vehemence of her loving sorrow. The holy man, at the same instant, saw her soul borne by Angels to the Bosom of God.

This is a striking example of what I want to say, but these things cannot be expressed. Dearest Mother, if weak and imperfect souls like mine felt what I feel, none would despair of reaching the summit of the Mountain of Love, since Jesus does not ask for great deeds, but only for gratitude and self-surrender.

He says: "I will not take the he-goats from out of the flocks, for all the beasts of the forests are mine, the cattle on the hills and the oxen. I know all the fowls of the air. If I were hungry, I would not tell thee, for the world is Mine, and the fulness thereof.

Shall I eat the flesh of bullocks, or shall I drink the blood of goats? Offer to God the sacrifice of praise and thanksgiving."[5]

This is all Our Lord claims from us. He has need of our love—He has no need of our works. The same God, Who declares that He has no need to tell us if He be hungry, did not disdain to beg a little water from the Samaritan woman. He was athirst, but when He said: "Give me to drink,"[6] He, the Creator of the Universe, asked for the love of His creature. He thirsted for love.

And this thirst of Our Divine Lord was ever on the increase. Amongst the disciples of the world, He meets with nothing but indifference and ingratitude, and alas! among His own, how few hearts surrender themselves without reserve to the infinite tenderness of His Love. Happy are we who are privileged to understand the inmost secrets of Our Divine Spouse. If you, dear Mother, would but set down in writing all you know, what wonders could you not unfold!

But, like Our Blessed Lady, you prefer to *keep all these things in your heart.*[7] To me you say that "It is honourable to reveal and confess the world of God."

[8] Yet you are right to keep silence, for no earthly words can convey the secrets of Heaven.

As for me, in spite of all I have written, I have not as yet begun. I see so many beautiful horizons, such infinitely varied tints, that the palette of the Divine Painter will alone, after the darkness of this life, be able to supply me with the colours wherewith I may portray the wonders that my soul descries. Since, however, you have expressed a desire to penetrate into the hidden sanctuary of my heart, and to have in writing what was the most consoling dream of my life, I will end this story of my soul, by an act of obedience. If you will allow me, it is to Jesus I will address myself, for in this way I shall speak more easily. You may find my expressions somewhat exaggerated, but I assure you there is no exaggeration in my heart—there all is calm and peace.

O my Jesus, who can say how tenderly and gently Thou dost lead my soul! The storm had raged there ever since Easter, the glorious feast of Thy triumph, until, in the month of May, there shone through the darkness of my night one bright ray of grace. . . . My mind dwelt on mysterious dreams sent sometimes to Thy favoured ones, and I thought how such a consolation was not to be mine—that for me, it was night, always the dark night. And in the midst of the storm I fell asleep. The following day, May 10, just at dawn, I dreamt that I was walking in a gallery alone with Our Mother. Suddenly, without knowing how they had entered, I perceived three Carmelites, in mantles and long veils, and I knew that they came from Heaven. "Ah!" I thought, "how glad I should be if I could but look on the face of one of these Carmelites!" And, as if my wish had been heard, I saw the tallest of the three Saints advance towards me. An inexpressible joy took possession of me as she raised her veil, and then covered me with it.

At once I recognised our Venerable Mother, Anne of Jesus, foundress of the Carmel in France.[9] Her face was beautiful with an unearthly beauty; no rays came from it, and yet, in spite of the thick veil which enveloped us, I could see it suffused by a soft light, which seemed to emanate from her heavenly countenance. She caressed me tenderly, and seeing myself the object of such affection, I made bold to say: "Dear Mother, I entreat you, tell me, will Our Lord leave me much longer in this world? Will He not soon come to fetch me?" She smiled sweetly, and answered, "Yes, soon . . . very soon . . . I promise you." "Dear Mother," I asked again, "tell me if He does not want more from me than these poor little acts and desires that I offer Him. Is He pleased with me?" Then our Venerable Mother's face shone with a new splendour, and her expression became still more gracious: "The Good God asks no more of you," she said, "He is pleased, quite pleased," and, taking my head between her hands, she kissed me so tenderly that it would be impossible to describe the joy I felt. My heart was overflowing with gladness, and, remembering my Sisters, I was about to beseech some favour for them, when, alas! I awoke. My happiness was too great for words. Many months have passed since I had this wonderful dream, and yet its memory is as fresh and delightful as ever. I can still picture the loving smiles of this holy Carmelite and feel her fond caresses. O Jesus! "Thou didst command the winds and the storm, and there came a great calm."[10]

On waking, I realised that Heaven does indeed exist, and that this Heaven is peopled with souls who cherish me as their child, and this impression still remains with me—all the sweeter, because, up to that time, I had but little devotion to the Venerable Mother Anne of Jesus. I had never sought her help, and but rarely heard her name. And now I know and understand how constantly I was in her thoughts, and the knowledge adds to my love for her and for all the dear ones in my Father's Home.

O my Beloved! this was but the prelude of graces yet greater which Thou didst desire to heap upon me. Let me remind Thee of them to-day, and forgive my folly if I venture to tell Thee once more of my hopes, and my heart's well nigh infinite longings—forgive me and grant my desire, that it may be well with my soul. To be Thy Spouse, O my Jesus, to be a daughter of Carmel, and by my union with Thee to be the mother of souls, should not all this content me? And yet other vocations make themselves felt —I feel called to the Priesthood and to the Apostolate—I would be a Martyr, a Doctor of the Church. I should like to accomplish the most heroic deeds—the spirit of the Crusader burns within me, and I long to die on the field of battle in defence of Holy Church.

The vocation of a Priest! With what love, my Jesus, would I bear Thee in my hand, when my words brought Thee down from Heaven! With what love would I give Thee to souls! And yet, while longing to be a Priest, I admire and envy the humility of St. Francis of Assisi, and am drawn to imitate him by refusing the sublime dignity of the

Priesthood. How reconcile these opposite tendencies?[11]

Like the Prophets and Doctors, I would be a light unto souls, I would travel to every land to preach Thy name, O my Beloved, and raise on heathen soil the glorious standard of Thy Cross. One mission alone would not satisfy my longings. I would spread the Gospel to the ends of the earth, even to the most distant isles. I would be a Missionary, not for a few years only, but, were it possible, from the beginning of the world till the consummation of time. Above all, I thirst for the Martyr's crown. It was the desire of my earliest days, and the desire has deepened with the years passed in the Carmel's narrow cell. But this too is folly, since I do not sigh for one torment; I need them all to slake my thirst. Like Thee, O Adorable Spouse, I would be scourged, I would be crucified! I would be flayed like St. Bartholomew, plunged into boiling oil like St. John, or, like St. Ignatius of Antioch, ground by the teeth of wild beasts into a bread worthy of God. [12]

With St. Agnes and St. Cecilia I would offer my neck to the sword of the executioner, and like Joan of Arc I would murmur the name of Jesus at the stake.

My heart thrills at the thought of the frightful tortures Christians are to suffer at the time of Anti-Christ, and I long to undergo them all. Open, O Jesus, the Book of Life, in which are written the deeds of Thy Saints: all the deeds told in that book I long to have accomplished for Thee. To such folly as this what answer wilt Thou make? Is there on the face of this earth a soul more feeble than mine? And yet, precisely because I am feeble, it has delighted Thee to accede to my least and most child-like desires, and to-day it is Thy good pleasure to realise those other desires, more vast than the Universe. These aspirations becoming a true martyrdom, I opened, one day, the Epistles of St. Paul to seek relief in my sufferings. My eyes fell on the 12th and 13th chapters of the First Epistle to the Corinthians. I read that all cannot become Apostles, Prophets, and Doctors; that the Church is composed of different members; that the eye cannot also be the hand. The answer was clear, but it did not fulfill my desires, or give to me the peace I sought. "Then descending into the depths of my nothingness, I was so lifted up that I reached my aim."[13]

Without being discouraged I read on, and found comfort in this counsel: "Be zealous for the better gifts. And I show unto you a yet more excellent way."[14] The Apostle then explains how all perfect gifts are nothing without Love, that Charity is the most excellent way of going surely to God. At last I had found rest.

Meditating on the mystical Body of Holy Church, I could not recognise myself among any of its members as described by St. Paul, or was it not rather that I wished to recognise myself in all? Charity provided me with the key to my vocation. I understood that since the Church is a body composed of different members, the noblest and most important of all the organs would not be wanting. I knew that the Church has a heart, that this heart burns with love, and that it is love alone which gives life to its members. I knew that if this love were extinguished, the Apostles would no longer preach the Gospel, and the Martyrs would refuse to shed their blood. I understood that love embraces all vocations, that it is all things, and that it reaches out through all the ages, and to the uttermost limits of the earth, because it is eternal.

Then, beside myself with joy, I cried out: "O Jesus, my Love, at last I have found my vocation. My vocation is love! Yes, I have found my place in the bosom of the Church, and this place, O my God, Thou hast Thyself given to me: in the heart of the

Church, my Mother, I will be LOVE! . . . Thus I shall be all things: thus will my dream be realised. . . ."

Why do I say I am beside myself with joy? This does not convey my thought. Rather is it peace which has become my portion—the calm peace of the sailor when he catches sight of the beacon which lights him to port. O luminous Beacon of Love! I know how to come even unto Thee, I have found the means of borrowing Thy Fires.

I am but a weak and helpless child, yet it is my very weakness which makes me dare to offer myself, O Jesus, as victim to Thy Love.

In olden days pure and spotless holocausts alone were acceptable to the Omnipotent God. Nor could His Justice be appeased, save by the most perfect sacrifices. But the law of fear has given place to the law of love, and Love has chosen me, a weak and imperfect creature, as its victim. Is not such a choice worthy of God's Love? Yea, for in order that Love may be fully satisfied, it must stoop even unto nothingness, and must transform that nothingness into fire. O my God, I know it—"Love is repaid by love alone."[15] Therefore I have sought, I have found, how to ease my heart, by rendering Thee love for love.

"Use the riches that make men unjust, to find you friends who may receive you into everlasting dwellings."[16] This, O Lord, is the advice Thou gavest to Thy disciples after complaining that "the children of this world are wiser in their generation than the children of light."[17]

Child of light, as I am, I understood that my desires to be all things, and to embrace all vocations, were riches that might well make me unjust; so I set to work to use them for the making of friends. Mindful of the prayer of Eliseus when he asked the Prophet Elias for his double spirit, I presented myself before the company of the Angels and Saints and addressed them thus: "I am the least of all creatures. I know my mean estate, but I know that noble and generous hearts love to do good. Therefore, O Blessed Inhabitants of the Celestial City, I entreat you to adopt me as your child. All the glory that you help me to acquire, will be yours; only deign to hear my prayer, and obtain for me a double portion of the love of God."

O my God! I cannot measure the extent of my request, I should fear to be crushed by the very weight of its audacity. My only excuse is my claim to childhood, and that children do not grasp the full meaning of their words. Yet if a father or mother were on the throne and possessed vast treasures, they would not hesitate to grant the desires of those little ones, more dear to them than life itself. To give them pleasure they will stoop even unto folly.

Well, I am a child of Holy Church, and the Church is a Queen, because she is now espoused to the Divine King of Kings. I ask not for riches or glory, not even the glory of Heaven—that belongs by right to my brothers the Angels and Saints, and my own glory shall be the radiance that streams from the queenly brow of my Mother, the Church. Nay, I ask for Love. To love Thee, Jesus, is now my only desire. Great deeds are not for me; I cannot preach the Gospel or shed my blood. No matter! My brothers work in my stead, and I, a little child, stay close to the throne, and love Thee for all who are in the strife.

But how shall I show my love, since love proves itself by deeds? Well! The little child will strew flowers . . . she will embrace the Divine Throne with their fragrance, she will sing Love's Canticle in silvery tones. Yes, my Beloved, it is thus my short life shall be spent in Thy sight. The only way I have of proving my love is to strew flowers before Thee —that is to say, I will let no tiny sacrifice pass, no look, no word. I wish to profit by the smallest actions, and to do them for Love. I wish to suffer for Love's sake, and for Love's sake even to rejoice: thus shall I strew flowers. Not one shall I find without scattering its petals before Thee . . . and I will sing . . . I will sing always, even if my roses must be gathered from amidst thorns; and the longer and sharper the thorns, the sweeter shall be my song.

But of what avail to thee, my Jesus, are my flowers and my songs? I know it well: this fragrant shower, these delicate petals of little price, these songs of love from a poor little heart like mine, will nevertheless be pleasing unto Thee. Trifles they are, but Thou wilt smile on them. The Church Triumphant, stooping towards her child, will gather up these scattered rose leaves, and, placing them in Thy Divine Hands, there to acquire an infinite value, will shower them on the Church Suffering to extinguish its flames, and on the Church Militant to obtain its victory.

O my Jesus, I love Thee! I love my Mother, the Church; I bear in mind that "the least act of pure love is of more value to her than all other works together."[18]

But is this pure love really in my heart? Are not my boundless desires but dreams—but foolishness?

If this be so, I beseech Thee to enlighten me; Thou knowest I seek but the truth. If my desires be rash, then deliver me from them, and from this most grievous of all martyrdoms. And yet I confess, if I reach not those heights to which my soul aspires, this very martyrdom, this foolishness, will have been sweeter to me than eternal bliss will be, unless by a miracle Thou shouldst take from me all memory of the hopes I entertained upon earth. Jesus, Jesus! If the mere desire of Thy Love awakens such delight, what will it be to possess it, to enjoy it for ever?

How can a soul so imperfect as mine aspire to the plenitude of Love? What is the key of this mystery? O my only Friend, why dost Thou not reserve these infinite longings to lofty souls, to the eagles that soar in the heights? Alas! I am but a poor little unfledged bird. I am not an eagle, I have but the eagle's eyes and heart! Yet, notwithstanding my exceeding littleless, I dare to gaze upon the Divine Sun of Love, and I burn to dart upwards unto Him! I would fly, I would imitate the eagles; but all that I can do is to lift up my little wings — it is beyond my feeble power to soar. What is to become of me? Must I die of sorrow because of my helplessness? Oh, no! I will not even grieve. With daring self-abandonment there will I remain until death, my gaze fixed upon that Divine Sun. Nothing shall affright me, nor wind nor rain. And should impenetrable clouds conceal the Orb of Love, and should I seem to believe that beyond this life there is darkness only, that would be the hour of perfect joy, the hour in which to push my confidence to its uttermost bounds. I should not dare to detach my gaze, well knowing that beyond the dark clouds the sweet Sun still shines.

So far, O my God, I understand Thy Love for me. But Thou knowest how often I forget this, my only care. I stray from Thy side, and my scarcely fledged wings become draggled in the muddy pools of earth; then I lament "like a young swallow,"[19] and my lament tells Thee all, and I remember, O Infinite Mercy! that "Thou didst not come to call the just, but sinners."[20]

Yet shouldst Thou still be deaf to the plaintive cries of Thy feeble creature, shouldst Thou still be veiled, then I am content to remain benumbed with cold, my wings bedraggled, and once more I rejoice in this well-deserved suffering.

O Sun, my only Love, I am happy to feel myself so small, so frail in Thy sunshine, and I am in peace

... I know that all the eagles of Thy Celestial Court have pity on me, they guard and defend me, they put to flight the vultures—the demons that fain would devour me. I fear them not, these demons, I am not destined to be their prey, but the prey of the Divine Eagle.

O Eternal Word! O my Saviour! Thou art the Divine Eagle Whom I love—Who lurest me. Thou Who, descending to this land of exile, didst will to suffer and to die, in order to bear away the souls of men and plunge them into the very heart of the Blessed Trinity—Love's Eternal Home! Thou Who, reascending into inaccessible light, dost still remain concealed here in our vale of tears under the snow-white semblance of the Host, and this, to nourish me with Thine own substance! O Jesus! forgive me if I tell Thee that Thy Love reacheth even unto folly. And in face of this folly, what wilt Thou, but that my heart leap up to Thee? How could my trust have any limits?

I know that the Saints have made themselves as fools for Thy sake; being 'eagles,' they have done great things. I am too little for great things, and my folly it is to hope that Thy Love accepts me as victim; my folly it is to count on the aid of Angels and Saints, in order that I may fly unto Thee with thine own wings, O my Divine Eagle! For as long a time as Thou willest I shall remain—my eyes fixed upon Thee. I long to be allured by Thy Divine Eyes; I would become Love's prey. I have the hope that Thou wilt one day swoop down upon me, and, bearing me away to the Source of all Love, Thou wilt plunge me at last into that glowing abyss, that I may become for ever its happy Victim.

O Jesus! would that I could tell all *little souls* of Thine ineffable condescension! I feel that if by any possibility Thou couldst find one weaker than my own, Thou wouldst take delight in loading her with still greater favours, provided that she abandoned herself with entire confidence to Thine Infinite Mercy. But, O my Spouse, why these desires of mine to make known the secrets of Thy Love? Is it not Thyself alone Who hast taught them to me, and canst Thou not unveil them to others? Yea! I know it, and this I implore Thee! . . .

I ENTREAT THEE TO LET THY DIVINE EYES REST UPON A VAST NUMBER OF
LITTLE SOULS, I ENTREAT THEE TO CHOOSE, IN THIS WORLD, A LEGION OF
LITTLE VICTIMS OF THY LOVE.

---

[1] Cant. 1:3.

[2] Cf. John 17.

[3] Luke 15:31.

[4] John 6:44.

[5] Ps. 49[50]:9-14.

[6] John 4:7.

[7] Cf. Luke 2:19.

[8] Tob. 12:7.

[9] The Venerable Mother Anne of Jesus—in the world, Anne of Lobera—was born in Spain in 1545. She entered the Carmelite Order in 1570, in the first convent of St. Joseph of Avila, and shortly afterwards became the counsellor and coadjutor of St. Teresa, who called her, "her daughter and her crown." St. John of the Cross, who was her spiritual director for fourteen years, described her as "a seraph incarnate," and her prudence and sanctity were held in such esteem that the most learned men consulted her in their doubts, and accepted her answers as oracles. She was always faithful to the spirit of St. Teresa, and had received from Heaven

the mission to restore the Carmel to its primitive perfection. Having founded three convents of the Reform in Spain, she established one in France, and another in Belgium. She died in the odor of sanctity in the Carmel of Brussels on March 4, 1621. On May 3, 1878, His Holiness Pope Leo XIII signed the Decree introducing the Cause of her Beatification.

[10] Matt. 8:10.

[11] St. Francis of Assisi, out of humility, refused to accept the sublime dignity of the Priesthood, and remained a Deacon until his death. [Ed.]

[12] An allusion to the beautiful words of the martyr St. Ignatius of Antioch, uttered when he heard the roar of the lions in the Roman arena. "I am the wheat of Christ; let me be ground by the teeth of the wild beasts, that I may become clean bread." [Ed.]

[13] St. John of the Cross.

[14] 1 Cor. 12:31.

[15] St. John of the Cross.

[16] Cf. Luke 16:9.

[17] Luke 16:8.

[18] St. John of the Cross.

[19] Isa. 38:14.

[20] Matt. 9:15.

END OF THE AUTOBIOGRAPHY

EPILOGUE: A VICTIM OF DIVINE LOVE

"Many pages of this story"—said its writer—"will never be read upon earth." It is necessary to repeat and emphasize her words. There are sufferings which are not to be disclosed here below; Our Lord has jealously reserved to Himself the right to reveal their merit and glory, in the clear vision where all veils shall be removed. "My God," she cried on the day of her religious profession, "give me martyrdom of soul or body . . . or rather give me both the one and the other!" And Our Lord Who, as she herself avowed, fulfilled all her desires, granted this one also, and in more abundant measure than the rest. He caused "the floods of infinite tenderness pent up in His Divine Heart to overflow into the soul of His little Spouse." This was the "Martyrdom of Love," so well described in her melodious song. But it was her own doctrine that, "to dedicate oneself as a Victim of Love is not to be dedicated to sweetness and consolations; it is to offer oneself to all that is painful and bitter, because Love lives only by sacrifice . . . and the more we would surrender ourselves to Love, the more we must surrender ourselves to suffering."

Therefore, because she desired to attain "the loftiest height of Love," the Divine Master led her thither by the rugged path of sorrow, and it was only on its bleak summit that she died a *Victim of Love*.

. . . .

We have seen how great was her sacrifice in leaving her happy home and the Father who loved her so tenderly. It may be imagined that this sacrifice was softened, because at the Carmel she found again her two elder and dearly loved sisters. On the contrary, this afforded the young postulant many an occasion for repressing her strong natural affections. The rules of solitude and silence were strictly observed, and she only saw her sisters at recreation. Had she been less mortified, she might often have sat beside them, but "by preference she sought out the company of those religious who were least agreeable to her," and no one could tell whether or not she bore a special affection towards her own sisters.

Some time after her entrance, she was appointed as "aid" to Sister Agnes of Jesus, her dear "Pauline"; this was a fresh occasion for sacrifice. Thérèse knew that all unnecessary conversation was forbidden, and therefore she never allowed herself even the least word. "O my little Mother," she said later, "how I suffered! I could not open my heart to you, and I thought you no longer knew me!"

After five years of this heroic silence, Sister Agnes of Jesus was elected Prioress. On the evening of the election Thérèse might well have rejoiced that henceforth she could speak freely to her "little Mother," and, as of old, pour out her soul. But sacrifice had become her daily food. If she sought one favour more than another, it was that she might be looked on as the lowest and the least; and, among all the religious, not one saw less of the Mother Prioress.

She desired to live the life of Carmel with all the perfection required by St. Teresa, and, although a martyr to habitual dryness, her prayer was continuous. On one occasion a novice, entering her cell, was struck by the heavenly expression of her countenance. She was sewing industriously, and yet seemed lost in deep contemplation. "What are you thinking of?" the young Sister asked. "I am meditating on the 'Our Father,'" Thérèse answered. "It is so sweet to call God, 'Our Father!'" . . . and tears glistened in her eyes. Another time she said, "I cannot well see what more I shall have in Heaven than I have now; I shall see God, it is true, but, as to being with Him, I am that already even on earth."

The flame of Divine Love consumed her, and this is what she herself relates: "A few days after the oblation of myself to God's Merciful Love, I was in the choir, beginning the Way of the Cross, when I felt myself suddenly wounded by a dart of fire so ardent that I thought I should die. I do not know how to explain this transport; there is no comparison to describe the intensity of that flame. It seemed as though an invisible force plunged me wholly into fire. . . . But oh! what fire! what sweetness!"

When Mother Prioress asked her if this rapture was the first she had experienced, she answered simply: "Dear Mother, I have had several transports of love, and one in particular during my Noviciate, when I remained for a whole week far removed from this world. It seemed as though a veil were thrown over all earthly things. But, I was not then consumed by a real fire. I was able to bear those transports of love without expecting to see the ties that bound me to earth give way; whilst, on the day of which I now speak, one minute—one second—more and my soul must have been set free. Alas! I found myself again on earth, and dryness at once returned to my heart." True, the Divine Hand had withdrawn the fiery dart—but the wound was unto death!

In that close union with God, Thérèse acquired a remarkable mastery over self. All sweet virtues flourished in the garden of her soul, but do not let us imagine that these wondrous flowers grew without effort on her part.

"In this world there is no fruitfulness without suffering—either physical pain, secret sorrow, or trials known sometimes only to God. When good thoughts and generous resolutions have sprung up in our souls through reading the lives of the Saints, we ought not to content ourselves, as in the case of profane books, with paying a certain tribute of admiration to the genius of their authors—we should rather consider the price which, doubtless, they have paid for that supernatural good they have produced."[1]

And, if to-day Thérèse transforms so many hearts, and the good she does on earth is beyond reckoning, we may well believe she bought it all at the price with which Jesus bought back our souls: by suffering and the Cross!

Not the least of these sufferings was the unceasing war she waged against herself, refusing every satisfaction to the demands of her naturally proud and impetuous nature. While still a child she had acquired the habit of never excusing herself or making a complaint; at the Carmel she strove to be the little servant of her Sisters in religion, and in that same spirit of humility she endeavoured to obey all without distinction.

One evening, during her illness, the Community had assembled in the garden to sing a hymn before an Altar of the Sacred Heart. Soeur Thérèse, who was already wasted by fever, joined them with difficulty, and, arriving quite exhausted, was obliged to sit down at once. When the hymn began, one of the Sisters made her a sign to stand up. Without hesitation, the humble child rose, and, in spite of the fever and great oppression from which she was suffering, remained standing to the end.

The Infirmarian had advised her to take a little walk in the garden for a quarter of an hour each day. This recommendation was for her a command. One afternoon a Sister, noticing what an effort it cost her, said: "Soeur Thérèse, you would do much better to rest; walking like this cannot do you any good. You only tire yourself!" "That is true," she replied, "but, do you know what gives me strength? I offer each step for some missionary. I think that possibly, over there, far away, one of them is weary and tired in his apostolic labours, and to lessen his fatigue I offer mine to the Good God."

She gave her novices some beautiful examples of detachment. One year the relations of the Sisters and the servants of the Convent had sent bouquets of flowers for Mother Prioress's feast. Thérèse was arranging them most tastefully, when a Lay-sister said crossly: "It is easy to see that the large bouquets have been given by your friends. I suppose those sent by the poor will again be put in the background!" . . . A sweet smile was the only reply, and notwithstanding the unpleasing effect, she immediately put the flowers sent by the servants in the most conspicuous place.

Struck with admiration, the Lay-sister went at once to the Prioress to accuse herself of her unkindness, and to praise the patience and humility shown by Soeur Thérèse.

After the death of Thérèse that same Sister, full of confidence, pressed her forehead against the feet of the saintly nun, once more asking forgiveness for her fault. At the same instant she felt herself cured of cerebral anæmia, from which she had suffered for many years, and which had prevented her from applying herself either to reading or mental prayer.

Far from avoiding humiliations, Soeur Thérèse sought them eagerly, and for that reason she offered herself as "aid" to a Sister who, she well knew, was difficult to please, and her generous proposal was accepted. One day, when she had suffered much from this Sister, a novice asked her why she looked so happy. Great was her surprise on receiving the reply: "It is because Sister N. has just been saying disagreeable things to me. What pleasure she has given me! I wish I could meet her now, and give her a sweet smile." . . . As she was still speaking, the

Sister in question knocked at the door, and the astonished novice could see for herself how the Saints forgive. Soeur Thérèse acknowledged later on, she "soared so high above earthly things that humiliations did but make her stronger."

To all these virtues she joined a wonderful courage. From her entrance into the Carmel, at the age of fifteen, she was allowed to follow all the practices of its austere Rule, the fasts alone excepted. Sometimes her companions in the noviciate, seeing how pale she looked, tried to obtain a dispensation for her, either from the Night Office, or from rising at the usual hour in the morning, but the Mother Prioress would never yield to these requests. "A soul of such mettle," she would say, "ought not to be dealt with as a child; dispensations are not meant for her. Let her be, for God sustains her. Besides, if she is really ill, she should come and tell me herself."[2]

But it was always a principle with Thérèse that "We should go to the end of our strength before we complain." How many times did she assist at Matins suffering from vertigo or violent headaches! "I am able to walk," she would say, "and so I ought to be at my duty." And, thanks to this undaunted energy, she performed acts that were heroic.

It was with difficulty that her delicate stomach accustomed itself to the frugal fare of the Carmel. Certain things made her ill, but she knew so well how to hide this, that no one ever suspected it. Her neighbour at table said that she had tried in vain to discover the dishes that she preferred, and the kitchen Sisters, finding her so easy to please, invariably served her with what was left. It was only during her last illness, when she was ordered to say what disagreed with her, that her mortifications came to light. "When Jesus wishes us to suffer," she said at that time, "there can be no evading it. And so, when Sister Mary of the Sacred Heart[3] was procuratrix, she endeavoured to look after me with a mother's tenderness. To all appearances, I was well cared for, and yet what mortifications did she not impose upon me! for she served me according to her own taste, which was entirely opposed to mine."

Thérèse's spirit of sacrifice was far-reaching; she eagerly sought what was painful and disagreeable, as her rightful share. All that God asked she gave Him without hesitation or reserve.

"During my postulancy," she said, "it cost me a great deal to perform certain exterior penances, customary in our convents, but I never yielded to these repugnances; it seemed to me that the image of my Crucified Lord looked at me with beseeching eyes, and begged these sacrifices."

Her vigilance was so keen, that she never left unobserved any little recommendations of the Mother Prioress, or any of the small rules which render the religious life so meritorious. One of the old nuns, having remarked her extraordinary fidelity on this point, ever afterwards regarded her as a Saint. Soeur Thérèse was accustomed to say that she never did any great penances. That was because her fervour counted as nothing the few that were allowed her. It happened, however, that she fell ill through wearing for too long a time a small iron Cross, studded with sharp points, that pressed into her flesh. "Such a trifle would not have caused this," she said afterwards, "if God had not wished thus to make me understand that the greater austerities of the Saints are not meant for me—nor for the souls that walk in the path of 'spiritual childhood.'"

. . . .

"The souls that are the most dear to My Father," Our Lord once said to Saint Teresa, "are those He tries the most, and the greatness of their trials is the measure of His Love." Thérèse was a soul most dear to God, and He was about to fill up the measure of His Love by making her pass through a veritable martyrdom. The reader will remember the call on Good Friday, April 3, 1896, when, to use her own expression, she heard the "distant murmur which announced the approach of the Bridegroom"; but she had still to endure long months of pain before the blessed hour of her deliverance.

On the morning of that Good Friday, she made so little of the hæmorrhage of the previous night, that Mother Prioress allowed her to practise all the penances prescribed by the Rule for that day. In the afternoon, a novice saw her cleaning windows. Her face was livid, and, in spite of her great energy, it was evident that her strength was almost spent. Seeing her fatigue, the novice, who loved her dearly, burst into tears, and begged leave to obtain her some little reprieve. But the young novice-mistress strictly forbade her, saying that she was quite able to bear this slight fatigue on the day on which Jesus had suffered and died.

Soon a persistent cough made the Mother Prioress feel anxious; she ordered Soeur Thérèse a more strengthening diet, and the cough ceased for some time. "Truly sickness is too slow a liberator," exclaimed our dear little Sister, "I can only rely upon Love."

She was strongly tempted to respond to the appeal of the Carmelites of Hanoï, who much desired to have her, and began a novena to the Venerable Théophane Vénard[4] to obtain her cure, but alas! that novena proved but the beginning of a more serious phase of her malady.

Like her Divine Master, she passed through the world doing good; like Him, she had been forgotten and unknown, and now, still following in His Footsteps, she was to climb the hill of Calvary. Accustomed to see her always suffering, yet always joyous and brave, Mother Prioress, doubtless inspired by God, allowed her to take part in the Community exercises, some of which tired her extremely. At night, she would courageously mount the stairs alone, pausing at each step to take breath. It was with difficulty that she reached her cell, and then in so exhausted a state, that sometimes, as she avowed later, it took her quite an hour to undress. After all this exertion it was upon a hard pallet that she took her rest. Her nights, too, were very bad, and when asked if she would not like someone to be near her in her hours of pain, she replied: "Oh, no! on the contrary, I am only too glad to be in a cell away from my Sisters, that I may not be heard. I am content to suffer alone—as soon as I am pitied and loaded with attentions, my happiness leaves me."

What strength of soul these words betray! Where we find sorrow she found joy. What to us is to hard to bear—being overlooked and ignored by creatures—became to her a source of delight. And her Divine Spouse knew well how to provide that bitter joy she found so sweet. Painful remedies had often to be applied. One day, when she had suffered from them more than usual, she was resting in her cell during recreation, and overheard a Sister in the kitchen speaking of her thus: "Soeur Thérèse will not live long, and really sometimes I wonder what our Mother Prioress will find to say about her when she dies.[5] She will be sorely puzzled, for this little Sister, amiable as she is, has certainly never done anything worth speaking about." The Infirmarian, who had also overheard the remark, turned to Thérèse and said: "If you relied upon the opinion of creatures you would indeed be disillusioned today." "The opinion of creatures!" she replied; "happily God has given me the grace to be absolutely indifferent to that. Let me tell you something which showed me, once and for all, how much it is worth. A few days after my Clothing, I went to our dear Mother's room, and one of the Sisters who happened to be there, said on seeing me: 'Dear Mother, this novice certainly does you credit. How well she looks! I hope she may be able to observe the Rule for many years to come.' I was feeling decidedly pleased at this compliment when another Sister came in, and, looking at me, said: 'Poor little Soeur Thérèse, how very tired you seem! You quite alarm me. If you do not soon improve, I am afraid you will not be able to keep the Rule very long.' I was then only sixteen, but this little incident made such an impression on me, that I never again set store on the varying opinion of creatures."

On another occasion someone remarked: "It is said that you have never suffered much." Smiling, she pointed to a glass containing medicine of a bright red colour. "You see this little glass?" she said. "One would suppose that it contained a most delicious draught, whereas, in reality, it is more bitter than anything else I take. It is the image of my life. To others it has been all rose colour; they have thought that I continually drank of a most delicious wine; yet to me it has been full of bitterness. I say bitterness, and yet my life has not been a bitter one, for I have learned to find my joy and sweetness in all that is bitter."

"You are suffering very much just now, are you not?" "Yes, but then I have so longed to suffer."

"How it distresses us to see you in such pain, and to think that it may increase!" said her novices.

"Oh! Do not grieve about me. I have reached a point where I can no longer suffer, because all suffering is become so sweet. Besides, it is quite a mistake to trouble yourselves as to what I may still have to undergo. It is like meddling with God's work. We who run in the way of Love must never allow ourselves to be disturbed by anything. If I did not simply live from one moment to another, it would be impossible for me to be patient; but I only look at the present, I forget the past, and I take good care not to forestall the future. When we yield to discouragement or despair, it is usually because we think too much about the past and the future. But pray much for me, for it is often just when I cry to Heaven for help that I feel most abandoned."

"How do you manage not to give way to discouragement at such times?" "I turn to God and all His Saints, and thank them notwithstanding; I believe they want to see how far my trust may extend. But the words of Job have not entered my heart in vain: 'Even if God should kill me, I would still trust in Him.'[6] I own it has taken a long time to arrive at this degree of self-abandonment; but I have reached it now, and it is the Lord Himself Who has brought me there."

Another time she said: "Our Lord's Will fills my heart to the brim, and hence, if aught else is added, it cannot penetrate to any depth, but, like oil on the surface of limpid waters, glides easily across. If my heart were not already brimming over, and must needs be filled by the feelings of joy and sadness that alternate so rapidly, then indeed would it be flooded by a wave of bitter pain; but these quick-succeeding changes scarcely ruffle the surface of my soul, and in its depths there reigns a peace that nothing can disturb."

And yet her soul was enveloped in thick darkness, and her temptations against Faith, ever conquered but ever returning, were there to rob her of all feeling of happiness at the thought of her approaching death. "Were it not for this trial, which is impossible to understand," she would say, "I think I should die of joy at the prospect of soon leaving this earth."

By this trial, the Divine Master wished to put the finishing touches to her purification, and thus enable her not only to walk with rapid steps, but to run in her little way of confidence and abandonment. Her words repeatedly proved this. "I desire neither death nor life. Were Our Lord to offer me my choice, I would not choose. I only will what He wills; it is what He does that I love. I do not fear the last struggle, nor any pains—however great—my illness may bring. God has always been my help. He has led me by the hand from my earliest childhood, and on Him I rely. My agony may reach the furthest limits, but I am convinced He will never forsake me."

Such confidence in God, of necessity stirred the fury of the devil—of him who, at life's close, tries every ruse to sow the seeds of despair in the hearts of the dying.

"Last night I was seized with a terrible feeling of anguish," she confessed to Mother Agnes of Jesus on one occasion; "I was lost in darkness, and from out of it came an accursed voice: 'Are you certain God loves you? Has He Himself told you so? The opinion of creatures will not justify you in His sight.' These thoughts had long tortured me, when your little note, like a message from Heaven, was brought to me. You recalled to me, dear Mother, the special graces Jesus had lavished upon me, and, as though you had had a revelation concerning my trial, you assured me I was deeply loved by God, and was on the eve of receiving from His Hands my eternal crown. Immediately peace and joy were restored to my heart. Yet the thought came to me, 'It is my little Mother's affection that makes her write these words.' Straightway I felt inspired to take up the Gospels, and, opening the book at random, I lighted on a passage which had hitherto escaped me: 'He whom God hath sent speaketh the Words of God, for God doth not give the Spirit by measure.'[7] Then I fell asleep fully consoled. It was you, dear Mother, whom the Good God sent me, and I must believe you, because you speak the Words of God."

For several days, during the month of August, Thérèse remained, so to speak, beside herself, and implored that prayers might be offered for her. She had never before been seen in this state, and in her inexpressible anguish she kept repeating: "Oh! how necessary it is to pray for the agonising! If one only knew!"

One night she entreated the Infirmarian to sprinkle her bed with Holy Water, saying: "I am besieged by the devil. I do not see him, but I feel him; he torments me and holds me with a grip of iron, that I may not find one crumb of comfort; he augments my woes, that I may be driven to despair.

". . . And I cannot pray. I can only look at Our Blessed Lady and say: 'Jesus!' How needful is that prayer we use at Compline: 'Procul recedant somnia et noctium phantasmata!' ('Free us from the phantoms of the night.') Something mysterious is happening within me. I am not suffering for myself, but for some other soul, and satan is angry." The Infirmarian, startled, lighted a blessed candle, and the spirit of darkness fled, never to return; but the sufferer remained to the end in a state of extreme anguish.

One day, while she was contemplating the beautiful heavens, some one said to her: "soon your home will be there, beyond the blue sky. How lovingly you gaze at it!" She only smiled, but afterwards she said to the Mother Prioress: "Dear Mother, the Sisters do not realise my sufferings. Just now, when looking at the sky, I merely admired the beauty of the material heaven—the true Heaven seems more than ever closed against me. At first their words troubled me, but an interior voice whispered: 'Yes, you were looking to Heaven out of love. Since your soul is entirely delivered up to love, all your actions, even the most indifferent, are marked with this divine seal.' At once I was consoled."

In spite of the darkness which enveloped her, her Divine Saviour sometimes left the door of her prison ajar. Those were moments in which her soul lost itself in transports of confidence and love. Thus it happened that on a certain day, when walking in the garden supported by one of her own sisters, she stopped at the charming spectacle of a hen sheltering its pretty little ones under its wing. Her eyes filled with tears, and, turning to her companion, she said: "I cannot remain here any longer, let us go in!" And even when she reached her cell, her tears continued to fall, and it was some time before she could speak. At last she looked at her sister with a heavenly expression, and said: "I was thinking of Our Lord, and the beautiful comparison He chose in order to make us understand His ineffable tenderness. This is what He has done for me all the days of my life. He has completely hidden me under His Wing. I cannot express all that has just stirred my heart; it is well for me that God conceals Himself, and lets me see the effects of His Mercy but rarely, and as it were from 'behind the lattices.' Were it not so I could never bear such sweetness."

. . . .

Disconsolate at the prospect of losing their treasure, the Community began a novena to Our Lady of Victories on June 5, 1897, in the fervent hope that she would once again miraculously raise the drooping Little Flower. But her answer was the same as that given by the blessed Martyr, Théophane Vénard, and they were forced to accept with generosity the bitterness of the coming separation.

At the beginning of July, her state became very serious, and she was at last removed to the Infirmary. Seeing her empty cell, and knowing she would never return to it, Mother Agnes of Jesus said to her: "When you are no longer with us, how sad I shall feel when I look at this cell!"

"For consolation, little Mother, you can think how happy I am up there, and remember that much of my happiness was acquired in that little cell; for," she added, raising her beautiful eyes to Heaven, "I have suffered so much there, and I should have been happy to die there."

As she entered the Infirmary she looked towards the miraculous statue of Our Lady, which had been brought thither. It would be impossible to describe that look. "What is it you see?" said her sister Marie, the witness of her miraculous cure as a child. And Thérèse answered: "Never has she seemed to me so beautiful . . . but to-day it is the statue, whereas that other day, as you well know, it was not the statue!" And from that time she often received similar consolations.

One evening she exclaimed: "Oh, how I love Our Blessed Lady! Had I been a Priest, how I would have sung her praises! She is spoken of as unapproachable, whereas she should be represented as easy of imitation. . . . She is more Mother than Queen. I have heard it said that her splendour eclipses that of all the Saints as the rising sun makes all the stars disappear. It sounds so strange. That a Mother should take away the glory of her children! I think quite the reverse. I believe that she will greatly increase the splendour of the elect . . . Our Mother Mary! Oh! how simple her life must have been!" and, continuing her discourse, she drew such a sweet and delightful picture of the Holy Family that all present were lost in admiration.

A very heavy cross awaited her before going to join her Spouse. From August 16 to September 30, the happy day of her death, she was unable to receive Holy Communion, because of her continual sickness. Few have hungered for the Bread of Angels like this seraph of earth. Again and again during that last winter of her life, after nights of intolerable pain, she rose at early morn to partake of the Manna of Heaven, and she thought no price too heavy to pay for the bliss of feeding upon God. Before depriving her altogether of this Heavenly Food, Our Lord often visited her on her bed of pain. Her Communion on July 16, the feast of Our Lady of Mount Carmel, was specially touching. During the previous night she composed some verses which were to be sung before Communion.

Thou know'st the baseness of my soul, O Lord, Yet fearest not to stoop and enter me. Come to my heart, O Sacrament adored! Come to my heart . . . it craveth but for Thee! And when Thou comest, straightway let me die Of very love for Thee; this boon impart! Oh, hearken Jesus, to my suppliant cry: Come to my heart!

In the morning, when the Holy Viaticum was carried to the Infirmary, the cloisters were thickly strewn with wild flowers and rose-petals. A young Priest, who was about to say his first Mass that day in the Chapel of the Carmel, bore the Blessed Sacrament to the dying Sister; and at her desire,

Sister Mary of the Eucharist—whose voice was exceptionally sweet—sang the following couplet:

Sweet martyrdom! to die of love's keen fire:
The martyrdom of which my heart is fain!
Hasten, ye Cherubim, to tune your lyre;
I shall not linger long in exile's pain!
. . . .

Fulfill my dream, O Jesus, since I sigh
Of love to die!

A few days later Thérèse grew worse, and on July 30 she received Extreme Unction. Radiant with delight the little Victim of Love said to us: "The door of my dark prison is ajar. I am steeped in joy, especially since our Father Superior has assured me that to-day my soul is like unto that of a little child after Baptism."

No doubt she thought she was quickly to join the white-robed band of the Holy Innocents. She little knew that two long months of martyrdom had still to run their course. "Dear Mother," she said, "I entreat you, give me leave to die. Let me offer my life for such and such an intention"—naming it to the Prioress. And when the permission was refused, she replied: "Well, I know that just at this moment

Our Lord has such a longing for a tiny bunch of grapes—which no one will give Him—that He will perforce have to come and steal it. . . . I do not ask anything; this would be to stray from my path of self-surrender. I only beseech Our Lady to remind her Jesus of the title of *Thief,* which He takes to Himself in the Gospels, so that He may not forget to come and carry me away."

. . . .

One day Soeur Thérèse took an ear of corn from a sheaf they had brought her. It was so laden with grain that it bent on its stalk, and after gazing upon it for some time she said to the Mother Prioress: "Mother, that ear of corn is the image of my soul. God has loaded it with graces for me and for many others. And it is my dearest wish ever to bend beneath the weight of God's gifts, acknowledging that all comes from Him."

She was right. Her soul was indeed laden with graces, and it was easy to discern the Spirit of God speaking His praises out of the mouth of that innocent child.

Had not this Spirit of Truth already dictated these words to the great Teresa of Avila:

"Let those souls who have reached to perfect union with God hold themselves in high esteem, with a humble and holy presumption. Let them keep unceasingly before their eyes the remembrance of the good things they have received, and beware of the thought that they are practising humility in not recognising the gifts of God. Is it not clear that the constant remembrance of gifts bestowed serves to increase the love of the giver? How can he who ignores the riches he possesses, spend them generously upon others?"

But the above was not the only occasion on which the "little Thérèse of Lisieux"[8] gave utterance to words that proved prophetic. In the month of April, 1895, while she was still in excellent health, she said in confidence to one of the older nuns: "I shall die soon. I do not say that it will be in a few months, but in two or three years at most; I know it because of what is taking place in my soul."

The novices betrayed surprise when she read their inmost thoughts. "This is my secret," she said to them: "I never reprimand you without first invoking Our Blessed Lady, and asking her to inspire me as to what will be most for your good, and I am often astonished myself at the things I teach you. At such times I feel that I make no mistake, and that it is Jesus Who speak by my lips."

During her illness one of her sisters had experienced some moments of acute distress, amounting almost to discouragement, at the thought of the inevitable parting. Immediately afterwards she went to the Infirmary, but was careful not to let any sign of grief be seen. What was her surprise when Thérèse, in a sad and serious tone, thus addressed her: "We ought not to weep like those who have no hope."

One of the Mothers, having come to visit her, did her a trifling service. "How happy I should be," thought the Mother, "if this Angel would only say: 'I will repay you in Heaven!' At that instant Soeur Thérèse, turning to her, said: "Mother, I will repay you in Heaven!"

But more surprising than all, was her consciousness of the mission for which Our Lord had destined her. The veil which hides the future seemed lifted, and more than once she revealed to us its secrets, in prophecies which have already been realised.

"I have never given the Good God aught but love; it is with Love
He will repay.

AFTER MY DEATH I WILL LET FALL A SHOWER OF ROSES."

At another time she interrupted a Sister, who was speaking to her of the happiness of Heaven, by the sublime words: "It is not that which attracts me."

"And what attracts you?" asked the other. "Oh! it is Love! To love, to be beloved, and *to return to earth to win love for our Love!*"

One evening, she welcomed Mother Agnes of Jesus with an extraordinary expression of joy: "Mother!" she said, "some notes from a concert far away have just reached my ears, and have made me think that soon I shall be listening to the wondrous melodies of Paradise. The thought, however, gave me but a moment's joy—one hope alone makes my heart beat fast: the Love that I shall receive and the Love I shall be able to give!

"I feel that my mission is soon to begin—my mission to make others love God as I love Him . . . to each souls my *little way* . . .

I WILL SPEND MY HEAVEN IN DOING GOOD UPON EARTH.

Nor is this impossible, since from the very heart of the Beatific Vision, the Angels keep watch over us. No, there can be no rest for me until the end of the world. But when the Angel shall have said: 'Time is no more!' then I shall rest, then I shall be able to rejoice, because the number of the elect will be complete."

"And what is this *little way* that you would teach to souls?"

"IT IS THE WAY OF SPIRITUAL CHILDHOOD, THE WAY OF TRUST AND ABSOLUTE SELF-SURRENDER.

I want to point out to them the means that I have always found so perfectly successful, to tell them that there is but one thing to do here below: we must offer Jesus *the flowers of little sacrifices* and win Him by a caress. That is how I have won Him, and that is why I shall be made so welcome."

"Should I guide you wrongly by my *little way* of love," she said to a novice, "do not fear that I shall allow you to continue therein; I should soon come back to the earth, and tell you to take another road. If I do not return, then believe in the truth of these my words: We can never have too much confidence in the Good God, He is so mighty, so merciful. As we hope in Him so shall we receive."

On the eve of the feast of Our Lady of Mount Carmel, a novice said to her: "I think that if you were to die to-morrow, after Holy Communion, I should be quite consoled—it would be such a beautiful death!" Thérèse answered quickly: "Die after Holy Communion! Upon a great feast! Nay, not so. *In my 'little way' everything is most ordinary; all that I do, little souls must be able to do likewise.*"

And to one of her missionary brothers she wrote: "What draws me to my Heavenly Home is the summons of my Lord, together with the hope that at length I shall love Him as my heart desires, and shall be able to make Him loved by a multitude of souls who will bless Him throughout eternity."

And in another letter to China: "I trust fully that I shall not remain idle in Heaven; my desire is to continue my work for the Church and for souls. I ask this of God, and I am convinced He will hear my prayer. You see that if I quit the battle-field so soon, it is not from a selfish desire of repose. For a long time now, suffering has been my Heaven here upon earth, and I can hardly conceive how I shall become acclimatised to a land where joy is unmixed with sorrow. Jesus will certainly have to work a complete change in my soul—else I could never support the ecstasies of Paradise."

It was quite true, suffering had become her Heaven upon earth—she welcomed it as we do happiness. "When I suffer much," she would say, "when something painful or disagreeable happens to me, instead of a melancholy look, I answer by a smile. At first I did not always succeed, but now it has become a habit which I am glad to have acquired."

A certain Sister entertained doubts concerning the patience of Thérèse. One day, during a visit, she remarked that the invalid's face wore an expression of unearthly joy, and she sought to know the reason. "It is because the pain is so acute just now," Thérèse replied; "I have always forced myself to love suffering and to give it a glad welcome." "Why are you so bright this morning?" asked Mother Agnes of Jesus. "Because of two little crosses. Nothing gives me 'little joys' like 'little crosses.'" And another time: "You have had many trials to-day?" "Yes, but I love them! . . . I love all the Good God sends me!" "Your sufferings are terrible!" "No —they are not terrible: can a little Victim of Love find anything terrible that is sent by her Spouse? Each moment He sends me what I am able to bear, and nothing more, and if He increase the pain, my strength is increased as well. But I could never ask for greater sufferings—I am too little a soul. They would then be of my own choice. I should have to bear them all without Him, and I have never been able to do anything when left to myself."

Thus spoke that wise and prudent Virgin on her deathbed, and her lamp, filled to the brim with the oil of virtue, burned brightly to the end. If, as the Holy Spirit reminds us in the Book of Proverbs: "*A man's doctrine is proved by his patience,*"[9] those who have heard her may well believe in her doctrine, for she has proved it by a patience no test could overcome.

At each visit the doctor expressed his admiration. "If only you knew what she has to endure! I have never seen any one suffer so intensely with such a look of supernatural joy. . . . I shall not be able to cure her; she was not made for this earth." In view of her extreme weakness, he ordered some strengthening remedies. Thérèse was at first distressed because of their cost, but she afterwards admitted: "I am no longer troubled at having to take those expensive remedies, for I have read that when they were given to St. Gertrude, she was gladdened by the thought that it would redound to the good of our benefactors, since Our Lord Himself has said: 'Whatever you do to the least of My little ones, you do unto Me.'"[10] "I am convinced that medicines are powerless to cure me," she added, "but I have made a covenant with God that the poor missionaries who have neither time nor means to take care of themselves may profit thereby."

She was much moved by the constant gifts of flowers made to her by her friends outside the Convent, and again by the visits of a sweet little redbreast that loved to play about her bed. She saw in these things the Hand of God. "Mother, I feel deeply the many touching proofs of God's Love for me. I am laden with them . . . nevertheless, I continue in the deepest gloom! . . . I suffer much . . . very much! and yet my state is one of profound peace. All my longings have been realised . . . I am full of confidence."

Shortly afterwards she told me this touching little incident: "One evening, during the 'Great Silence,' the Infirmarian brought me a hot-water bottle for my feet, and put tincture of iodine on my chest. I was in a burning fever, and parched with thirst, and, whilst submitting to these remedies, I could not help saying to Our Lord: 'My Jesus, Thou seest I am already burning, and they have brought me more heat and fire. Oh! if they had brought me even half a glass of water, what a comfort it would have been! . . . My Jesus! Thy little child is so thirsty. But she is glad to have this opportunity of resembling Thee more closely, and thus helping Thee to save souls.' The Infirmarian soon left me, and I did not expect to see her again until the following morning. What was my surprise when she returned a few minutes later with a refreshing drink! 'It has just struck me that you may be thirsty,' she said, 'so I shall bring you something every evening.' I looked at her astounded, and when I was once more alone, I melted into tears. Oh! how good Jesus is! how tender and loving! How easy it is to reach His Heart!"

. . . .

On September 6, the little Spouse of Jesus received a touching proof of the loving thought of His Sacred Heart. She had frequently expressed a wish to possess a relic of her special patron, the Venerable Théophane Vénard, but as her desire was not realised, she said no more. She was quite overcome, therefore, when Mother Prioress brought her the longed-for treasure—received that very day.

She kissed it repeatedly, and would not consent to part with it.

It may be asked why she was so devoted to this young Martyr. She herself explained the reason in an affectionate interview with her own sisters: "Théophane Vénard is a *little* saint; his life was not marked by anything extraordinary. He had an ardent devotion to Our Immaculate Mother and a tender love of his own family." Dwelling on these words she added: "And I, too, love my family with a tender love; I fail to understand those Saints who do not share my feelings. As a parting gift I have copied for you some passages from his last letters home. His soul and mine have many points of resemblance, and his words do but re-echo my thoughts."

We give here a copy of that letter, which one might have believed was composed by Thérèse herself:

"I can find nothing on earth that can make me truly happy; the desires of my heart are too vast, and nothing of what the world calls happiness can satisfy it. Time for me will soon be no more, my thoughts are fixed on Eternity. My heart is full of peace, like a tranquil lake or a cloudless sky. I do not regret this life on earth. I thirst for the waters of Life Eternal.

"Yet a little while and my soul will have quitted this earth, will have finished her exile, will have ended her combat. I go to Heaven. I am about to enter the Abode of the Blessed—to see what the eye hath never seen, to hear what the ear hath never heard, to enjoy those things the heart of man hath not conceived . . . I have reached the hour so coveted by us all. It is indeed true that Our Lord chooses the little ones to confound the great ones of this earth. I do not rely upon my own strength but upon Him Who, on the Cross, vanquished the powers of hell.

"I am a spring flower which the Divine Master culls for His pleasure. We are all flowers, planted on this earth, and God will gather us in His own good time—some sooner, some later . . . I, little flower of one day, am the first to be gathered! But we shall meet again in Paradise, where lasting joy will be our portion.

"Sister Teresa of the Child Jesus, using the words of the angelic martyr—Théophane Vénard."

Toward the end of September, when something was repeated to her that had been said at recreation, concerning the responsibility of those who have care of souls, she seemed to revive a little and gave utterance to these beautiful words: "To him that is little, mercy is granted.[11] It is possible to remain *little* even in the most responsible position, and is it not written that, at the last day, 'the Lord will arise to save the meek and lowly ones of the earth'?[12] He does not say 'to judge,' but 'to save!'"

As time went on, the tide of suffering rose higher and higher, and she became so weak, that she was unable to make the slightest movement without assistance. Even to hear anyone whisper increased her discomfort; and the fever and oppression were so extreme that it was with the greatest difficulty she was able to articulate a word. And yet a sweet smile was always on her lips. Her only fear was lest she should give her Sisters any extra trouble, and until two days before her death she would never allow any one to remain with her during the night. However, in spite of her entreaties, the Infirmarian would visit her from time to time. On one occasion she found Thérèse with hands joined and eyes raised to Heaven. "What are you doing?" she asked; "you ought to try and go to sleep." "I cannot, Sister, I am suffering too much, so I am praying. . . ." "And what do you say to Jesus?" "I say nothing—I only love Him!"

"Oh! how good God is!" . . . she sometimes exclaimed. "Truly He must be very good to give me strength to bear all I have to suffer." One day she said to the Mother Prioress: "Mother, I would like to make known to you the state of my soul; but I cannot, I feel too much overcome just now." In the evening Thérèse sent her these lines, written in pencil with a trembling hand:

"O my God! how good Thou art to the little Victim of Thy Merciful Love! Now, even when Thou joinest these bodily pains to those of my soul, I cannot bring myself to say: 'The anguish of death hath encompassed me.'[13] I rather cry out in my gratitude: 'I have gone down into the valley of the shadow of death, but I fear no evil, because Thou, O Lord, art with me.'"[14]

Her little Mother said to her: "Some think that you are afraid of death." "That may easily come to pass," she answered; "I do not rely on my own feelings, for I know how frail I am. It will be time enough to bear that cross if it comes, meantime I wish to rejoice in my present happiness. When the

Chaplain asked me if I was resigned to die, I answered: 'Father, I need rather to be resigned to live—I feel nothing but joy at the thought of death.' Do not be troubled, dear Mother, if I suffer much and show no sign of happiness at the end. Did not Our Lord Himself die 'a Victim of Love,' and see how great was His Agony!"

. . . .

At last dawned the eternal day. It was Thursday, September 30, 1897. In the morning, the sweet Victim, her eyes fixed on Our Lady's statue, spoke thus of her last night on earth: "Oh! with what fervour I have prayed to her! . . . And yet it has been pure agony, without a ray of consolation. . . . Earth's air is failing me: when shall I breathe the air of Heaven?"

For weeks she had been unable to raise herself in bed, but, at half-past two in the afternoon, she sat up and exclaimed: "Dear Mother, the chalice is full to overflowing! I could never have believed that it was possible to suffer so intensely. . . . I can only explain it by my extreme desire to save souls. . . ." And a little while after: "Yes, all that I have written about my thirst for suffering is really true! I do not regret having surrendered myself to Love."

She repeated these last words several times. A little later she added: "Mother, prepare me to die well." The good Mother Prioress encouraged her with these words: "My child, you are quite ready to appear before God, for you have always understood the virtue of humility." Then, in striking words, Thérèse bore witness to herself:

"Yes, I feel it; my soul has ever sought the truth. . . . I have understood humility of heart!"

. . . .

At half-past four, her agony began — the agony of this "Victim of Divine Love." When the Community gathered round her, she thanked them with the sweetest smile, and then, completely given over to love and suffering, the Crucifix clasped in her failing hands, she entered on the final combat. The sweat of death lay heavy on her brow . . . she trembled . . . but, as a pilot, when close to harbour, is not dismayed by the fury of the storm, so this soul, strong in faith, saw close at hand the beacon-lights of Heaven, and valiantly put forth every effort to reach the shore.

As the convent bells rang the evening Angelus, she fixed an inexpressible look upon the statue of the Immaculate Virgin, the Star of the Sea. Was it not the moment to repeat her beautiful prayer:

"O thou who camest to smile on me in the morn of my life, come once again and smile, Mother, for now it is eventide!"[15]

A few minutes after seven, turning to the Prioress, the poor little Martyr asked: "Mother, is it not the agony? . . . am I not going to die?" "Yes, my child, it is the agony, but Jesus perhaps wills that it be prolonged for some hours." In a sweet and plaintive voice she replied: "Ah, very well then . . . very well . . . I do not wish to suffer less!"

Then, looking at her crucifix:

"Oh! . . . I love Him! . . . My God, I . . . love . . . Thee!"

These were her last words. She had scarcely uttered them when, to our great surprise, she sank down quite suddenly, her head inclined a little to the right, in the attitude of the Virgin Martyrs offering themselves to the sword; or rather, as a Victim of Love, awaiting from the Divine Archer the fiery shaft, by which she longs to die.

Suddenly she raised herself, as though called by a mysterious voice; and opening her eyes, which shone with unutterable happiness and peace, fixed her gaze a little above the statue of Our Lady. Thus she remained for about the space of a *Credo*, when her blessed soul, now become the prey of the "Divine Eagle," was borne away to the heights of Heaven.

. . . .

A few days before her death, this little Saint had said: "The death of Love which I so much desire is that of Jesus upon the Cross." Her prayer was fully granted. Darkness enveloped her, and her soul was steeped in anguish. And yet, may we not apply to her also that sublime prophecy of St. John of the Cross, referring to souls consumed by the fire of Divine Love: "They die Victims of the onslaughts of Love, in raptured ecstasies—like the swan, whose song grows sweeter as death draws nigh. Wherefore the Psalmist declared: 'Precious in the sight of the Lord is the death of His Saints.'[16] For then it is that the rivers of love burst forth from the soul and are whelmed in the Ocean of Divine Love."

No sooner had her spotless soul taken its flight than the joy of that last rapture imprinted itself on her brow, and a radiant smile illumined her face. We placed a palm-branch in her hand; and the lilies and roses that adorned her in death were figures of her white robe of baptism made red by her Martyrdom of Love.

On the Saturday and Sunday a large crowd passed before the grating of the nuns' chapel, to gaze on the mortal remains of the "Little Flower of Jesus." Hundreds of medals and rosaries were brought to touch the "Little Queen" as she lay in the triumphant beauty of her last sleep.

. . . .

On October 4, the day of the funeral, there gathered in the Chapel of the Carmel a goodly company of Priests. The honour was surely due to one who had prayed so earnestly for those called to that sacred office. After a last solemn blessing, this grain of priceless wheat was cast into the furrow by the hands of Holy Mother Church.

Who shall tell how many ripened ears have sprung forth since, how many the sheaves that are yet to come? "Amen, amen, I say to you, unless the grain of wheat, falling into the ground, die, itself remaineth alone. But if it die, it bringeth forth much fruit."[17] Once more the word of the Divine Reaper has been magnificently fulfilled.

THE PRIORESS OF THE CARMEL.

---

[1] Dom Guéranger.

[2] Mother Mary of Gonzaga died Dec. 17, 1904, at the age of 71. Mother Agnes of Jesus (Pauline) was at that time Prioress. The former—herself of the line of St. Antony of Padua—recognized in Soeur Thérèse "an heroic soul, filled with holiness, and capable of becoming one day an excellent Prioress." With this end in view, she trained her with a strictness for which the young Saint was most grateful. In the arms of Mother Mary of Gonzaga the "Little Flower of Jesus" was welcomed to the Carmel, and in those arms she died—"happy," she declared, "not to have in that hour as Superioress her 'little Mother,' in order the better to exercise her spirit of faith in authority." [Ed.]

[3] As will be remembered, this was Marie, her eldest sister. [Ed.]

[4] The Blessed Théophane Vénard was born at St. Loup, in the diocese of Poitiers, on the Feast of

the Presentation of Our Lady, Nov. 21, 1829. He was martyred at Kecho, Tong-King, on the Feast of the Presentation of Our Lord, Feb. 2, 1861, at the age of 32. A long and delightful correspondence with his family, begun in his college days and completed from his "cage" at Kecho, reveals a kinship of poesy as well as of sanctity and of the love of home, between the two "spring flowers." The beauty of his soul was so visible in his boyish face that he was spared all torture during his two months in the "cage." In 1909, the year in which Thérèse became "Servant of God" by the commencement of the Episcopal Process, her patron received the honours of Beatification. Another child of France—Joan, its "Martyr-Maid"—whose praises have been sung in affectionate verse by the Saints of St. Loup and Lisieux, was beatified that same year. [Ed.]

[5] An allusion to the obituary notice sent to each of the French Carmels when a Carmelite nun dies in that country. In the case of those who die in the odour of sanctity these notices sometimes run to considerable length. Four notices issued from the Carmel of Lisieux are of great interest to the clients of Soeur Thérèse, and are in course of publication at the Orphans' Press, Rochdale; those of the Carmel's saintly Foundress, Mother Genevieve of St. Teresa,

whose death is referred to in Chapter VIII; Mother Mary of Gonzaga, the Prioress of Thérèse; Sister Mary of the Eucharist (Marie Guérin), the cousin of Thérèse (Chapter III); and most interesting of all, the long sketch, partly autobiographical, of Mother Mary of St. Angelus (Marie Ange), the "trophy of Thérèse," brought by her intercession to the Carmel in 1902—where the writer made her acquaintance in the following spring; she became Prioress in 1908, dying eighteen months later in the odour of sanctity, aged only 28. [Ed.]

[6] Cf. Job 13:15.

[7] John 3:34.

[8] When asked before her death how they should pray to her in Heaven, Soeur Thérèse, with her wonted simplicity, made answer: "You will call me 'Little Thérèse'—*petite Thérèse*." And at Gallipoli, on the occasion of her celebrated apparition in the Carmel there, when the Prioress, taking her to be St. Teresa of Avila, addressed her as "our holy Mother," the visitor, adopting her then official title, replied: —"Nay, I am not our holy Mother, I am the Servant of God, *Soeur Thérèse of Lisieux*." This, her own name of Soeur Thérèse, has been retained in the present edition, unless where it was advisable to set down

her name in full—Sister Teresa of the Child Jesus and of the Holy Face. The name of the "Little Flower," borrowed by her from the Blessed Théophane Vénard, and used so extensively in the pages of her manuscript, is the one by which she is best known in English-speaking lands. [Ed.]

[9] Cf. Prov. 19:11.

[10] Matt. 25:49.

[11] Wisdom 6:7.

[12] Cf. Ps. 75[76]:10.

[13] Cf. Ps. 17[18]:5.

[14] Cf. Ps. 22[23]:4.

[15] From the last poem written by Soeur Thérèse.

[16] Ps. 115[116]:15.

[17] John 12:24, 25.

COUNSELS AND REMINISCENCES OF SOEUR THÉRÈSE, THE LITTLE FLOWER OF JESUS

Most of what follows has been gathered from the conversations of Soeur Thérèse with her novices. Her advice cannot but prove helpful to souls within the cloister, and likewise to many in the world who may be attracted by her simple and easy *little way* to God.

* * * * * *

One of the novices, greatly discouraged at the thought of her imperfections, tells us that her mistress spoke to her as follows:

"You make me think of a little child that is learning to stand but does not yet know how to walk. In his desire to reach the top of the stairs to find his mother, he lifts his little foot to climb the first step. It is all in vain, and at each renewed effort he falls. Well, be like that little child. Always keep lifting your foot to climb the ladder of holiness, and do not imagine that you can mount even the first step. All God asks of you is good will. From the top of the ladder He looks lovingly upon you, and soon, touched by your fruitless efforts, He will Himself come down, and, taking you in His Arms, will carry you to His Kingdom never again to leave Him. But should you cease to raise your foot, you will be left for long on the earth."

* * * * * *

"The only way to advance rapidly in the path of love is to remain always very little. That is what I did, and now I can sing with our holy Father, St. John of the Cross:

'Then I abased myself so low, so very low, That I ascended to such heights, such heights indeed, That I did overtake the prey I chased!'"

* * * * * *

Under a temptation which seemed to me irresistible, I said to her: "This time, I cannot surmount it." She replied: "Why seek to surmount it? Rather pass beneath. It is all well for great souls to soar above the clouds when the storm rages; we have simply to suffer the showers. What does it matter if we get wet? We shall dry ourselves in the sunshine of love.

"It recalls a little incident of my childhood. One day a horse was standing in front of the garden gate, and preventing us from getting through. My companions talked to him and tried to make him move off, but while they were still talking I quietly slipped between his legs . . . Such is the advantage of remaining small."

* * * * * *

Our Lord said to the mother of the sons of Zebedee: 'To sit on my right or left hand is for them for whom it is prepared by my Father.'[1] I imagine that these chosen places, which have been refused alike to great Saints and Martyrs, will be reserved for little children; and did not David foretell it when he said, that 'the little Benjamin will preside amidst the assemblies[2] of the Saints.'"

* * * * * *

"You are wrong to find fault with this thing and with that, or to try and make everyone see things as you see them. We desire to be 'as little children,' and little children do not know what is best: to them all seems right. Let us imitate their ways. Besides, there is no merit in doing what reason dictates."

* * * * * *

"My patrons and my special favourites in Heaven are those who, so to speak, stole it, such as the Holy Innocents and the Good Thief. The great Saints won it by their works; I wish to be like the thieves and to win it by stratagem—a stratagem of love which will open its gates both to me and to poor sinners. In the Book of Proverbs the Holy Ghost encourages me, for He says: 'Come to me, little one, to learn subtlety!'"[3]

* * * * * *

"What would you do if you could begin over again your religious life?"

"I think I should do as I have already done."

"Then you do not share the feeling of the hermit who said: 'While a quarter of an hour, or even a breath of life still remains to me, I shall fear the fires of hell even though I should have spent long years in penance'?"

"No, I do not share that fear; I am too small. Little children are not damned."

"You are ever seeking to be as little children are, but tell us what must be done to obtain that childlike spirit. 'Remaining little'—what does it mean?"

"'Remaining little' means—to recognise one's nothingness, to await everything from the Goodness of God, to avoid being too much troubled at our faults; finally, not to worry over amassing spiritual riches, not to be solicitous about anything. Even amongst the poor, while a child is still small, he is given what is necessary; but, once he is grown up, his father will no longer feed him, and tells him to seek work and support himself. Well, it was to avoid hearing this, that I have never wished to grow up, for I feel incapable of earning my livelihood, which is Life Eternal!"

* * * * * *

In imitation of our saintly Mistress I also wished never to grow up; she called me therefore "the little one," and during a retreat she wrote to me the following notes:

"Do not fear to tell Jesus that you love him, even though you may not feel that love. In this way you will compel Him to come to your aid, and to carry you like a little child who is too weak to walk.

"It is indeed a great source of trial, when everything looks black, but this does not depend entirely on yourself. Do all in your power to detach your heart from earthly cares, especially from creatures; then be assured Our Lord will do the rest. He could not permit you to fall into the abyss. Be comforted, little one! In Heaven everything will no longer look black, but dazzling white. There all will be clothed in the Divine radiance of Our Spouse—the Lily of the Valley. Together we will follow Him whithersoever He goeth. Meantime we must make good use of this life's brief day. Let us give Our Lord pleasure, let us by self-sacrifice give Him souls! Above all, let us be little—so little that everyone might tread us underfoot without our even seeming to suffer pain.

"I am not surprised at the failures of the little one; she forgets that in her rôle of missionary and warrior she ought to forgo all childish consolations. It is wrong to pass one's time in fretting, instead of sleeping on the Heart of Jesus.

"Should the little one fear the dark of the night, or complain at not seeing Him who carries her, let her shut her eyes. It is the one sacrifice God asks. By remaining thus, the dark will cease to terrify, because she will not see it, and before long, peace—if not joy—will re-enter her soul."

* * * * * *

To help me accept a humiliation she confided to me what follows:

"If I had not been received into the Carmel, I would have entered a Refuge, and lived there unknown and despised among the poor 'penitents.' My joy would have been to pass for one, and I would have become an apostle among my companions, telling them my thoughts on the Infinite Mercy of God."

"But how could you have hidden your innocence from your Confessor?"

"I would have told him that while still in the world I made a general confession, and that it was forbidden me to repeat it."

* * * * * *

"Oh! When I think of all I have to acquire!"

"Or rather to lose! It is Jesus Who takes upon Himself to fill your soul according as you rid it of imperfections. I see clearly that you are mistaking the road, and that you will never arrive at the end of your journey. You want to climb the mountain, whereas God wishes you to descend it. He is awaiting you in the fruitful valley of humility."

* * * * * *

"To me it seems that humility is truth. I do not know whether I am humble, but I do know that I see the truth in all things."

* * * * * *

"Indeed you are a Saint!"

"No, I am not a Saint. I have never wrought the works of a Saint. *I am but a tiny soul whom Almighty God has loaded with His favours.*

"The truth of what I say will be made known to you in Heaven."

"But have you not always been faithful to those favours?"

"Yes, *from the age of three I have never refused our Good God anything.* Still I cannot glorify myself. See how this evening the tree-tops are gilded by the setting sun. So likewise my soul appears to you all shining and golden because it is exposed to the rays of Love. But should the Divine Sun no longer shine thereon, it would instantly be sunk in gloom."

"We too would like to become all golden—what must we do?"

"You must practise the little virtues. This is sometimes difficult, but God never refuses the first grace—courage for self-conquest; and if the soul correspond to that grace, she at once finds herself in God's sunlight. The praise given to Judith has always struck me: 'Thou hast done manfully, and thy heart has been strengthened.'[4] In the onset we must act with courage. By this means the heart gains strength, and victory follows victory."

* * * * * *

In conformity with the Rule, Soeur Thérèse never raised her eyes in the refectory, and, as I found great difficulty in this observance, she composed for me the following prayer. It reveals her exceeding humility, because in it she asked a grace of which I alone stood in need:

"O Jesus, in honour and in imitation of the example Thou gavest in the house of Herod, Thy two little Spouses resolve to keep their eyes cast down in the refectory. When that impious king scoffed at Thee, O Infinite Beauty, no complaint came from Thy Lips. Thou didst not even deign to fix on him Thy Adorable Eyes. He was not worthy of the favour, but we who are Thy Spouses, we desire to draw Thy Divine Gaze upon ourselves. As often as we refrain from raising our eyes, we beg Thee to reward us by a glance of love, and we even dare ask Thee not to refuse this sweet glance when we fail in our self-control, for we will humble ourselves most sincerely before Thee."

* * * * * *

I confided to her that I made no progress, and that consequently I had lost heart.

"Up to the age of fourteen," she said, "I practised virtue without tasting its sweetness. I desired suffering, but I did not think of making it my joy; that grace was vouchsafed me later. My soul was like a beautiful tree the flowers of which had scarcely opened when they fell.

"Offer to God the sacrifice of never gathering any fruit. If He will that throughout your whole life you should feel a repugnance to suffering and humiliation—if He permit that all the flowers of your desires and of your good will should fall to the ground without any fruit appearing, do not worry. At the hour of death, in the twinkling of an eye, He will cause fair fruits to ripen on the tree of your soul.

"We read in the Book of Ecclesiasticus: 'There is an inactive man that wanteth help, is very weak in ability, and full of poverty: yet the Eye of God hath looked upon him for good, and hath lifted him up from his low estate, and hath exalted his head: and many have wondered at him, and have glorified God. . . . Trust in God, and stay in thy place. For it is easy in the Eyes of God, on a sudden, to make the poor man rich. The blessing of God maketh haste to reward the just, and in a swift hour His blessing beareth fruit.'"[5]

"But if I fall, I shall always be found imperfect; whereas you are looked upon as holy."

"That is, perhaps, because I have never desired to be considered so. . . . But that you should be found imperfect is just what is best. Here is your harvest. To believe oneself imperfect and others perfect — this is true happiness. Should earthly creatures think you devoid of holiness, they rob you of nothing, and you are none the poorer: it is they who lose. For is there anything more sweet than the inward joy of thinking well of our neighbour?

"As for myself I am glad and rejoice, not only when I am looked upon as imperfect, but above all when I feel that it is true. Compliments, on the contrary, do but displease me."

* * * * * *

"God has a special love for you since He entrusts souls to your care."

"That makes no difference, and I am really only what I am in His Eyes. It is not because He wills me to be His interpreter among you, that He loves me more; rather, He makes me your little handmaid. It is for you, and not for myself, that He has bestowed upon me those charms and those virtues which you see.

"I often compare myself to a little bowl filled by God with good things. All the kittens come to eat from it, and they sometimes quarrel as to which will have the largest share. But the Holy Child Jesus keeps a sharp watch. 'I am willing you should feed from My little bowl,' He says, 'but take heed lest you upset and break it.'

"In truth there is no great danger, because I am already on the ground. Not so with Prioresses; set, as they are, on tables, they run far more risks. Honours are always dangerous. What poisonous food is served daily to those in high positions! What deadly fumes of incense! A soul must be well detached from herself to pass unscathed through it all."

* * * * * *

"It is a consolation for you to do good and to procure the Glory of God. I wish I were equally favoured."

"What if God does make use of me, rather than of another, to procure His Glory! Provided His Kingdom be established among souls, the instrument matters not. Besides, He has no need of anyone.

"Some time ago I was watching the flicker, almost invisible, of a tiny night-light, when one of the Sisters drew near, and, lighting her candle in the dying flame, passed it round to light all those of the Community. 'Who dare glory in his own good works?' I reflected. 'From one faint spark such as this, it would be possible to set the whole earth on fire.' We often think we receive graces and are divinely illumined by means of brilliant candles.

But from whence comes their light? From the prayers, perhaps, of some humble, hidden soul, whose inward shining is not apparent to human eyes; a soul of unrecognised virtue and, in her own sight, of little value—a dying flame.

"What mysteries will yet be unveiled to us! I have often thought that perhaps I owe all the graces with which I am laden, to some little soul whom I shall know only in Heaven.

"It is God's Will that in this world souls shall dispense to each other, by prayer, the treasures of Heaven, in order that when they reach their Everlasting Home they may love one another with grateful hearts, and with an affection far in excess of that which reigns in the most perfect family on earth.

"There no looks of indifference will meet us, because all the Saints will be mutually indebted to each other. No envious glances will be cast, for the happiness of each one of the Blessed will be the happiness of all. With the Doctors of the Church we shall be like unto Doctors; with the Martyrs, like unto Martyrs; with the Virgins, like unto Virgins; and just as the members of one family are proud one of the other, so without the least jealousy shall we take pride in our brothers and sisters.

"When we see the glory of the great Saints, and know that through the secret working of Providence we have contributed to it, who knows whether the joy we shall feel will not be as intense, perhaps sweeter, than the happiness they themselves possess?

"And do you not think that the great Saints, on their side, seeing what they owe to all little souls, will love them with a love beyond compare? The friendships of Paradise will be both sweet and full of surprise, of this I am certain. The familiar friend of an Apostle, or of a great Doctor of the Church, may be a shepherd boy, and a simple little child may be united in closest intimacy with a Patriarch. . . . I long to enter that Kingdom of Love!"

* * * * * *

"Believe me, the writing of pious books, the composing of the sublimest poetry, all that does not equal the smallest act of self-denial. When, however, our inability to do good gives us pain, our only resource is to offer up the good works of others, and in this lies the benefit of the

Communion of Saints. Recall to mind that beautiful verse of the canticle of our Father, St. John of the Cross:

'Return, my dove! See on the height The wounded Hart, To whom refreshment brings The breeze, stirred by thy wings.'

"Thus the Spouse, the wounded Hart, is not attracted by the height, but only by the breeze from the pinions of the dove—a breeze which one single stroke of wing is sufficient to create."

* * * * * *

"The one thing which is not open to envy is the lowest place. Here alone, therefore, there is neither vanity nor affliction of spirit. Yet, 'the way of a man is not his own,'[6] and sometimes we find ourselves wishing for what dazzles. In that hour let us in all humility take our place among the imperfect, and look upon ourselves as little souls who at every instant need to be upheld by the goodness of God. From the moment He sees us fully convinced of our nothingness, and hears us cry out: 'My foot stumbles, Lord, but Thy Mercy is my strength,'[7] He reaches out His Hand to us. But, should we attempt great things, even under pretext of zeal, He deserts us. It suffices, therefore, to humble ourselves, to bear with meekness our imperfections. Herein lies — for us — true holiness."

* * * * * *

One day I was complaining of being more tired than my Sisters, for, besides the ordinary duties, I had other work unknown to the rest. Soeur Thérèse replied:

"I should like always to see you a brave soldier, never grumblng at hardships, but considering the wounds of your companions as most serious, and your own as mere scratches. You feel this fatigue so much because no one is aware of it.

"Now the Blessed Margaret Mary, at the time she had two whitlows, confessed that she really suffered from the hidden one only. The other, which she was unable to hide, excited her Sisters' pity and made her an object of compassion. This is indeed a very natural feeling, the desire that people should know of our aches and pains, but in giving way to it we play the coward."

* * * * * *

"When we are guilty of a fault we must never attribute it to some physical cause, such as illness or the weather. We must ascribe it to our own imperfections, without being discouraged thereby. 'Occasions do not make a man frail, but show what he is.'"[8]

* * * * * *

"God did not permit that our Mother should tell me to write my poems as soon as I had composed them, and, fearful of committing a sin against poverty, I would not ask leave. I had therefore to wait for some free time, and at eight o'clock in the evening I often found it extremely difficult to remember what I had composed in the morning.

"True, these trifles are a species of martyrdom; but we must be careful not to alleviate the pain of the martyrdom by permitting ourselves, or securing permission for, a thousand and one things which would tend to make the religious life both comfortable and agreeable."

* * * * * *

One day, as I was in tears, Soeur Thérèse told me to avoid the habit of allowing others to see the trifles that worried me, adding that nothing made community life more trying than unevenness of temper.

"You are indeed right," I answered, "such was my own thought. Henceforward my tears will be for God alone. I shall confide my worries to One Who will understand and console me."

"Tears for God!" she promptly replied, "that must not be. Far less to Him than to creatures ought you to show a mournful face. Our Divine Master has only our monasteries where He may obtain some solace for His Heart. He comes to us in search of rest—to forget the unceasing complaints of His friends in the world, who, instead of appreciating the value of the Cross, receive it far more often with moans and tears. Would you then be as the mediocre souls? Frankly, this is not disinterested love. . . . *It is for us to console our Lord, and not for Him to console us.* His Heart is so tender that if you cry He will dry your tears; but thereafter He will go away sad, since you did not suffer Him to repose tranquilly within you. Our Lord loves the glad of heart, the children that greet Him with a smile. When will you learn to hide your troubles from Him, or to tell Him gaily that you are happy to suffer for Him?"

"The face is the mirror of the soul," she said once, "and yours, like that of a contented little child, should always be calm and serene. Even when alone, be cheerful, remembering always that you are in the sight of the Angels."

* * * * * *

I was anxious she should congratulate me on what, in my eyes, was an heroic act of virtue; but she said to me:

"Compare this little act of virtue with what our Lord has the right to expect of you! Rather should you humble yourself for having lost so many opportunities of proving your love."

Little satisfied with this answer, I awaited an opportunity of finding out how Soeur Thérèse herself would act under trial, and the occasion was not long in coming. Reverend Mother asked us to do some extremely tiring work which bristled with difficulties, and, on purpose, I made it still more difficult for our Mistress.

Not for one second, however, could I detect her in fault, and, heedless of the fatigue involved, she remained gracious and amiable, eager throughout to help others at her own expense. At last I could resist no longer, and I confessed to her what my thoughts had been.

"How comes it," I said, "that you can be so patient? You are ever the same—calm and full of joy." "It was not always the case with me," she replied, "but since I have abandoned all thought of self-seeking, I live the happiest life possible."

* * * * * *

Our dear Mistress used to say that during recreation, more than at any other time, we should find opportunities for practising virtue.

"If your desire be to draw great profit, do not go with the idea of procuring relaxation, but rather with the intention of entertaining others and practising complete detachment from self. Thus, for instance, if you are telling one of the Sisters something you think entertaining, and she should interrupt to tell you something else, show yourself interested, even though in reality her story may not interest you in the least. Be careful, also, not to try to resume what you were saying. In this way you will leave recreation filled with a great interior peace and endowed with fresh strength for the practice of virtue, because you have not sought to please yourself, but others. If only we could realise what we gain by self-denial in all things!"

"You realise it, certainly, for you have always practised self-denial."

"Yes, I have forgotten myself, and I have tried not to see myself in anything."

* * * * * *

"When some one knocks at our door, or when we are rung for, we must practise mortification and refrain from doing even another stitch before answering. I have practised this myself, and I assure you that it is a source of peace."

After this advice, and according as occasion offered, I promptly answered every summons. One day, during her illness, she was witness of this, and said:

"At the hour of death you will be very happy to find this to your account. You have just done something more glorious than if, through clever diplomacy, you had procured the good-will of the Government for all religious communities and had been proclaimed throughout France as a second Judith."

* * * * * *

Questioned as to her method of sanctifying meals, she answered:

"In the refectory we have but one thing to do: perform a lowly action with lofty thoughts. I confess that the sweetest aspirations of love often come to me in the refectory. Sometimes I am brought to a standstill by the thought that were Our Lord in my place He would certainly partake of those same dishes which are served to me. It is quite probable that during His lifetime He tasted of similar food — He must have eaten bread and fruit.

"Here are my little rubrics:

"I imagine myself at Nazareth, in the house of the Holy Family. If, for instance, I am served with salad, cold fish, wine, or anything pungent in taste, I offer it to St. Joseph. To our Blessed Lady I offer hot foods and ripe fruit, and to the Infant Jesus our feast-day fare, especially rice and preserves. Lastly, when I am served a wretched dinner I say cheerfully: 'To-day, my little one, it is all for you!'"

Thus in many pretty ways she hid her mortifications. One fast-day, however, when our Reverend Mother ordered her some special food, I found her seasoning it with wormwood because it was too much to her taste. On another occasion I saw her drinking very slowly a most unpleasant medicine. "Make haste," I said, "drink it off at once!" "Oh, no!" she answered; "must I not profit of these small opportunities for penance since the greater ones are forbidden me?"

Toward the end of her life I learned that, during her noviciate, one of our Sisters, when fastening the scapular for her, ran the large pin through her shoulder, and for hours she bore the pain with joy. On another occasion she gave me proof of her interior mortification. I had received a most interesting letter which was read aloud at recreation, during her absence. In the evening she expressed the wish to read it, and I gave it to her. Later on, when she returned it, I begged her to tell me what she thought of one of the points of the letter which I knew ought to have charmed her. She seemed rather confused, and after a pause she answered: "God asked of me the sacrifice of this letter because of the eagerness I displayed the other day . . . so I have not read it."

* * * * * *

When speaking to her of the mortifications of the Saints, she remarked: "It was well that Our Lord warned us: 'In My Father's House there are many mansions, otherwise I would have told you.'[9] For, if every soul called to perfection were obliged to perform these austerities in order to enter Heaven, He would have told us, and we should have willingly undertaken them. But He has declared that, 'there are many mansions in His House.' If there are some for great souls, for the Fathers of the Desert and for Martyrs of penance, there must also be one for little children. And in that one a place is kept for us, if we but love Him dearly together with Our Father and the Spirit of Love."

* * * * * *

"While in the world, I used, on waking, to think of all the pleasant or unpleasant things which might happen throughout the day, and if I foresaw nothing but worries I got up with a heavy heart. Now it is quite the reverse. I think of the pains and of the sufferings awaiting me, and I rise, feeling all the more courageous and light of heart in proportion to the opportunities I foresee of proving my love for Our Lord, and of gaining—mother of souls as I am—my children's livelihood. Then I kiss my crucifix, and, laying it gently on my pillow, I leave it there while I dress, and I say: 'My Jesus, Thou hast toiled and wept enough during Thy three-and-thirty years on this miserable earth. Rest Thee, to-day! It is my turn to suffer and to fight.'"

* * * * * *

One washing-day I was sauntering towards the laundry, and looking at the flowers as I passed. Soeur Thérèse was following, and quickly overtook me: "Is that," she said quietly, "how people hurry themselves when they have children, and are obliged to work to procure them food?"

* * * * * *

"Do you know which are my Sundays and feast-days? They are the days on which God tries me the most."

* * * * * *

I was distressed at my want of courage, and Soeur Thérèse said to me: "You are complaining of what should be your greatest happiness. If you fought only when you felt eagerness, where would be your merit? What does it matter, even if you are devoid of courage, provided you act as though you possessed it? If you feel too lazy to pick up a bit of thread, and yet do so for love of Jesus, you acquire more merit than for a much nobler action done in a moment of fervour. Instead of grieving, be glad that, by allowing you to feel your own weakness, Our Lord is furnishing you with an opportunity of saving a greater number of souls."

* * * * * *

I asked her whether Our Lord were not displeased at the sight of my many failings. This was her answer: "Be comforted, for He Whom you have chosen as your Spouse has every imaginable perfection; but—dare I say it?—He has one great infirmity too—He is blind! And there is a science about which He knows nothing—addition! These two great defects, much to be deplored in an earthly bridegroom, do but make ours infinitely more lovable. Were it necessary that He should be clear-sighted, and familiar with the science of figures, do you not think that, confronted with our many sins, He would send us back to our nothingness? But His Love for us makes him actually blind.

"If the greatest sinner on earth should repent at the moment of his death, and draw His last breath in an act of love, neither the many graces he had abused, nor the multiplied crimes he had committed, would stand in his way. Our Lord would see nothing, count nothing, but the sinner's last prayer, and without delay He would receive him into the arms of His Mercy.

"But, to make Him thus blind and to prevent Him doing the smallest sum of addition, we must approach Him through His Heart—on that side He is vulnerable and defenceless."

* * * * * *

I had grieved her, and had gone to ask her pardon: "If you but knew what I feel!" she exclaimed. "Never have I more clearly understood the love with which Jesus receives us when we seek His forgiveness. If I, His poor little creature, feel so tenderly towards you when you come back to me, what must pass through Our Lord's Divine Heart when we return to Him? Far more quickly than I have just done will He blot out our sins from His memory. . . . Nay, He will even love us more tenderly than before we fell."

* * * * * *

I had an immense dread of the judgments of God, and no argument of Soeur Thérèse could remove it. One day I put to her the following objection: "It is often said to us that in God's sight the angels themselves are not pure. How, therefore, can you expect me to be otherwise than filled with fear?"

She replied: "There is but one means of compelling God not to judge us, and it is—to appear before Him empty-handed." "And how can that be done?" "It is quite simple: lay nothing by, spend your treasures as you gain them. Were I to live to be eighty, I should always be poor, because I cannot economise. All my earnings are immediately spent on the ransom of souls.

"Were I to await the hour of death to offer my trifling coins for valuation, Our Lord would not fail to discover in them some base metal, and they would certainly have to be refined in Purgatory. Is it not recorded of certain great Saints that, on appearing before the Tribunal of God, their hands laden with merit, they have yet been sent to that place of expiation, because in God's Eyes all our justice is unclean?"

"But," I replied, "if God does not judge our good actions, He will judge our bad ones." "Do not say that! Our Lord is Justice itself, and if He does not judge our good actions, neither will He judge our bad ones. It seems to me, that for Victims of Love there will be no judgment. God will rather hasten to reward with eternal delights His own Love which He will behold burning in their hearts."

"To enjoy such a privilege, would it suffice to repeat that Act of Oblation which you have composed?" "Oh, no! words do not suffice. To be a true Victim of Love we must surrender ourselves entirely. . . . *Love will consume us only in the measure of our self-surrender.*"

* * * * * *

I was grieving bitterly over a fault I had committed. "Take your
Crucifix," she said, "and kiss it." I kissed the Feet.

"Is that how a child kisses its father? Throw your arms at once round His Neck and kiss His Face." When I had done so, she continued: "That is not sufficient—He must return your caress." I had to press the Crucifix to both my cheeks, whereupon she added: "Now, all is forgiven."

* * * * * *

I told her one day that if I must be reproached I preferred deserving it to being unjustly accused. "For my part," she replied, "I prefer to be charged unjustly, because, having nothing to reproach myself with, I offer gladly this little injustice to God. Then, humbling myself, I think how easily I might have deserved the reproach. The more you advance, the fewer the combats; or rather, the more easy the victory, because the good side of things will be more visible. Then your soul will soar above creatures. As for me, I feel utterly indifferent to all accusations because I have learned the hollowness of human judgment."

She added further: "When misunderstood and judged unfavourably, what benefit do we derive from defending ourselves? Leave things as they are, and say nothing. It is so sweet to allow ourselves to be judged anyhow, rightly or wrongly.

"It is not written in the Gospel that Saint Mary Magdalen put forth excuses when charged by her sister with sitting idle at Our Lord's Feet. She did not say: 'Martha, if you knew the happiness that is mine and if you heard the words that I hear, you too would leave everything to share my joy and my repose.' No, she preferred to keep silent. . . . Blessed silence which giveth such peace to the soul!"

* * * * * *

At a moment of temptation and struggle I received this note: "'The just man shall correct me in mercy and shall reprove me; but let not the oil of the sinner perfume my head.'[10] It is only by the just that I can be either reproved or corrected, because all my Sisters are pleasing to God. It is less bitter to be rebuked by a sinner than by a just man; but through compassion for sinners, to obtain their conversion, I beseech Thee, O my God, to permit that I may be well rebuked by those just souls who surround me. I ask also that the *oil of praise,* so sweet to our nature, *may not perfume my head,* that is to say, my mind, by making me believe that I possess virtues when I have merely performed a few good actions.

"Jesus! 'Thy Name is as oil poured out,'[11] and it is into this divine perfume that I desire wholly to plunge myself, far from the gaze of mankind."

* * * * * *

"It is not playing the game to argue with a Sister that she is in the wrong, even when it is true, because we are not answerable for her conduct. We must not be *Justices of the peace,* but *Angels of peace* only."

* * * * * *

"You give yourselves up too much to what you are doing," she used to say to us; "you worry about the future as though it were in your hands. Are you much concerned at this moment as to what is happening in other Carmelite convents, and whether the nuns there are busy or otherwise? Does their work prevent you praying or meditating? Well, just in the same way, you ought to detach yourselves from your own personal labours, conscientiously spending on them the time prescribed, but with perfect freedom of heart. We read that the Israelites, while building the walls of Jerusalem, worked with one hand and held a sword in the other.[12] This is an image of what we should do: avoid being wholly absorbed in our work."

* * * * * *

"One Sunday," Thérèse relates, "I was going toward the chestnut avenue, full of rejoicing, for it was spring-time, and I wanted to enjoy nature's beauties. What a bitter disappointment! My dear chestnuts had been pruned, and the branches, already covered with buds, now lay on the ground. On seeing this havoc, and thinking that three years must elapse before it could be repaired, my heart felt very sore. But the grief did not last long. 'If I were in another convent,' I reflected, 'what would it matter to me if the chestnut-trees of the Carmel at Lisieux were entirely cut down?' I will not worry about things that pass. God shall be my all. I will take my walks in the wooded groves of His Love, whereon none dare lay hands."

* * * * * *

A novice asked her Sisters to help her shake some blankets. As they were somewhat liable to tear because of their worn condition, she insisted, rather sharply, on their being handled with care. "What would you do," said Thérèse to the impatient one, "if it were not your duty to mend these blankets? There would be no thought of self in the matter, and if you did call attention to the fact that they are easily torn, it would be done in quite an impersonal way. In all your actions, you should avoid the least trace of self-seeking."

* * * * * *

Seeing one of our Sisters very much fatigued, I said to Soeur Thérèse: "It grieves me to see people suffer, especially those who are holy." She instantly replied: "I do not feel as you do. Saints who suffer never excite my pity. I know they have strength to bear their sufferings, and that through them they are giving great glory to God. But I compassionate greatly those who are not Saints, and who do not know how to profit by suffering. They indeed awake my pity. I would strain every nerve to help and comfort them."

* * * * * *

"Were I to live longer, it is the office of Infirmarian that would most please me. I would not ask for it, but were it imposed through obedience, I should consider myself highly favoured. I think I should fulfill its duties with much affection, always mindful of Our Lord's words: 'I was sick, and you visited Me.'[13] The infirmary bell should be for you as heavenly music, and you ought purposely to pass by the windows of the sick that it might be easy for them to summon you. Consider yourself as a little slave whom everyone has the right to command. Could you but see the Angels who from the heights of Heaven watch your combats in the arena! They are awaiting the end of the fight to crown you and cover you with flowers. You know that we claim to rank as *little Martyrs* . . . . but we must win our palms.

"God does not despise these hidden struggles with ourselves, so much richer in merit because they are unseen: 'The patient man is better than the valiant, and he that ruleth his spirit than he that taketh cities.'[14] Through our little acts of charity, practised in the dark, as it were, we obtain the conversion of the heathen, help the missionaries, and gain for them plentiful alms, thus building both spiritual and material dwellings for Our Eucharistic God."

* * * * * *

I had seen Mother Prioress showing, as I thought, more confidence and affection to one of our Sisters than she extended to me. Expecting to win sympathy, I told my trouble to Soeur Thérèse, and great was my surprise when she put me the question: "Do you think you love our Mother very much?" "Certainly! otherwise I should be indifferent if others were preferred to me."

"Well, I shall prove that you are absolutely mistaken, and that it is not our Mother that you love, but yourself. When we really love others, we rejoice at their happiness, and we make every sacrifice to procure it. Therefore if you had this true, disinterested affection, and loved our Mother for her own sake, you would be glad to see her find pleasure even at your expense; and since you think she has less satisfaction in talking with you than with another Sister, you ought not to grieve at being apparently neglected."

* * * * * *

I was distressed at my many distractions during prayers: "I also have many," she said, "but as soon as I am aware of them, I pray for those people the thought of whom is diverting my attention, and in this way they reap benefit from my distractions. . . . I accept all for the love of God, even the wildest fancies that cross my mind."

* * * * * *

I was regretting a pin which I had been asked for, and which I had found most useful. "How rich you are," said Thérèse, "you will never be happy!"

* * * * * *

The grotto of the Holy Child was in her charge, and, knowing that one of our Mothers greatly disliked perfumes, she never put any sweet-smelling flowers there, not even a tiny violet. This cost her many a real sacrifice. One day, just as she had placed a beautiful artificial rose at the foot of the statue, the Mother called her. Soeur Thérèse, surmising that it was to bid her remove the rose, was anxious to spare her any humiliation. She therefore took the flower to the good Sister, and, forestalling all observations, said: "Look, Mother, how well nature is imitated nowadays: would you not think this rose had been freshly gathered from the garden?"

* * * * * *

"There are moments," she told us, "when we are so miserable within, that there is nothing for it but to get away from ourselves. At those times God does not oblige us to remain at home. He even permits our own company to become distasteful to us in order that we may leave it. Now I know no other means of exit save through the doorway of charitable works, on a visit to Jesus and Mary."

* * * * * *

"When I picture the Holy Family, the thought that does me most good is—the simplicity of their home-life. Our Lady and St. Joseph were well aware that Jesus was God, while at the same time great wonders were hidden from them, and—like us—they lived by faith. You have heard those words of the Gospel: 'They understood not the word that He spoke unto them';[15] and those others no less mysterious: 'His Father and Mother were wondering at those things which were spoken concerning Him.'[16] They seemed to be learning something new, for this word 'wondering' implies a certain amount of surprise."

* * * * * *

"There is a verse in the Divine Office which I recite each day with reluctance: 'I have inclined my heart to do Thy justifications for ever, because of the reward.'[17] I hasten to add in my heart: 'My Jesus, Thou knowest I do not serve Thee for sake of reward, but solely out of love, and a desire to win Thee souls."

* * * * * *

"In Heaven only shall we be in possession of the clear truth. On earth, even in matters of Holy Scripture, our vision is dim. It distresses me to see the differences in its translations, and had I been a Priest I would have learned Hebrew, so as to read the Word of God as He deigned to utter it in human speech."

* * * * * *

Soeur Thérèse often spoke to me of a well-known toy with which she had amused herself when a child. This was the kaleidoscope, shaped like a small telescope, through which, as it is made to revolve, one perceives an endless variety of pretty-coloured figures.

"This toy," she said, "excited my admiration, and I wondered what could provide so charming a phenomenon, when one day, after a lengthy examination, I found that it consisted simply of tiny bits of paper and cloth scattered inside. A further examination revealed that there were three mirrors inside the tube, and the problem was solved. It became for me the illustration of a great truth.

"So long as our actions, even the most trivial, remain within Love's kaleidoscope, so long the Blessed Trinity, figured by the three mirrors, imparts to them a wonderful brightness and beauty. The eye-piece is Jesus Christ, and He, looking from outside through Himself into the kaleidoscope, finds perfect all our works. But, should we leave that ineffable abode of Love, He would see but the rags and chaff of unclean and worthless deeds."

* * * * * *

I told Soeur Thérèse of the strange phenomena produced by magnetism on persons who surrender their will to the hypnotiser. It seemed to interest her greatly, and next day she said to me: "Your conversation yesterday did me so much good! How I long to be hypnotised by Our Lord! It was my waking thought, and verily it was sweet to surrender Him my will. I want Him to take possession of my faculties in such wise that my acts may no more be mine, or human, but Divine— inspired and guided by the Spirit of Love."

* * * * * *

Before my profession I received through my saintly Novice-mistress a very special grace. We had been washing all day. I was worn-out with fatigue and harassed with spiritual worries. That night, before meditation, I wanted to speak to her, but she dismissed me with the remark: "That is the bell for meditation, and I have not time to console you; besides, I see plainly that it would be useless trouble. For the present, God wishes you to suffer alone." I followed her to meditation so discouraged that, for the first time, I doubted of my vocation. I should never be able to be a Carmelite. The life was too hard.

I had been kneeling for some minutes, when all at once, in the midst of this interior struggle—without having asked or even wished for peace—I felt a sudden and extraordinary change of soul. I no longer knew myself. My vocation appeared to me both lovely and lovable. I saw the sweetness and priceless value of suffering. All the privations and fatigues of the religious life appeared to me infinitely preferable to worldly pleasures, and I came away from my meditation completely transformed.

Next day I told my Mistress what had taken place, and, seeing she was deeply touched, I begged to know the reason. "God is good," she exclaimed. "Last evening you inspired me with such profound pity that I prayed incessantly for you at the beginning of meditation. I besought Our Lord to bring you comfort, to change your dispositions, and show you the value of suffering. He has indeed heard my prayers."

* * * * * *

Being somewhat of a child in my ways, the Holy Child—to help me in the practice of virtue—inspired me with the thought of amusing myself with Him, and I chose the game of *ninepins*. I imagined them of all sizes and colours, representing the souls I wished to reach. The ball was—*love*.

In December, 1896, the novices received, for the benefit of the Foreign Missions, various trifles towards a Christmas tree, and at the bottom of the box containing them was a *top*—a rare thing in a Carmelite convent. My companions remarked: "What an ugly thing!—of what use will it be?" But I, who knew the game, caught hold of it, exclaiming: "Nay, what fun! it will spin a whole day without stopping if it be well whipped"; and thereupon I spun it around to their great surprise.

Soeur Thérèse was quietly watching us, and on Christmas night, after midnight Mass, I found in our cell the famous top, with a delightful letter addressed as follows:

To My Beloved Little Spouse

Player of Ninepins on the Mountain of Carmel

Christmas Night, 1896.

MY BELOVED LITTLE SPOUSE,—I am well pleased with thee! All the year round thou hast amused Me by playing at *ninepins*. I was so overjoyed that the whole court of Angels was surprised and charmed. Several little cherubs have asked me why I did not make them children. Others wanted to know if the melody of their instruments were not more pleasing to me than thy joyous laugh when a ninepin fell at the stroke of thy love-ball. My answer to them was, that they must not regret they are not children, since one day they would play with thee in the meadows of Heaven. I told them also that thy smiles were certainly more sweet to Me than their harmonies, because these smiles were purchased by suffering and forgetfulness of self.

And now, my cherished Spouse, it is my turn to ask something of thee. Thou wilt not refuse Me — thou lovest Me too much. Let us change the game. Ninepins amuse me greatly, but at present I should like to play at spinning a top, and, if thou dost consent, thou shalt be the top. I give thee one as a model. Thou seest that it is ugly to look at, and would be kicked aside by whosoever did not know the game. But at the sight of it a child would leap for joy and shout: "What fun! it will spin a whole day without stopping!"

Although thou too art not attractive, I — the little Jesus — love thee, and beg of thee to keep always spinning to amuse Me. True, it needs a whip to make a top spin. Then let thy Sisters supply the whip, and be thou most grateful to those who shall make thee turn fastest. When I shall have had plenty of fun, I will bring thee to join Me here, and our games shall be full of unalloyed delight.—Thy little Brother,

JESUS.

* * * * * *

I had the habit of constantly crying about the merest trifles, and this was a source of great pain to Soeur Thérèse. One day a bright idea occurred to her: taking a mussel-shell from her painting table, and, holding my hands lest I should prevent her, she gathered my tears in the shell, and soon they were turned into merry laughter.

"There," she said, "from this onwards I permit you to cry as much as you like on condition that it is into the shell!"

A week, however, before her death I spent a whole evening in tears at the thought of her fast-approaching end. She knew it, and said: "You have been crying. Was it into the shell?" I was unable to tell an untruth, and my answer grieved her. "I am going to die," she continued, "and I shall not be at rest about you unless you promise to follow faithfully my advice. I consider it of the utmost importance for the good of your soul."

I promised what she asked, begging leave, however, as a favour, to be allowed to cry at her death. "But," she answered, "why cry at my death? Those tears will certainly be useless. You will be bewailing my happiness! Still I have pity on your weakness, and for the first few days you have leave to cry, though afterwards you must again take up the shell."

It has cost me some heroic efforts, but I have been faithful. I have kept the shell at hand, and each time the wish to cry overcame me, I laid hold of the pitiless thing. However urgent the tears, the trouble of passing it from one eye to the other so distracted my thoughts, that before very long this ingenious method entirely cured me of my sensibility.

* * * * * *

Owing to a fault which had caused Soeur Thérèse much pain, but of which I had deeply repented, I intended to deprive myself of Holy Communion. I wrote to her of my resolution, and this was her reply: "Little flower, most dear to Jesus, by this humiliation your roots are feeding upon the earth. You must now open wide your petals, or rather lift high your head, so that the Manna of the Angels may, like a divine dew, come down to strengthen you and supply all your wants. Good-night, poor little flower! Ask of Jesus that all the prayers offered for my cure may serve to increase the fire which ought to consume me."

* * * * * *

"At the moment of Communion I sometimes liken my soul to that of a little child of three or four, whose hair has been ruffled and clothes soiled at play. This is a picture of what befalls me in my struggling with souls. But Our Blessed Lady comes promptly to the rescue, takes off *my soiled pinafore,* and arranges my hair, adorning it with a pretty ribbon or a simple flower. . . . Then I am quite nice, and able, without any shame, to seat myself at the Banquet of Angels."

* * * * * *

In the infirmary we scarcely waited for the end of her thanksgiving before seeking her advice. At first, this somewhat distressed her, and she would make gentle reproaches, but soon she yielded to us, saying: "I must not wish for more rest than Our Lord. When He withdrew into the desert after preaching, the crowds would come and intrude upon His solitude. Come, then, to me as much as you like; I must die sword in hand—'the sword of the Spirit, which is the Word of God.'"[18]

* * * * * *

"Advise us," we said to her, "how to profit by our spiritual instructions." "Go for guidance with great simplicity, not counting too much on help which may fail you at any moment. You would then have to say with the Spouse in the Canticles: 'The keepers took away my cloak and wounded me; when I had a little passed by them, I found Him whom my soul loveth.'[19] If you ask with humility and with detachment after your Beloved, the *keepers* will tell you. More often, you will find Jesus only when you have passed by all creatures. Many times have I repeated this verse of the Spiritual Canticle of St. John of the Cross:

'Messengers, I pray, no more Between us send, who know not how To tell me what my spirit longs to know. For they Thy charms who read—For ever telling of a thousand more—Make all my wounds to bleed, While deeper then before Doth an—I know not what!—my spirit grieve With stammerings vague, and of all life bereave.'"

* * * * * *

"If, supposing the impossible, God Himself could not see my good actions, I would not be troubled. I love Him so much I would like to give Him joy without His knowing who gave. When He sees the gift being made, He is, as it were, obliged to make a return. . . . I should wish to spare Him the trouble."

* * * * * *

"Had I been rich, I could never have seen a poor person hungry without giving him to eat. This is my way also in the spiritual life. There are many souls on the brink of hell, and as my earnings come to hand they are scattered among these sinners. The time has never yet been when I could say: 'Now I am going to work for myself.'"

* * * * * *

"There are people who make the worst of everything. As for me, I do just the contrary. I always see the good side of things, and even if my portion be suffering, without a glimmer of solace, well, I make it my joy."

* * * * * *

"Whatever has come from God's Hands has always pleased me, even those things which have seemed to me less good and less beautiful than the gifts made to others."

* * * * * *

"When staying with my aunt, while I was still a little girl, I was given a certain book to read. In one of the stories great praise was bestowed on a schoolmistress who by her tact escaped from every difficulty without hurting anyone's feelings. Her method of saying to one person: 'You are right,' and to another: 'You are not wrong,' struck me particularly, and as I read I reflected that I would not have acted in that way because we should always tell the truth. And this I always do, though I grant it is much more difficult. It would be far less trouble for us, when told of a worry, to cast the blame on the absent. Less trouble . . . nevertheless I do just the contrary, and if I am disliked it cannot be helped. Let the novices not come to me if they do not want to learn the truth."

* * * * * *

"Before a reproof[20] bear fruit it must cost something and be free from the least trace of passion. Kindness must not degenerate into weakness. When we have had good reason for finding fault, we must leave it, and not allow ourselves to worry over having given pain. To seek out the delinquent for the purpose of consoling her, is to do more harm than good. Left alone, she is compelled to look beyond creatures, and to turn to God; she is forced to see her faults and to humble herself. Otherwise she would become accustomed to expect consolation after a merited rebuke, and would act like a spoilt child who stamps and screams, knowing well that by this means its mother will be forced to return and dry its tears."

* * * * * *

"'Let the sword of the Spirit, which is the Word of God, be ever in your mouth and in your hearts.'[21] If we find any one particular person disagreeable we should never be disheartened, much less cease our endeavour to reform that soul. We should wield *the sword of the Spirit,* and so correct her faults. Things should never be allowed to pass for the sake of our own ease. We must carry on the war even when there is no hope of victory. Success matters nothing, and we must fight on and never complain:

'I shall gain nothing from that soul, she does not understand, there is nothing for it but to abandon her.' That would be the act of a coward. We must do our duty to the very end."

* * * * * *

"Formerly, if any of my friends were in trouble, and I did not succeed in consoling them when they came to see me, I left the parlour quite heart-broken. Soon, however, Our Lord made me understand how incapable I was of bringing comfort to a soul, and from that day I no longer grieved when my visitors went away downcast. I confided to God the sufferings of those so dear to me, and I felt sure that He heard my prayer. At their next visit I learned that I was not mistaken. After this experience, I no longer worry when I have involuntarily given pain. ... I simply ask Our Lord to make amends."

* * * * * *

"What do you think of all the graces that have been heaped upon you?" — "I think 'the Spirit of God breatheth where He will.'"[22]

* * * * * *

"Mother," she one day said to the Prioress, "were I unfaithful, were I to commit even the smallest infidelity, I feel that my soul would be plunged into the most terrible anguish, and I should be unable to welcome death."

Mother Prioress evinced surprise at hearing her speak in this strain, and she continued: "I am speaking of infidelity in the matter of pride. If, for example, I were to say: 'I have acquired such or such a virtue and I can practise it'; or again: 'My God, Thou knowest I love Thee too much to dwell on one single thought against faith,' straightway I should be assailed by the most dangerous temptations and should certainly yield. To prevent this misfortune I have but to say humbly and from my heart: 'My God, I beseech Thee not to let me be unfaithful.'

"I understand clearly how St. Peter fell. He placed too much reliance on his own ardent nature, instead of leaning solely on the Divine strength. Had he only said: 'Lord, give me strength to follow Thee unto death!' the grace would not have been refused him.

"How is it, Mother, that Our Lord, knowing what was about to happen, did not say to him: 'Ask of Me the strength to do what is in thy mind?' I think His purpose was to give us a twofold lesson—first: that He taught His Apostles nothing by His presence which He does not teach us through the inspirations of grace; and secondly: that, having made choice of St. Peter to govern the whole Church, wherein there are many sinners, He wished him to test in himself what man can do without God's help. This is why Jesus said to him before his fall: 'Thou being once converted confirm thy brethren';[23] that is, 'Tell them the story of thy sin—show them by thy own experience, how necessary it is for salvation to rely solely upon Me.'"

* * * * * *

I was much afflicted at seeing her ill, and I often exclaimed: "Life is so dreary!" "Life is not dreary"—she would immediately say; "on the contrary, it is most gay. Now if you said: 'Exile is dreary,' I could understand. It is a mistake to call 'life' that which must have an end. Such a word should be only used of the joys of Heaven—joys that are unfading—and in this true meaning life is not sad but gay—most gay...."

Her own gaiety was a thing of delight. For several days she had been much better, and we were saying to her: "We do not yet know of what disease you will die. . . ." "But," she answered, "I shall die of death! Did not God tell Adam of what he would die when He said to him: 'Thou shalt die of death'?"[24]

"Then death will come to fetch you?"—"No, not death, but the Good God. Death is not, as pictures tell us, a phantom, a horrid spectre. The Catechism says that it is the separation of soul and body—no more! Well, I do not fear a separation which will unite me for ever to God."

"Will the *Divine Thief*," some one asked, "soon come to steal His little bunch of grapes?" "I see Him in the distance, and I take good care not to cry out: 'Stop thief!' Rather, I call to Him: 'This way, this way!'"

* * * * * *

Asked under what name we should pray to her in Heaven, she answered humbly: "Call me *Little Thérèse.*"

* * * * * *

I was telling her that the most beautiful angels, all robed in white, would bear her soul to Heaven: "Fancies like those," she answered, "do not help me, and my soul can only feed upon truth. God and His Angels are pure spirits. No human eye can see them as they really are. That is why I have never asked extraordinary favours. I prefer to await the Eternal Vision."

"To console me at your death I have asked God to send me a beautiful dream."—"That is a thing I would never do . . . ask for consolations. Since you wish to resemble me, you know what are my ideas on this:

'Fear not, O Lord, that I shall waken Thee: I shall await in peace the Heavenly Shore.'

"It is so sweet to serve God in the dark night and in the midst of trial. After all, we have but this life in which to live by faith."

* * * * * *

"I am happy at the thought of going to Heaven, but when I reflect on these words of Our Lord: 'I come quickly, and My reward is with Me, to render to every man according to his works,'[25] I think that He will find my case a puzzle: I have no works. . . . Well, He will render unto me *according to His own works!*"

* * * * * *

"The chief plenary indulgence, which is within reach of everybody, and can be gained without the ordinary conditions, is that of charity—which 'covereth a multitude of sins.'"[26]

* * * * * *

"Surely you will not even pass through Purgatory. If such a thing should happen, then certainly nobody goes straight to Heaven."—"That gives me little thought. I shall be quite content with the Merciful God's decision. Should I go to Purgatory, I shall—like the three Hebrew children in the furnace—walk amid the flames singing the Canticle of Love."

* * * * * *

"In Heaven you will be placed among the Seraphim." "If so, I shall not imitate them. At the sight of God *they cover themselves with their wings*[27]: I shall take good care not to hide myself with mine."

* * * * * *

I showed her a picture which represented Joan of Arc being comforted in prison by her Voices, and she remarked: "I also am comforted by an interior voice. From above, the Saints encourage me, saying: 'So long as thou art a captive in chains, thou canst not fulfill thy mission, but later on, after thy death, will come thy day of triumph.'"

* * * * * *

"In Heaven, God will do all I desire, because on earth I have never done my own will."

* * * * * *

"You will look down upon us from Heaven, will you not?"—"No, I will come down."

* * * * * *

Some months before the death of Soeur Thérèse, *The Life of St. Aloysius* was being read in the refectory, and one of the Mothers was struck by the mutual and tender affection which existed between the young Saint and the aged Jesuit, Father Corbinelli.

"You are little Aloysius," she said to Thérèse, "and I am old Father Corbinelli—be mindful of me when you enter Heaven." "Would you like me to fetch you thither soon, dear Mother?" "No, I have not yet suffered enough." "Nay, Mother, I tell you that you have suffered quite enough." To which Mother Hermance replied: "I dare not say Yes. . . . In so grave a matter I must have the sanction of authority." So the request was made to Mother Prioress, who, without attaching much importance to it, gave her sanction.

Now, on one of the last days of her life, Soeur Thérèse, scarcely able to speak owing to her great weakness, received through the infirmarian a bouquet of flowers. It had been gathered by Mother Hermance, and was accompanied by an entreaty for one word of affection. The message: "Tell Mother Hermance of the Heart of Jesus that during Mass this morning I saw Father Corbinelli's grave close to that of little Aloysius."

"That is well," replied the good Mother, greatly touched; "tell Soeur Thérèse that I have understood. . . ." And from that moment she felt convinced her death was near. It took place just one year later, and, according to the prediction of the "Little Aloysius," the two graves lie side by side.

* * * * * *

The last words penned by the hand of Soeur Thérèse were: "O Mary, were I Queen of Heaven, and wert thou Thérèse, I should wish to be Thérèse, that I might see thee Queen of Heaven!"

---

[1] Cf. Matt. 20:23.

[2] Cf. Ps. 67[68]:28.

[3] Cf. Prov. 1:4.

[4] Judith 15:11.

[5] Ecclus. 11:12, 13, 22, 23, 24.

[6] Jer. 10:23.

[7] Cf. Psalm 93[94]:18.

[8] *Imit.*, I, xvi. 4.

[9] John 14:2.

[10] Cf. Psalm 111[112]:5.

[11] Cant. 1:2.

[12] Cf. 2 Esdras 4:17.

[13] Matt. 25:36.

[14] Prov. 16:32.

[15] Luke 2:50.

[16] Luke 2:33.

[17] Ps. 118[119]:112.

[18] Ephes. 6:17.

[19] Cf. Cant. 5:7, 3:4.

[20] In this and the following "counsel" it should be remembered that it is a Novice-Mistress who is speaking. [Ed.]

[21] Cf. Ephes. 6:17; Isaias 61:21.

[22] Cf. John 3:8.

[23] Luke 22:32.

[24] Cf. Gen. 2:17. A play on the French: *Tu mourras de mort*. [Ed.]

[25] Apoc. 22:12.

[26] Prov. 10:12.

[27] Cf. Isaias 6:2.

LETTERS OF SOEUR THÉRÈSE THE LITTLE FLOWER OF JESUS

LETTERS OF SOEUR THÉRÈSE TO HER SISTER CÉLINE

I

J.M.J.T.

May 8, 1888.

DEAREST CÉLINE,—There are moments when I wonder whether I am really and truly in the Carmel; sometimes I can scarcely believe it. What have I done for God that He should shower so many graces upon me?

A whole month has passed since we parted; but why do I say parted? Even were the wide ocean between us, our souls would remain as one. And yet I know that not to have me is real suffering, and if I listened to myself I should ask Jesus to let me bear the sadness in your stead! I do not listen, as you see; I should be afraid of being selfish in wishing for myself the better part—I mean the suffering. You are right—life is often burdensome and bitter. It is painful to begin a day of toil, especially when Jesus hides Himself from our love. What is this sweet Friend about? Does He not see our anguish and the burden that weighs us down? Why does He not come and comfort us?

Be not afraid. . . . He is here at hand. He is watching, and it is He who begs from us this pain, these tears. . . . He needs them for souls, for our souls, and He longs to give us a magnificent reward. I assure you that it costs Him dear to fill us with bitterness, but He knows that it is the only means of preparing us to know Him as He knows Himself, and to become ourselves Divine! Our soul is indeed great and our destiny glorious. Let us lift ourselves above all things that pass, and hold ourselves far from the earth! Up above, the air is so pure. . . . Jesus may hide Himself, but we know that He is there.

II

October 20, 1888.

MY DEAREST SISTER,—Do not let your weakness make you unhappy. When, in the morning, we feel no courage or strength for the practice of virtue, it is really a grace: it is the time to "lay the axe to the root of the tree,"[1] relying upon Jesus alone. If we fall, an act of love will set all right, and Jesus smiles. He helps us without seeming to do so; and the tears which sinners cause Him to shed are wiped away by our poor weak love. Love can do all things. The most impossible tasks seem to it easy and sweet. You know well that Our Lord does not look so much at the greatness of our actions, nor even at their difficulty, as at the love with which we do them. What, then, have we to fear?

You wish to become a Saint, and you ask me if this is not attempting too much. Céline, I will not tell you to aim at the seraphic holiness of the most privileged souls, but rather to be "perfect as your Heavenly Father is perfect."[2] You see that your dream—that our dreams and our desires—are not fancies, since Jesus Himself has laid their realisation upon us as a commandment.

III

January, 1889.

MY DEAR LITTLE CÉLINE,—Jesus offers you the cross, a very heavy cross, and you are afraid of not being able to carry it without giving way. Why? Our Beloved Himself fell three times on the way to Calvary, and why should we not imitate our Spouse? What a favour from Jesus, and how He must love us to send us so great a sorrow! Eternity itself will not be long enough to bless Him for it. He heaps his favours upon us as upon the greatest Saints. What, then, are His loving designs for our souls? That is a secret which will only be revealed to us in our Heavenly Home, on the day when "the Lord shall wipe away all our tears."[3]

Now we have nothing more to hope for on earth —"the cool evenings are passed"[4]—for us suffering alone remains! Ours is an enviable lot, and the Seraphim in Heaven are jealous of our happiness.

The other day I came across this striking passage: "To be resigned and to be united to the will of God are not the same; there is the same difference between them as that which exists between union and unity; in union there are still two, in unity there is but one."[5] Yes, let us be one with God even in this life; and for this we should be more than resigned, we should embrace the Cross with joy.

IV

February 28, 1889.

MY DEAR LITTLE SISTER,—Jesus is "a Spouse of blood."[6] He wishes for Himself all the blood of our hearts. You are right—it costs us dear to give Him what He asks. But what a joy that it does cost! It is happiness to bear our crosses, and to feel our weakness in doing so.

Céline, far from complaining to Our Lord of this cross which He sends us, I cannot fathom the Infinite Love which had led Him to treat us in this way. Our dear Father must indeed be loved by God to have so much suffering given to him. I know that by humiliation alone can Saints be made, and I also know that our trial is a mine of gold for us to turn to account. I, who am but a little grain of sand, wish to set to work, though I have neither courage nor strength. Now this very want of power will make my task easier, for I wish to work for love. Our martyrdom is beginning . . . Let us go forth to suffer together, dear sister, and let us offer our sufferings to Jesus for the salvation of souls.

V

March 12, 1899.

. . . I must forget this world. Here everything wearies me—I find only one joy, that of suffering, and this joy, which is not one of sense, is above all joy. Life is passing, and eternity is drawing near. Soon we shall live the very life of God. After we have been filled at the source of all bitterness, our thirst will be quenched at the very Fountain of all sweetness.

"The figure of this world passeth away"[7]—soon we shall see new skies—a more radiant sun will light with its splendour crystal seas and infinite horizons. We shall no longer be prisoners in a land of exile, all will have passed away, and with our Heavenly Spouse we shall sail upon boundless seas. Now, "our harps are hanging on the willows which grow by the rivers of Babylon,"[8] but in the day of our deliverance what harmonies will they not give forth, how joyfully shall we make all their strings vibrate! Now, "we shed tears as we remember Sion, for how can we sing the songs of the Lord in a land of exile?"[9] The burden of our song is suffering. Jesus offers us a chalice of great bitterness. Let us not withdraw our lips from it, but suffer in peace. He who says *peace* does not say *joy,* or at least sensible joy: to suffer in peace it is enough to will heartily all that Our Lord wills. Do not think we can find love without suffering, for our nature remains and must be taken into account; but it puts great treasures within our reach. Suffering is indeed our very livelihood, and is so precious that Jesus came down upon earth on purpose to possess it. We should like to suffer generously and nobly; we should like never to fall. What an illusion! What does it matter to me if I fall at every moment! In that way I realise my weakness, and I gain thereby. My God, Thou seest how little I am good for, when Thou dost carry me in Thy Arms; and if Thou leavest me alone, well, it is because it pleases Thee to see me lie on the ground. Then why should I be troubled?

If you are willing to bear in peace the trial of not being pleased with yourself, you will be offering the Divine Master a home in your heart. It is true that you will suffer, because you will be like a stranger to your own house; but do not be afraid—the poorer you are, the more Jesus will love you. I know that He is better pleased to see you stumbling in the night upon a stony road, than walking in the full light of day upon a path carpeted with flowers, because these flowers might hinder your advance.

VI

July 14, 1889.

MY DARLING SISTER,—I am ever with you in spirit. Yes, it is very hard to live upon this earth, but to-morrow, in a brief hour, we shall be at rest. O my God, what shall we then see? What is this life which will have no end? Our Lord will be the soul of our soul. O unsearchable mystery! "Eye hath not seen nor ear heard, neither hath it entered into the heart of man what things God hath prepared for them that love Him."[10] And all this will come soon—very soon—if we love Jesus ardently. It seems to me that God has no need of years to perfect His labour of love in a soul. One ray from His Heart can in an instant make His flower blossom forth, never to fade. . . . Céline, during the fleeting moments that remain to us, let us save souls! I feel that Our Spouse asks us for souls—above all, for the souls of Priests. . . . It is He Who bids me tell you this.

There is but one thing to be done here below: to love Jesus, and to save souls for Him that He may be more loved. We must not let slip the smallest opportunity of giving Him joy. We must refuse Him nothing. He is in such need of love.

We are His chosen lilies. He dwells as a King in our midst—He lets us share the honours of His Royalty—His Divine Blood bedews our petals—and His Thorns as they wound us spread abroad the perfume of our love.

VII

October 22, 1889.

MY DEAREST CÉLINE,—I send you a picture of the Holy Face. The contemplation of this Divine subject seems to me to belong in a special way to my little sister, truly the sister of my soul. May she be another Veronica, and wipe away all the Blood and Tears of Jesus, her only Love! May she give Him souls! May she force her way through the soldiers—that is, the world—to come close to His side. . . . Happy will she be when she sees in Heaven the value of that mysterious draught with which she quenched the thirst of her Heavenly

Spouse; when she sees His Lips, once parched with burning thirst, speaking to her the one eternal word — love, and the thanks which shall have no end. . . .

Good-bye, dear little Veronica;[11] to-morrow, no doubt, your Beloved will ask some new sacrifice, a fresh relief for His thirst . . . but "let us go and die with Him!"

VIII

July 18, 1890.

MY DEAR LITTLE SISTER,—I send you a passage from Isaias which will comfort you. Long ago the Prophet's soul was filled with the thought of the hidden beauties of the Divine Face, as our souls are now. Many a century has passed since then. It makes me wonder what is Time. Time is but a mirage, a dream. Already God sees us in glory, and rejoices in our everlasting bliss. How much good I derive from this thought! I understand now why He allows us to suffer.

Since Our Beloved has "trodden the wine-press alone,"[12] the wine-press from which He gives us to drink — on our side let us not refuse to be clothed in blood-stained garments, or to tread out for Jesus a new wine which may quench His thirst! When "He looks around Him," He will not be able to say now that "He is alone"[13] — we shall be there to help Him.

"His look as it were hidden."[14] Alas! it is so even to this day, and no one understands His Tears. "Open to Me, My Sister, My Spouse," he says to us, "for My Head is full of dew and My Locks of the drops of the night."[15] Thus Jesus complains to our souls when He is deserted and forgotten . . . *To be forgotten.* It is this, I think, which gives Him most pain.

And our dear Father! — it is heartrending, but how can we repine since Our Lord Himself was looked upon "as one struck by God and afflicted"? [16] In this great sorrow we should forget ourselves, and pray for Priests — our lives must be entirely devoted to them. Our Divine Master makes me feel more and more that this is what He asks of you and me.

IX

September 23, 1890.

O Céline, how can I tell you all that is happening within me? What a wound I have received! And yet I feel it is inflicted by a loving Hand, by a Hand divinely jealous.

All was ready for my espousals;[17] but do you not think that something was still wanting to the feast? It is true, Jesus had already enriched me with many jewels, but no doubt there was one of incomparable beauty still missing; this priceless diamond He has given me to-day . . . Papa will not be here to-morrow! Céline, I confess that I have cried bitterly. . . . I am still crying so that I can scarcely hold my pen.

You know how intensely I longed to see our dearest Father again; but now I feel that it is God's Will that he should not be at my feast. God has allowed it simply to try our love. Jesus wishes me to be an orphan . . . to be alone, with Him alone, so that He may unite Himself more closely to me. He wishes, too, to give me back in Heaven this joy so lawfully desired, but which He has denied me here on earth.

To-day's trial is one of those sorrows that are difficult to understand: a joy was set before us, one most natural and easy of attainment. We stretched forth our hands . . . and the coveted joy was withdrawn. But it is not the hand of man which has done this thing—it is God's work. Céline, understand your Thérèse, and let us accept cheerfully the thorn which is offered us. Tomorrow's feast will be one of tears, but I feel that Jesus will be greatly consoled. . . .

X

October 14, 1890.

MY DARLING SISTER,—I know quite well all you are suffering. I know your anguish, and I share it. Oh! If I could but impart to you the peace which Jesus has put into my soul amid my most bitter tears. Be comforted—all passes away. Our life of yesterday is spent; death too will come and go, and then we shall rejoice in life, true life, for countless ages, for evermore. Meanwhile let us make of our heart a garden of delights where Our sweet Saviour may come and take His rest. Let us plant only lilies there, and sing with St. John of the Cross:

"There I remained in deep oblivion, My head reposing upon Him I love, Lost to myself and all! I cast my cares away And let them, heedless, mid the lilies lie."[18]

XI

April 26, 1891.

MY DEAR LITTLE SISTER,—Three years ago our hearts had not yet been bruised, and life was one glad smile. Then Jesus looked down upon us, and all things were changed into an ocean of tears . . . but likewise into an ocean of grace and of love. God has taken from us him whom we loved so tenderly —was it not that we might be able to say more truly than ever: "Our Father Who art in heaven"? How consoling is this divine word, and what vast horizons it opens before us!

My darling Céline, you who asked me so many questions when we were little, I wonder how it was you never asked: "Why has God not made me an Angel?" Well, I am going to tell you. Our Lord wishes to have His Court here on earth, as He has in Heaven; He wishes for angel-martyrs and angel-apostles; and if He has not made you an Angel in Heaven, it is because He wishes you to be an Angel of earth, so that you may be able to suffer for His Love.

Dearest sister, the shadows will soon disappear, the rays of the Eternal Sun will thaw the hoar frost of winter. . . . A little longer, and we shall be in our true country, and our childhood's joys—those Sunday evenings, those outpourings of the heart— will be given back to us for ever!

XII

August 15, 1892.

MY DEAR LITTLE SISTER,—To write to you today I am obliged to steal a little time from Our Lord. He will forgive, because it is of Him that we are going to speak together. The vast solitudes and enchanting views which unfold themselves before you ought to uplift your soul. I do not see those things, and I content myself by saying with St. John of the Cross in his Spiritual Canticle:

In Christ I have the mountains, The quiet, wooded valleys.

Lately I have been thinking what I could undertake for the salvation of souls, and these simple words of the Gospel have given me light. Pointing to the fields of ripe corn, Jesus once said to His disciples: "Lift up your eyes and see the fields, for they are already white with the harvest";[19] and again: "The harvest indeed is great, but the labourers are few; pray ye therefore the Lord of the harvest that He send forth labourers."[20]

Here is a mystery indeed! Is not Jesus all-powerful? Do not creatures belong to Him who made them? Why does He deign to say: "Pray ye the Lord of the harvest that He send forth labourers"? It is because His Love for us is so unsearchable, so tender, that He wishes us to share in all He does. The Creator of the Universe awaits the prayer of a poor little soul to save a multitude of other souls, ransomed, like her, at the price of His Blood.

Our vocation is not to go forth and reap in Our Father's fields. Jesus does not say to us: "Look down and reap the harvest." Our mission is even more sublime. "Lift up your eyes and see," saith our Divine Master, "see how in Heaven there are empty thrones. It is for you to fill them. . . . You are as Moses praying on the mountain, so ask Me for labourers and they shall be sent. I only await a prayer, a sigh! Is not the apostolate of prayer—so to speak—higher than that of the spoken word? It is for us by prayer to train workers who will spread the glad tidings of the Gospel and who will save countless souls—the souls to whom we shall be the spiritual Mothers. What, then, have we to envy in the Priests of the Lord?

XIII

MY DARLING SISTER,—The affection of our childhood days has changed into a closest union of mind and heart. Jesus has drawn us to Him together, for are you not already His? He has put the world beneath our feet. Like Zaccheus we have climbed into a tree to behold Him—mysterious tree, raising us high above all things, from whence we can say: "All is mine, all is for me: the Earth and the Heavens are mine, God Himself is mine, and the Mother of my God is for me."[21]

Speaking of that Blessed Mother, I must tell you of one of my simple ways. Sometimes I find myself saying to her: "Dearest Mother, it seems to me that I am happier than you. I have you for my Mother, and you have no Blessed Virgin to love. . . . It is true, you are the Mother of Jesus, but you have given Him to me; and He, from the Cross, has given you to be our Mother—thus we are richer than you!

Long ago, in your humility, you wished to become the little handmaid of the Mother of God; and I—poor little creature—am not your handmaid but your child! You are the Mother of Jesus, and you are also *mine!*"

Our greatness in Jesus is verily marvellous, my Céline. He has unveiled for us many a mystery by making us climb the mystical tree of which I spoke above. And now what science is He going to teach? Have we not learned all things from Him?

"Make haste to come down, for this day I must abide in thy house."[22] Jesus bids us come down. Where, then, must we go? The Jews asked Him: "Master, where dwellest thou?"[23] And He answered, "The foxes have holes and the birds of the air nests, but the Son of Man hath not where to lay His Head."[24] If we are to be the dwelling-place of Jesus, we must come down even to this—we must be so poor that we have not where to lay our heads.

This grace of light has been given to me during my retreat. Our Lord desires that we should receive Him into our hearts, and no doubt they are empty of creatures. Alas! mine is not empty of self; that is why He bids me come down. And I shall come down even to the very ground, that Jesus may find within my heart a resting-place for His Divine Head, and may feel that there at least He is loved and understood.

XIV

April 25, 1893.

MY LITTLE CÉLINE,—I must come and disclose the desires of Jesus with regard to your soul. Remember that He did not say: "I am the flower of the gardens, a carefully-tended Rose"; but, "I am the Flower of the fields and the Lily of the valleys."[25] Well, you must be always as a drop of dew hidden in the heart of this beautiful Lily of the valley.

The dew-drop—what could be simpler, what more pure? It is not the child of the clouds; it is born beneath the starry sky, and survives but a night. When the sun darts forth its ardent rays, the delicate pearls adorning each blade of grass quickly pass into the lightest of vapour. . . . There is the portrait of my little Céline! She is a drop of dew, an offspring of Heaven—her true Home. Through the night of this life she must hide herself in the *Field-*

flower's golden cup; no eye must discover her abode.

Happy dewdrop, known to God alone, think not of the rushing torrents of this world! Envy not even the crystal stream which winds among the meadows. The ripple of its waters is sweet indeed, but it can be heard by creatures. Besides, the Field-flower could never contain it in its cup. One must be so little to draw near to Jesus, and few are the souls that aspire to be little and unknown. "Are not the river and the brook," they urge, "of more use than a dewdrop? Of what avail is it? Its only purpose is to refresh for one moment some poor little field-flower."

Ah! They little know the true *Flower of the field.* Did they know Him they would understand better Our Lord's reproach to Martha. Our Beloved needs neither our brilliant deeds nor our beautiful thoughts. Were He in search of lofty ideas, has He not His Angels, whose knowledge infinitely surpasses that of the greatest genius of earth? Neither intellect nor other talents has He come to seek among us. . . . He has become the *Flower of the field* to show how much He loves simplicity.

The Lily of the valley asks but a single dewdrop, which for one night shall rest in its cup, hidden from all human eyes. But when the shadows shall begin to fade, when the *Flower of the field* shall have become the *Sun of Justice,*[26] then the dewdrop—the humble sharer of His exile—will rise up to Him as love's vapour. He will shed on her a ray of His light, and before the whole court of Heaven she will shine eternally like a precious pearl, a dazzling mirror of the Divine Sun.

XV

August 2, 1893.

MY DEAR CÉLINE,—What you write fills me with joy; you are making your way by a royal road. The Spouse in the Canticles, unable to find her Beloved in the time of repose, went forth to seek Him in the city. But in vain . . . it was only without the walls she found Him. It is not in the sweetness of repose that Jesus would have us discover His Adorable Presence. He hides Himself and shrouds Himself in darkness. True, this was not His way with the multitude, for we read that all the people were carried away as soon as He spoke to them.

The weaker souls He charmed by His divine eloquence with the aim of strengthening them against the day of temptation and trial, but His faithful friends were few that day when "He was silent"[27] in the presence of His judges. Sweet melody to my heart is that silence of the Divine Master!

He would have us give Him alms as to a poor man, and puts Himself—so to speak—at our mercy. He will take nothing that is not cheerfully given, and the veriest trifle is precious in His Divine Eyes. He stretches forth His Hand to receive a little love, that in the radiant day of the Judgment He may speak to us those ineffably sweet words: "Come, ye blessed of My Father, for I was hungry and you gave Me to drink, I was a stranger and you took Me in, I was sick and you visited Me, I was in prison and you came to Me."[28]

Dearest Céline, let us rejoice in the lot that is ours! Let us give and give again, and give royally, never forgetting that Our Beloved is a hidden Treasure which few souls know how to find. Now to discover that which is hidden we must needs hide ourselves in the hiding-place. Let our life, then, be one of concealment. The author of the *Imitation* tells us:

"If thou would'st know and learn something to the purpose, love to be unknown, and to be esteemed as nothing . . . [29] Having forsaken all things, a man should forsake himself. . . [30] Let this man glory in this and another in that, but thou for thy part rejoice neither in this nor in that, but in the contempt of thyself."[31]

XVI

MY DEAR CÉLINE, — You tell me that my letters do good to you. I am indeed glad, but I assure you that I am under no misapprehension: "Unless the Lord build the house, they labour in vain who build it." [32] The greatest eloquence cannot call forth a single act of love without that grace which touches the heart.

Think of a beautiful peach with its delicate tint of rose, with its flavour so sweet that no human skill could invent such nectar. Tell me, Céline, is it for the peach's own sake that God created that colour so fair to the eye, that velvety covering so soft to the touch? Is it for itself that He made it so sweet? Nay, it is for us; the only thing that is all its own and is essential to its being, is the stone; it possesses nothing beyond.

Thus also it pleases Jesus to lavish His gifts on certain souls in order to draw yet others to Himself; in His Mercy He humbles them inwardly and gently compels them to recognise their nothingness and His Almighty Power. Now this sentiment of humility is like a kernel of grace which God hastens to develop against that blessed day, when, clothed with an imperishable beauty, they will be placed, without danger, on the banqueting-table of Paradise. Dear little sister, sweet echo of my soul, Thérèse is far from the heights of fervour at this moment; but when I am in this state of spiritual dryness, unable to pray, or to practise virtue, I look for little opportunities, for the smallest trifles, to please my Jesus: a smile or a kind word, for instance, when I would wish to be silent, or to show that I am bored. If no such occasion offer, I try at least to say over and over again that I love Him. This is not hard, and it keeps alive the fire in my heart. Even should the fire of love seem dead, I would still throw my tiny straws on the ashes, and I am confident it would light up again.

It is true I am not always faithful, but I never lose courage. I leave myself in the Arms of Our Lord. He teaches me to draw profit from everything, from the good and from the bad which He finds in me.[33]

He teaches me to speculate in the Bank of Love, or rather it is He Who speculates for me, without telling me how He does it—that is His affair, not mine. I have but to surrender myself wholly to Him, to do so without reserve, without even the satisfaction of knowing what it is all bringing to me. ... After all, I am not the prodigal child, and Jesus need not trouble about a feast for me, *because I am always with Him.*[34]

I have read in the Gospel that the Good Shepherd leaves the faithful ones of His flock in the desert to hasten after the lost sheep. This confidence touches me deeply. You see He is sure of them. How could they stray away? They are prisoners of Love. In like manner does the Beloved Shepherd of our souls deprive us of the sweets of His Presence, to give His consolations to sinners; or if He lead us to Mount Thabor it is but for one brief moment . . . the pasture land is nearly always in the valleys, "it is there that He takes His rest at mid-day."[35]

XVII

October 20, 1893.

MY DEAR SISTER,—I find in the Canticle of Canticles this passage which may be fitly applied to you: "What dost thou see in thy beloved but a band of musicians in an armed camp?"[36] Through suffering, your life has in truth become a battlefield, and there must be a band of musicians, so you shall be the little harp of Jesus. But no concert is complete without singing, and if Jesus plays, must not Céline make melody with her voice? When the music is plaintive, she will sing the songs of exile; when the music is gay, she will lilt the airs of her Heavenly Home. . . .

Whatever may happen, all earthly events, be they happy or sad, will be but distant sounds, unable to awake a vibration from the harp of Jesus. He reserves to Himself alone the right of lightly touching its strings.

I cannot think without delight of that sweet saint, Cecilia. What an example she gives us! In the midst of a pagan world, in the very heart of danger, at the moment when she was to be united to a man whose love was so utterly of earth, it seems to me as if she should have wept and trembled with fear. But instead, "during the music of the marriage-feast Cecilia kept singing in her heart."[37] What perfect resignation! No doubt she heard other melodies than those of this world; her Divine Spouse too was singing, and the Angels repeated in chorus the refrain of Bethlehem's blessed night: "Glory to God in the highest, and on earth peace to men of goodwill."[38]

The Glory of God! St. Cecilia understood it well, and longed for it with all her heart. She guessed that her Jesus was thirsting for souls . . . and that is why her whole desire was to bring to Him quickly the soul of the young Roman, whose only thought was of human glory. This wise Virgin will make of him a Martyr, and multitudes will follow in his footsteps. She knows no fear: the Angels in their song made promise of peace. She knows that the Prince of Peace is bound to protect her, to guard her virginity, and to make her recompense. . . . "Oh, how beautiful is the chaste generation!"[39]

Dearest sister, I hardly know what I write; I let my pen follow the dictates of my heart. You tell me that you feel your weakness, but that is a grace. It is Our Lord Who sows the seeds of distrust of self in your soul. Do not be afraid! If you do not fail to give Him pleasure in small things, he will be obliged to help you in great ones.

The Apostles laboured long without Him, they toiled a whole night and caught no fish. Their labours were not inacceptable to him, but He wished to prove that He is the Giver of all things. So an act of humility was asked of the Apostles, and Our loving Lord called to them: "Children, have you anything to eat?"[40] St. Peter, avowing his helplessness, cried out: "Lord, we have laboured all the night, and have taken nothing."[41] It is enough, the Heart of Jesus is touched. . . . Had the Apostle caught some small fish, perhaps our Divine Master would not have worked a miracle; but he had caught *nothing,* and so through the power and goodness of God his nets were soon filled with great fishes. Such is Our Lord's way. He gives as God—with divine largesse—but He insists on humility of heart.

XVIII

July 7, 1894.

MY DEAR LITTLE SISTER,—I do not know if you are still in the same frame of mind as when you last wrote to me; I presume that you are, and I answer with this passage of the Canticle of Canticles, which explains so well the state of a soul in utter dryness, a soul which cannot find joy or consolation in anything: "I went down into the garden of nut-trees to see the fruits of the valleys, and to look if the vineyard had flourished, and the pomegranates were in bud. I no longer knew where I was: my soul was troubled because of the chariots of Aminadab." [42]

There is the true picture of our souls. Often we go down in the fertile valleys where our heart loves to find its nourishment; and the vast fields of Holy Scripture, which have so often opened to yield us richest treasures, now seem but an arid and waterless waste. We no longer even know where we stand. In place of peace and light, all is sorrow and darkness. But, like the Spouse in the Canticles, we know the cause of this trial: "My soul was troubled because of the chariots of Aminadab." We are not as yet in our true country, and as gold is tired in the fire so must our souls be purified by temptation. We sometimes think we are abandoned. Alas! *the chariots*—that is to say, the idle clamours which beset and disturb us—are they within the soul or without? We cannot tell, but Jesus knows; He sees all our grief, and in the night, on a sudden, His

Voice is heard: "Return, return, O Sulamitess: return, return, that we may behold thee."[43]

O gracious call! We dared no longer even look upon ourselves, the sight filled us with horror, and Jesus calls us that He may look upon us at leisure. He wills to see us; He comes, and with Him come the other two Persons of the Adorable Trinity to take possession of our soul.

Our Lord had promised this, when, with unspeakable tenderness, He had said of old: "If anyone love Me he will keep My word, and My Father will love him, and We will come to him, and will make Our abode with him."[44] To keep the word of Jesus, then, is one condition of our happiness, the proof of our love for Him; and this word seems to me to be His very Self, for He calls Himself the Uncreated *Word* of the Father.

In the same Gospel of St. John He makes the sublime prayer: "Sanctify them by Thy word, Thy word is truth."[45] And in another passage Jesus teaches us that He is "the Way and the Truth and the Life."[46] We know, then, what is this word which must be kept; we cannot say, like Pilate: "What is truth?"[47] We possess the Truth, for our Beloved dwells in our hearts.

Often *this Beloved is to us a bundle of myrrh.*[48] We share the chalice of His sufferings; but how sweet it will be to us one day to hear these gentle words: "You are they who have continued with Me in My temptations, and I dispose to you, as My Father hath disposed to Me, a kingdom."[49]

XIX

August 19, 1894.

This is perhaps the last time that I need have recourse to writing in order to talk to you, my dear little sister. God in His goodness has granted my dearest wish. Come, and we will suffer together . . . Then Jesus will take one of us, and the others will remain in exile yet a little longer. Now, listen well to what I am going to say: God will never, never separate us; and if I die before you, do not think that I shall be far away — never shall we have been more closely united. You must not be grieved at my childish prophecy. I am not ill, I have an iron constitution; but the Lord can break iron as if it were clay.

Our dear Father makes his presence felt in a way which touches me deeply. After a death lasting for five long years, what joy to find him as he used to be, nay, more a father than ever! How well he is going to repay you for the care you so generously bestowed on him! You were his Angel, now he will be yours. He has only been one month in heaven, and already, through the power of his intercession, all your plans are succeeding. It is easy for him now to arrange matters for us, and he has had less to suffer on Céline's account than he had for his poor little Queen.

For a long time you have been asking me for news about the noviciate, especially about my work, and now I am going to satisfy you. In my dealings with the novices I am like a setter on the scent of game. The rôle gives me much anxiety because it so very exacting. You shall decide for yourself if this be not the case. All day long, from morn till night, I am in pursuit of game. Mother Prioress and the Novice Mistress play the part of sportsmen—but sportsmen are too big to be creeping through the cover, whereas a little dog can push its way in anywhere ... and then its scent is so keen! I keep a close watch upon my little rabbits; I do not want to do them any harm, but I tell them gently: "You must keep your fur glossy, and must not look foolishly about as does a rabbit of the warren." In fact, I try to make them such as the Hunter of Souls would have them, simple little creatures that go on browsing heedless of everything else.

I laugh now, but seriously I am quite convinced that one of these rabbits—you know which one I mean—is worth a hundred times more than the setter; it has run through many a danger, and I own that, had I been in its place, I should have long since been lost for ever in the great forest of the world.

XX

I am so glad, dearest Céline, that you do not feel any particular attraction at the thought of entering the Carmel. This is really a mark of Our Lord's favour, and shows that He looks for a gift from your hands. He knows that it is so much sweeter to give than to receive. What happiness to suffer for Him Who loves us even unto folly, and to pass for fools in the eyes of the world! We judge others by ourselves, and, as the world will not hearken to reason, it calls us unreasonable too.

We may console ourselves, we are not the first. Folly was the only crime with which Herod could reproach Our Lord . . . and, after all, Herod was right. Yes, indeed, it was folly to come and seek the poor hearts of mortal men to make them thrones for Him, the King of Glory, Who sitteth above the Cherubim! Was He not supremely happy in the company of His Father and the Holy Spirit of Love? Why, then, come down on earth to seek sinners and make of them His closest friends? Nay, our folly could never exceed His, and our deeds are quite within the bounds of reason. The world may leave us alone. I repeat, it is the world that is *insane*, because it heeds not what Jesus has done and suffered to save it from eternal damnation.

We are neither idlers nor spendthrifts. Our Divine Master has taken our defence upon Himself. Remember the scene in the house of Lazarus: Martha was serving, while Mary had no thought of food but only of how she could please her Beloved. And "she broke her alabaster box, and poured out upon her Saviour's Head the precious spikenard, [50] and the house was filled with the odour of the ointment."[51]

The Apostles murmured against Magdalen. This still happens, for so do men murmur against us. Even some fervent Catholics think our ways are exaggerated, and that—with Martha—we ought to wait upon Jesus, instead of pouring out on Him the odorous ointment of our lives. Yet what does it matter if these ointment-jars—our lives—be broken, since Our Lord is consoled, and the world in spite of itself is forced to inhale the perfumes they give forth? It has much need of these perfumes to purify the unwholesome air it breathes.

For a while only, good-bye, dearest sister. Your barque is near to port. The breezes filling its sails are the zephyrs of Love—breezes that speed more swiftly than the lightning-flash. Good-bye! in a few days we shall be together within these Carmel walls . . . and in the after days together in Paradise. Did not Jesus say during His Passion: "Hereafter you shall see the Son of Man sitting on the right hand of the power of God and coming in the clouds of heaven"?[52] . . . We shall be there!

THÉRÈSE. _____

[1] Matt. 3:10.

[2] Matt. 5:48.

[3] Apoc. 21:4.

[4] St. John of the Cross.

[5] Mme. Swetchine.

[6] Exodus 4:25.

[7] I Cor. 7:31.

[8] Cf. Ps. 136:2.

[9] Cf. Ps. 136:1, 4.

[10] I Cor. 2:9.

[11] It is remarkable that Soeur Thérèse applied this name to her sister Céline, who, under her inspiration, was later to reproduce so faithfully the true likeness of Our Lord, from the Holy Winding Sheet of Turin. [Ed.] [Remainder of long footnote, discussing this likeness, its reproduction, and related matters, omitted from this electronic edition.]

[12] Isa. 63:3.

[13] Cf. Isa. 63:5.

[14] Isa. 53:3.

[15] Cant. 5:2.

[16] Is. 53:4.

[17] Soeur Thérèse received the veil on September 24, 1890.

[18] St. John of the Cross: *The Night of the Soul,* 8th stanza.

[19] John 4:35.

[20] Matt. 9:37, 38.

[21] St. John of the Cross.

[22] Luke 19:5.

[23] John 1:38.

[24] Luke 9:58.

[25] Cant. 2:1.

[26] Malachias 4:2.

[27] Matt. 26:23.

[28] Matt. 25:34-36.

[29] *Imit.,* Bk. I, ch. ii. 3.

[30] *Ib.,* Bk. II, ch. xi. 4.

[31] *Ib.,* Bk. III, ch. xlix. 7.

[32] Ps. 126[127]:1.

[33] St. John of the Cross.

[34] Cf. Luke 15:31.

[35] Cant. 1:6.

[36] Cf. Cant. 7:1.

[37] Office of St. Cecilia.

[38] Luke 2:14.

[39] Wisdom 4:1.

[40] John 21:5.

[41] Luke 5:5. Soeur Thérèse joins in one the two miraculous draughts of fishes. [Ed.]

[42] Cf. Cant. 6:10, 11.

[43] Cant. 6:12.

[44] John 14:23.

[45] Cf. John 17:17.

[46] John 14:6.

[47] John 18:38.

[48] Cf. Cant. 1:12.

[49] Luke 22:28, 29.

[50] Cf. Mark 14:3.

[51] John 12:3.

[52] Matt. 26:64.

LETTERS TO MOTHER AGNES OF JESUS

Selections

I

(Written in 1887, shortly before Thérèse entered the Carmel.)

MY DARLING LITTLE MOTHER,—You are right when you tell me that every cup must contain its drop of gall. I find that trials are a great help towards detachment from the things of earth: they make one look higher than this world. Nothing here can satisfy, and we can find rest only in holding ourselves ready to do God's will.

My frail barque has great difficulty in reaching port. I sighted it long since, and still I find myself afar off. Yet Jesus steers this little barque, and I am sure that on His appointed day it will come safely to the blessed haven of the Carmel. O Pauline! when Jesus shall have vouchsafed me this grace, I wish to give myself entirely to Him, to suffer always for Him, to live for Him alone. I do not fear His rod, for even when the smart is keenest we feel that it is His sweet Hand which strikes.

It is such joy to think that for each pain cheerfully borne we shall love God more through eternity. Happy should I be if at the hour of my death I could offer Jesus a single soul. There would be one soul less in hell, and one more to bless God in Heaven.

II

(Written during her retreat before receiving the habit.)

January, 1889.

Dryness and drowsiness—such is the state of my soul in its intercourse with Jesus! But since my Beloved wishes to sleep I shall not prevent Him. I am only too happy that He does not treat me as a stranger, but rather in a homely way. He riddles his "little ball" with pin-pricks that hurt indeed, though when they come from the Hand of this loving Friend, the pain is all sweetness, so gentle in His touch. How different the hand of man!

Yet I am happy, most happy to suffer! If Jesus Himself does not pierce me, He guides the hand which does. Mother! If you knew how utterly indifferent to earthly things I desire to be, and of how little concern to me are all the beauties of creation. I should be wretched were I to possess them. My heart seems so vast when I think of the goods of earth—all of them together unable to fill it. But by the side of Jesus how small does it appear! He is full good to me—this God who soon will be my Spouse. He is divinely lovable for not permitting me to be the captive of any passing joy. He knows well that if He sent me but a shadow of earthly happiness I should cling to it with all the intense ardour of my heart, and He refuses even this shadow . . . He prefers to leave me in darkness, rather than afford me a false glimmer which would not be Himself.

I do not wish creatures to have one atom of my love. I wish to give all to Jesus, since He makes me understand that He alone is perfect happiness. All! —all shall be for Him! And even when I have nothing, as is the case to-night, I will give Him this nothing . . .

III

1889.

. . . .

I have a longing for those heart-wounds, those pin-pricks which inflict so much pain. I know of no ecstasy to which I do not prefer sacrifice. There I find happiness, and there alone. The slender reed has no fear of being broken, for it is planted beside the waters of Love. When, therefore, it bends before the gale, it gathers strength in the refreshing stream, and longs for yet another storm to pass and sway its head. My very weakness makes me strong. No harm can come to me since, in whatever happens, I see only the tender Hand of Jesus . . . Besides, no suffering is too big a price to pay for the glorious palm.

IV

(Written during her retreat before profession.)

September, 1890.

MY DEAREST MOTHER,—Your little hermit must give you an account of her journey. Before starting, my Beloved asked me in what land I wished to travel, and what road I wished to take. I told him that I had only one desire, that of reaching the summit of the *Mountain of Love.*

Thereupon roads innumerable spread before my gaze, but so many of these were perfect that I felt incapable of choosing any of my own free will. Then I said to my Divine Guide: "Thou knowest where lies the goal of my desire, and for Whose sake I would climb the Mountain. Thou knowest Who possesses the love of my heart. For Him only I set out on this journey; lead me therefore by the paths of His choosing: my joy shall be full if only He is pleased."

And Our Lord took me by the hand, and led me through an underground passage where it is neither hot nor cold, where the sun shines not, and where neither wind nor rain can enter—a place where I see nothing but a half-veiled light, the light that gleams from the downcast Eyes of the Face of Jesus.

My Spouse speaks not a word, and I say nothing save that I love Him more than myself; and in the depths of my heart I know this is true, for I am more His than mine. I cannot see that we are advancing toward our journey's goal since we travel by a subterranean way; and yet, without knowing how, it seems to me that we are nearing the summit of the Mountain.

I give thanks to my Jesus for making me walk in darkness, and in this darkness I enjoy profound peace. Willingly do I consent to remain through all my religious life in this gloomy passage into which He has led me. I desire only that my darkness may obtain light for sinners. I am content, nay, full of joy, to be without all consolation. I should be ashamed if my love were like that of those earthly brides who are ever looking for gifts from their bridegrooms, or seeking to catch the loving smile which fills them with delight.

Thérèse, the little Spouse of Jesus, loves Him for Himself; she only looks on the Face of her Beloved to catch a glimpse of the Tears which delight her with their secret charm. She longs to wipe away those Tears, or to gather them up like priceless diamonds with which to adorn her bridal dress. *Jesus! . . . Oh! I would so love Him! Love Him as He has never yet been loved! . . .*

At all cost I must win the palm of St. Agnes; if it cannot be mine through blood, I must win it by Love.

V

1891.

Love can take the place of a long life. Jesus does not consider time, for He is Eternal. He only looks at the love. My little Mother, beg Him to bestow it upon me in full measure. I do not desire that thrill of love which I can feel; if Jesus feel its thrill, then that is enough for me. It is so sweet to love Him, to make Him loved. Ask Him to take me to Him on my profession-day, if by living on I should ever offend Him, because I wish to bear unsullied to Heaven the white robe of my second Baptism.[1]

Now Jesus can grant me the grace never to offend Him more, or rather never to commit any faults but those which do not offend Him or give Him pain; faults which serve but to humble me and strengthen my love. There is no one to lean on apart from Jesus. He alone faileth not, and it is exceeding joy to think that He can never change.

VI

1891.

MY DEAREST LITTLE MOTHER,—Your letter has done me such good. The sentence: "Let us refrain from saying a word which could raise us in the eyes of others," has indeed enlightened my soul. Yes, we must keep all for Jesus with jealous care. It is so good to work for Him alone. How it fills the heart with joy, and lends wings to the soul! Ask of Jesus that Thérèse—His *grain of sand*—may save Him a multitude of souls in a short space of time, so that she may the sooner behold His Adorable Face.

VII

1892.

Here is the dream of this "grain of sand": Love Jesus alone, and naught else beside! The grain of sand is so small that if it wished to open its heart to any other but Jesus, there would no longer be room for this Beloved.

What happiness to be so entirely hidden that no one gives us a thought—to be unknown even to those with whom we live! My little Mother, I long to be unknown to everyone of God's creatures! I have never desired glory amongst men, and if their contempt used to attract my heart, I have realized that even this is too glorious for me, and I thirst to be forgotten.

The Glory of Jesus—this is my sole ambition. I abandon my glory to Him; and if He seem to forget me, well, He is free to do so since I am no longer my own, but His. He will weary sooner of making me wait than I shall of waiting.

VIII

[One day when Soeur Thérèse was suffering acutely from feverishness, one of the Sisters urged her to help in a difficult piece of painting. For a moment Thérèse's countenance betrayed an inward struggle, which did not escape the notice of Mother Agnes of Jesus. That same evening Thérèse wrote her the following letter.]

May 28, 1897.

MY DEAREST MOTHER,—I have just been shedding sweet tears—tears of repentance, but still more of thankfulness and love. To-day I showed you the treasure of my patience, and how virtuous I am—I who preach so well to others! I am glad that you have seen my want of perfection. You did not scold me, and yet I deserved it. But at all times your gentleness speaks to me more forcibly than would severe words. To me you are the image of God's Mercy.

Sister N., on the contrary, is more often the image of God's severity. Well, I have just met her, and, instead of passing me coldly by, she embraced me and said: "Poor little Sister, I am so sorry . . . I do not want to tire you; it was wrong of me to ask your help; leave the work alone." In my heart I felt perfect sorrow, and I was much surprised to escape all blame. I know she must really deem me imperfect. She spoke in this way because she thinks I am soon to die. However that may be, I have heard nothing but kind and tender words from her;

and so I consider her most kind, and myself an unamiable creatures.

When I returned to our cell, I was wondering what Jesus thought, when all at once I remembered His words to the woman taken in adultery: "Hath no man condemned thee?"[2] With tears in my eyes, I answered Him: "No one, Lord, . . . neither my little Mother—the image of Thy Mercy—nor Sister N., the image of Thy Justice. I feel that I can go in peace, because neither wilt Thou condemn me."

I confess I am much happier because of my weakness than if—sustained by grace—I had been a model of patience. It does me so much good to see that Jesus is always sweet and tender towards me. Truly it is enough to make me die of grateful love.

My little Mother, you will understand how this evening the vessel of God's Mercy has overflowed for your child. . . . *Even now I know it! Yea, all my hopes will be fulfilled . . .*

VERILY THE LORD WILL WORK WONDERS FOR ME, AND THEY WILL INFINITELY SURPASS MY BOUNDLESS DESIRES.

[1] Soeur Thérèse here alludes to the probable opinion of theologians that—as in Baptism—all stain of sin is removed and all temporal punishment for sin remitted, by the vows taken on the day of religious profession. [Ed.]

[2] John 8:10.

LETTERS TO SISTER MARY OF THE SACRED HEART

I

February 21, 1888.

MY DEAR MARIE,—You cannot think what a lovely present Papa made me last week; I believe if I gave you a hundred or even a thousand guesses you would never find out what it was. Well, my dear Father bought me a new-born lamb, all white and fleecy. He said that before I entered the Carmel he wanted me to have this pleasure. We were all delighted, especially Céline. What touched me more than anything was Papa's thoughtfulness. Besides, a lamb is symbolic, and it made me think of Pauline.

So far, so good, but now for the sequel. We were already building castles in the air, and expected that in two or three days the lamb would be frisking round us. But the pretty creature died that same afternoon. Poor little thing, scarcely was it born when it suffered and died. It looked so gentle and innocent that Céline made a sketch of it, and then we laid it in a grave dug by Papa. It appeared to be asleep. I did not want the earth to be its covering, so we put snow upon our pet, and all was over.

You do not know, dearest Godmother, how this little creature's death has made me reflect. Clearly we must not become attached to anything, no matter how innocent, because it will slip from our grasp when least expected; nothing but the eternal can content us.

II

(Written during her retreat before receiving the habit.)

January 8, 1889.

Your little *Lamb*—as you love to call me, dearest sister—would borrow from you some strength and courage. I cannot speak to Our Lord, and He is silent too. Pray that my retreat may be pleasing to the Heart of Him Who alone reads the secrets of the soul.

Life is full of sacrifice, it is true, but why seek happiness here? For life is but "a night to be spent in a wretched inn," as our holy Mother St. Teresa says. I assure you my heart thirsts ardently for happiness, but I see clearly that no creature can quench that thirst. On the contrary, the oftener I would drink from these seductive waters the more burning will my thirst become. I know a source where "they that drink shall yet thirst,"[1] but with a delicious thirst, a thirst one can always allay. . . . That source is the suffering known to Jesus only.

III

August 14, 1889.

You ask for a word from your little Lamb. But what shall I say? Is it not you who have taught me? Remember those days when I sat upon your knee, and you talked to me of Heaven.

I can still hear you say: "Look at those who want to become rich, and see how they toil to obtain money. Now, my little Thérèse, through every moment of the day and with far less trouble, we can lay up riches in Heaven. Diamonds are so plentiful, we can gather them together as with a rake, and we do this by performing all our actions for the love of God." Then I would leave you, my heart overflowing with joy, and fully bent on amassing great wealth.

Time has flown since those happy hours spent together in our dear nest. Jesus has visited us, and has found us worthy to be tried in the crucible of suffering. God has said that on the last day "He will wipe away all tears from our eyes,"[2] and no doubt the more tears there are to dry, the greater will be the happiness.

Pray to-morrow for the little one who owes you her upbringing, and who, without you, might never have come to the Carmel.

IV

(During her retreat before profession)

September 4, 1890.

The heavenly music falls but faintly on the ear of your child, and it has been a dreary journey towards her Bridal Day. It is true her Betrothed has led her through fertile lands and gorgeous scenery, but the dark night has prevented her admiring, much less revelling in, the beauty all around. Perhaps you think this grieved her. Oh, no! she is happy to follow her Betrothed for His own sake, and not for the sake of His gifts. He is so ravishingly beautiful, even when silent—even when concealed. Weary of earthly consolation, your little child wishes for her Beloved alone. I believe that the work of Jesus during this retreat has been to detach me from everything but Himself. My only comfort is the exceeding strength and peace that is mine. Besides, I hope to be just what He wills I should be, and in this lies all my happiness.

Did you but know how great is my joy at giving pleasure to Jesus through being utterly deprived of all joy! . . . . Truly this is the very refinement of all joy—joy we do not feel.

V

September 7, 1890.

To-morrow I shall be the Spouse of Jesus, of Him Whose "look was as it were hidden and despised."

[3] What a future this alliance opens up! How can I thank Him, how render myself less unworthy of so great a favour?

I thirst after Heaven, that blessed abode where our love for Jesus will be without bounds. True, we must pass through suffering and tears to reach that home, but I wish to suffer all that my Beloved is pleased to send me; I wish to let Him do as He wills with His "little ball." You tell me, dearest Godmother, that my Holy Child is beautifully adorned for my wedding-day;[4] perhaps, however, you wonder why I have not put new rose-coloured candles. The old ones appeal to me more because they were lighted for the first time on my clothing-day. They were then fresh and of rosy hue. Papa had given them to me; he was there, and all was joyful. But now their tint has faded. Are there yet any rose-coloured joys on earth for your little Thérèse? No, for her there are only heavenly joys; joys where the hollowness of all things gives place to the Uncreated Reality.

VI

MY DEAREST SISTER,—I do not find it difficult to answer you. . . . How can you ask me if it be possible for you to love God as I love Him! My desire for martyrdom is as nothing; it is not to that I owe the boundless confidence that fills my heart. Such desires might be described as spiritual riches, which are *the unjust mammon*,[5] when one is complacent in them as in something great. . . . These aspirations are a consolation Jesus sometimes grants to weak souls like mine — and there are many such! But when He withholds this consolation, it is a special grace. Remember these words of a holy monk: "The martyrs suffered with joy, and the King of Martyrs in sorrow." Did not Jesus cry out: "My father, remove this chalice from Me"?[6] Do not think, then, that my desires are a proof of my love. Indeed I know well that it is certainly not these desires which make God take pleasure in my soul. What does please Him is to find me love my littleness, my poverty: it is the blind trust which I have in His Mercy. . . . There is my sole treasure, dearest Godmother, and why should it not be yours?

Are you not ready to suffer all that God wills? Assuredly; and so if you wish to know joy and to love suffering, you are really seeking your own consolation, because once we love, all suffering disappears. Verily, if we were to go together to martyrdom, you would gain great merit, and I should have none, unless it pleased Our Lord to change my dispositions.

Dear sister, do you not understand that to love Jesus and to be His Victim of Love, the more weak and wretched we are the better material do we make for this consuming and transfiguring Love? . . . The simple desire to be a Victim suffices, but we must also consent to ever remain poor and helpless, and here lies the difficulty: "Where shall we find one that is truly poor in spirit? We must seek him afar off," says the author of the *Imitation*.[7] He does not say that we must search among great souls, but "afar off"—that is to say, in abasement and in nothingness. Let us remain far from all that dazzles, loving our littleness, and content to have no joy. Then we shall be truly poor in spirit, and Jesus will come to seek us however far off we may be, and transform us into flames of Love. . . . I long to make you understand what I feel. Confidence alone must lead us to Love. . . . Does not fear lead to the thought of the strict justice that is threatened to sinners? But that is not the justice Jesus will show to such as love Him.

God would not vouchsafe you the desire to be the Victim of His Merciful Love, were this not a favour in store—or rather already granted, since you are wholly surrendered unto Him and long to be consumed by Him, and God never inspires a longing which He cannot fulfill.

The road lies clear, and along it we must run together. I feel that Jesus wishes to bestow on us the same graces; He wishes to grant us both a free entrance into His Heavenly Kingdom. Dearest Godmother, you would like to hear still more of the secrets which Jesus confides to your child, but human speech cannot tell what the human heart itself can scarcely conceive. Besides, Jesus confides His secrets to you likewise. This I know, for you it was who taught me to listen to His Divine teaching. On the day of my Baptism you promised in my name that I would serve Him alone. You were the Angel who led me and guided me in my days of exile and offered me to Our Lord. As a child loves its mother, I love you; in Heaven only will you realise the gratitude with which my heart is full to overflowing.

Your little daughter,

Teresa of the Child Jesus.

---

[1] Eccles. 24:29.

[2] Apoc. 21:4.

[3] Isa. 53:3.

[4] She alludes to the Statue of the Holy Child in the cloister, which was under her own special care. [Ed.]

[5] Luke 16:2.

[6] Luke 22:42.

[7] Cf. *Imit.*, II, xi. 4.

LETTERS TO SISTER FRANCES TERESA[1]

I

August 13, 1893.

DEAR LITTLE SISTER, — At last your desires are satisfied. Like the dove sent forth from the ark, you have been unable to find a spot on earth whereon to rest, and have long been on the wing seeking to re-enter the blessed abode where your heart had for ever fixed its home. Jesus has kept you waiting, but at last, touched by the plaintive cry of His dove, He has put forth His Divine Hand, and, taking hold of it, has set it in His Heart—that sanctuary of His Love.

It is quite a spiritual joy, this joy of mine. For I shall never look upon you again, never hear your voice as I outpour my heart into yours. Yet I know that earth is but a halting-place to us who journey towards a Heavenly Home. What matter if the routes we follow lie apart? Our goal is the same—that Heaven where we shall meet, no more to be separated. There we shall taste for ever the sweets of our earthly home. We shall have much to tell one another when this exile is ended. Speech here below is so inadequate, but a single glance will be enough for perfect understanding in our home beyond; and I believe that our happiness will be greater than if we had never been parted here.

Meanwhile we must live by sacrifice. Without it there would be no merit in the religious life. As someone told us in a conference: "The reason why the forest oak raises its head so high is because, hemmed in on all sides, it wastes no sap in putting forth branches underneath, but towers aloft. Thus in the religious life the soul, hedged in all around by the rule and by the practice of community life, of necessity finds there a means of lifting a high head towards Heaven."

Dearest sister, pray for your little Thérèse that she may draw profit from her exile on earth and from the plentiful means granted her of meriting Heaven.

II

January, 1895.

DEAR LITTLE SISTER,—How fruitful for Heaven has been the year that is gone! . . . Our dear Father has seen that which the eye of man cannot see, he has heard the minstrelsy of the angels . . . now his heart understands, and his soul enjoys "the things which God hath prepared for those who love Him." [2] . . . Our turn will come, and it is full sweet to think our sails are set towards the Eternal Shore.

Do you not find, as I do, that our beloved Father's death has drawn us nearer to Heaven? More than half of our loved ones already enjoy the Vision of God, and the five who remain in exile will follow soon. This thought of the shortness of life gives me courage, and helps me to put up with the weariness of the journey. What matters a little toil upon earth? We pass . . . "We have not here a lasting city."[3]

Think of your Thérèse during this month consecrated to the Infant Jesus, and beg of Him that she may always remain a very little child. I will offer the same prayer for you, because I know your desires, and that humility is your favourite virtue.

Which Thérèse will be the more fervent? . . . She who will be the more humble, the more closely united to Jesus, and the more faithful in making love the mainspring of every action. We must not let slip one single occasion of sacrifice, everything has such value in the religious life . . . Pick up a pin from a motive of love, and you may thereby convert a soul. Jesus alone can make our deeds of such worth, so let us love Him with every fibre of our heart.

III

July 12, 1896.

MY DEAR LITTLE LÉONIE,—I should have answered your letter last Sunday if it had been given to me, but you know that, being the youngest, I run the risk of not seeing letters for some considerable time after my sisters, and occasionally not at all. I only read yours on Friday, so forgive my delay.

You are right—Jesus is content with a tender look or a sigh of love. For my part, I find it quite easy to practise perfection, now that I realise it only means making Jesus captive through His Heart. Look at a little child who has just vexed its mother, either by giving way to temper or by disobedience. If it hides in a corner and is sulky, or if it cries for fear of being punished, its mother will certainly not forgive the fault. But should it run to her with its little arms outstreteched, and say; "Kiss me, Mother; I will not do it again!" what mother would not straightway clasp her child lovingly to her heart, and forget all it had done? . . . She knows quite well that her little one will repeat the fault—no matter, her darling will escape all punishment so long as it makes appeal to her heart.

Even when the law of fear was in force, before Our Lord's coming, the prophet Isaias said—speaking in the name of the King of Heaven: "Can a woman forget her babe? . . . And if she should forget, yet will I not forget thee."[4] What a touching promise! We who live under the law of Love, shall we not profit by the loving advances made by our

Spouse? How can anybody fear Him Who allows Himself to be made captive "with one hair of our neck"?[5]

Let us learn to keep Him prisoner—this God, the Divine Beggar of love. By telling us that a single hair can work this wonder, He shows us that the smallest actions done for His Love are those which charm His Heart. If it were necessary to do great things, we should be deserving of pity, but we are happy beyond measure, because Jesus lets Himself be led captive by the smallest action. . . . With you, dear Léonie, little sacrifices are never lacking. Is not your life made up of them? I rejoice to see you in presence of such wealth, especially when I remember that you know how to make profit thereby, not only for yourself but likewise for poor sinners. It is so sweet to help Jesus to save the souls which He has ransomed at the price of His Precious Blood, and which only await our help to keep them from the abyss.

It seems to me that if our sacrifices take Jesus captive, our joys make Him prisoner too. All that is needful to attain this end is, that instead of giving ourselves over to selfish happiness, we offer to our Spouse the little joys He scatters in our path, to charm our hearts and draw them towards Him.

You ask for news of my health. Well, my cough has quite disappeared. Does that please you? It will not prevent Our Lord from taking me to Himself whensoever He wishes. And I need not prepare for that journey, since my whole endeavour is to remain as a little child. Jesus Himself must pay all its expenses, as well as the price of my admission to Heaven.

Good-bye, dearest one, pray to Him without fail for the last and least of your sisters.

IV

July 17, 1897.

MY DEAR LÉONIE,—I am so pleased to be able to write to you again. Some days ago I thought I should never again have this consolation, but it seems God wishes to prolong somewhat the time of my exile. This does not trouble me—I would not enter Heaven one moment sooner through my own will. The only real happiness on earth is to strive always to think "how goodly is the chalice"[6] that Jesus give us. Yours is indeed a goodly one, dear Léonie. If you wish to be a Saint—and it will not be hard—keep only one end in view: give pleasure to Jesus, and bind yourself more closely to Him.

Good-bye, my dear sister, I should wish the thought of my entering Heaven to fill you with joy, because I shall then be better able to give you proof of my tender love. In the Heart of our Heavenly Spouse we shall live His very life, and through eternity I shall remain,

Your very little sister,

TERESA OF THE CHILD JESUS.

---

[1] Nearly all the letters written by Soeur Thérèse to her sister Léonie are lost. These few have been recovered. It will be remembered that Léonie entered the Convent of the Visitation at Caen. See note, page 113.

[2] Cf. I Cor. 2:9.

[3] Heb. 13:14.

[4] Isa. 49:15.

[5] Cant. 4:9.

[6] Ps. 22[23]:5.

LETTERS TO HER COUSIN MARIE GUÉRIN

I

1888.

Before you confided in me,[1] I felt you were suffering, and my heart was one with yours. Since you have the humility to ask advice of your little Thérèse, this is what she thinks: you have grieved me greatly by abstaining from Holy Communion, because you have grieved Our Lord. The devil must be very cunning to deceive a soul in this way. Do you not know, dear Marie, that by acting thus you help him to accomplish his end? The treacherous creature knows quite well that when a soul is striving to belong wholly to God he cannot cause her to sin, so he merely tries to persuade her that she has sinned. This is a considerable gain, but not enough to satisfy his hatred, so he aims at something more, and tries to shut out Jesus from a tabernacle which Jesus covets. Unable to enter this sanctuary himself, he wishes that at least it remain empty and without its God. Alas, what will become of that poor little heart? When the devil has succeeded in keeping a soul from Holy Communion he has gained all his ends . . . while Jesus weeps! . . .

Remember, little Marie, that this sweet Jesus is there in the Tabernacle expressly for you and you alone. Remember that He burns with the desire to enter your heart. Do not listen to satan. Laugh him to scorn, and go without fear to receive Jesus, the God of peace and of love.

"Thérèse thinks all this" — you say — "because she does not know my difficulties." She does know, and knows them well; she understands everything, and she tells you confidently that you can go without fear to receive your only true Friend. She, too, has passed through the martyrdom of scruples, but Jesus gave her the grace to receive the Blessed Sacrament always, even when she imagined she had committed great sins. I assure you I have found that this is the only means of ridding oneself of the devil. When he sees that he is losing his time he leaves us in peace.

In truth it is impossible that a heart which can only find rest in contemplation of the Tabernacle — and yours is such, you tell me — could so far offend Our Lord as not to be able to receive Him . . . What does offend Jesus, what wounds Him to the Heart, is want of confidence.

Pray much that the best portion of your life may not be overshadowed by idle fears. We have only life's brief moments to spend for the Glory of God, and well does satan know it. This is why he employs every ruse to make us consume them in useless labour. Dear sister, go often to Holy Communion, go very often — that is your one remedy.

II

1894

You are like some little village maiden who, when sought in marriage by a mighty king would not dare to accept him, on the plea that she is not rich enough, and is strange to the ways of a court. But does not her royal lover know better than she does, the extent of her poverty and ignorance?

Marie, though you are nothing, do not forget that Jesus is All. You have only to lose your own nothingness in that Infinite All, and thenceforth to think only of that All who alone is worthy of your love.

You tell me you wish to see the fruit of your efforts. That is exactly what Jesus would hide from you. He likes to contemplate by Himself these little fruits of our virtue. They console Him.

You are quite wrong, Marie, if you think that Thérèse walks eagerly along the way of Sacrifice: her weakness is still very great, and every day some new and wholesome experience brings this home more clearly. Yet Jesus delights to teach her how to *glory in her infirmities.*[2] It is a great grace, and I pray Him to give it to you, for with it come peace and tranquillity of heart. When we see our misery we do not like to look at ourselves but only upon our Beloved.

You ask me for a method of obtaining perfection. I know of Love—and Love only! Our hearts are made for this alone. Sometimes I endeavour to find some other word for love; but in a land of exile "words which have a beginning and an end"[3] are quite unable to render adequately the emotions of the soul, and so we must keep to the one simple word—LOVE.

But on whom shall our poor hearts lavish this love, and who will be worthy of this treasure? Is there anyone who will understand it and—above all

—is there anyone who will be able to repay? Marie, Jesus alone understands love: He alone can give back all—yea, infinitely more than the utmost we can give. _____

[1] The allusion is to the scruples from which Marie suffered. Having read this letter—which is a strong plea for Frequent Communion—Pope Pius X declared it "most opportune." Thérèse was but fifteen when she wrote it. [Ed.]

[2] 2 Cor. 11:5.

[3] St. Augustine.

LETTER TO HER COUSIN, JEANNE GUÉRIN (MADAME LA NÉELE)

August, 1895.

It is a very great sacrifice that God has asked of you, my dear Jeanne, in calling your little Marie to the Carmel; but remember that He has promised a hundredfold to anyone who for His Love hath left father or mother or *sister*.[1] Now, for love of Jesus, you have not hesitated to part with a sister dearer to you than words can say, and therefore He is bound to keep His promise. I know that these words are generally applied to those who enter the religious life, but my heart tells me they were spoken, too, for those whose generosity is such that they will sacrifice to God even the loved ones they hold dearer than life itself.

[1] Mark 10:30.

LETTERS TO HER BROTHER MISSIONARIES

I

1895.

Our Divine Lord asks no sacrifice beyond our strength. At times, it is true, He makes us taste to the full the bitterness of the chalice He puts to our lips. And when He demands the sacrifice of all that is dearest on earth, it is impossible without a very special grace not to cry out as He did during His Agony in the Garden: "My Father, let this chalice pass from me!" But we must hasten to add: "Yet not as I will, but as Thou wilt."[1] It is so consoling to think that Jesus, "the Strong God,"[2] has felt all our weaknesses and shuddered at the sight of the bitter chalice—that very chalice He had so ardently desired.

Your lot is indeed a beautiful one, since Our Lord has chosen it for you, and has first touched with His own Lips the cup which He holds out to yours. A Saint has said: "The greatest honour God can bestow upon a soul is not to give to it great things, but to ask of it great things." Jesus treats you as a privileged child. It is His wish you should begin your mission even now,[3] and save souls through the Cross. Was it not by suffering and death that He ransomed the world? I know that you aspire to the happiness of laying down your life for Him; but the martyrdom of the heart is not less fruitful than the shedding of blood, and this martyrdom is already yours. Have I not, then, good reason to say that your lot is a beautiful one—worthy an apostle of Christ?

II

1896.

Let us work together for the salvation of souls! We have but the one day of this life to save them, and so give to Our Lord a proof of our love. Tomorrow will be Eternity, then Jesus will reward you a hundredfold for the sweet joys you have given up for Him. He knows the extent of your sacrifice. He knows that the sufferings of those you hold dear increase your own; but He has suffered this same martyrdom for our salvation. He, too, left His Mother; He beheld that sinless Virgin standing at the foot of the Cross, her heart pierced through with a sword of sorrow, and I hope he will console your own dear mother. . . . I beg Him most earnestly to do so.

Ah! If the Divine Master would permit those you are about to leave for His Love but one glimpse of the glory in store, and the vast retinue of souls that will escort you to Heaven, already they would be repaid for the great sacrifice that is at hand.

III

February 24, 1896.

Please say this little prayer for me each day; it sums up all my desires:

"Merciful Father, in the name of Thy sweet Jesus, of the Blessed Virgin, and all the Saints, I beg Thee to consume my sister with Thy spirit of love, and to grant her the grace to make Thee greatly loved."

If Our Lord takes me soon to Himself, I ask you still to continue this prayer, because my longing will be the same in Heaven as upon earth: *to love Jesus and to make Him loved.*

IV

. . . .

All I desire is God's Holy Will, and if in Heaven I could no longer work for His glory, I should prefer exile to Home.

V

June 21, 1897

You may well sing of the Mercies of God! They shine forth in you with splendour. You love St.

Augustine and St. Mary Magdalen, those souls to whom many sins were forgiven because they loved much. I love them too; I love their sorrow, and especially their audacious love. When I see Mary Magdalen come forth before all Simon's guests to wash with her tears her Master's Feet—those Feet that for the first time she touches—I feel her heart has fathomed that abyss of love and mercy, the Heart of Jesus; and I feel, too, that not only was He willing to forgive, but even liberally to dispense the favours of a Divine and intimate friendship, and to raise her to the loftiest heights of prayer.

My Brother, since I also have been given to understand the Love of the Heart of Jesus, I confess that all fear has been driven from mine. The remembrance of my faults humbles me; and it helps me never to rely upon my own strength—which is but weakness—but more than all, it speaks to me of mercy and of love. When a soul with childlike trust casts her faults into Love's all-devouring furnace, how shall they escape being utterly consumed?

I know that many Saints have passed their lives in the practice of amazing penance for the sake of expiating their sins. But what of that? "In my Father's house there are many mansions."[4] These are the words of Jesus, and therefore I follow the path He marks out for me; I try to be nowise concerned about myself and what Jesus deigns to accomplish in my soul.

VI

1897.

On this earth where everything changes, one thing alone does never change—our Heavenly King's treatment of His friends. From the day He raised the standard of the Cross, in its shadow all must fight and win. "The life of every missionary abounds in crosses," said Théophane Vénard. And again: "True happiness consists in suffering, and in order to live we must die."

Rejoice, my Brother, that the first efforts of your Apostolate are stamped with the seal of the Cross. Far more by suffering and by persecution than by eloquent discourses does Jesus wish to build up His Kingdom.

You are still—you tell me—a little child who cannot speak. Neither could Father Mazel, who was ordained with you, and yet he has already won the palm . . . Far beyond our thoughts are the thoughts of God! When I learnt that this young missionary had died before he had set foot on the field of his labours, I felt myself drawn to invoke him. I seemed to see him amidst the glorious Martyr choir. No doubt, in the eyes of men he does not merit the title of Martyr, but in the eyes of God this inglorious death is no less precious than the sacrifice of him who lays down his life for the Faith.

Though one must be exceeding pure before appearing in the sight of the All-Holy God, still I know that He is infinitely just, and this very Justice which terrifies so many souls is the source of all my confidence and joy. Justice is not only stern severity towards the guilty; it takes account of the good intention, and gives to virtue its reward. Indeed I hope as much from the Justice of God as from His Mercy. It is because He is just, that "He is compassionate and merciful, longsuffering, and plenteous in mercy. For He knoweth our frame, He remembereth that we are dust. As a father hath compassion on his children, so hath the Lord compassion on us."[5]

O my Brother, after these beautiful and consoling words of the
Royal Prophet, how can we doubt God's power to open the gates of
His Kingdom to His children who have loved Him

unto perfect sacrifice, who have not only left home and country so as to make Him known and loved, but even long to lay down their lives for Him? . . . Jesus said truly there is no greater love than this. Nor will He be outdone in generosity. How could He cleanse in the flames of Purgatory souls consumed with the fire of Divine Love?

I have used many words to express my thought, and yet I fear I have failed. What I wish to convey is, that in my opinion all missionaries are Martyrs by will and desire, and not even one should pass through the purifying flames.

This, then, is what I think about the Justice of God; my own way is all confidence and love, and I cannot understand those souls who are afraid of so affectionate a Friend. Sometimes, when I read books in which perfection is put before us with the goal obstructed by a thousand obstacles, my poor little head is quickly fatigued. I close the learned treatise, which tires my brain and dries up my heart, and I turn to the Sacred Scriptures. Then all becomes clear and lightsome—a single word opens out infinite vistas, perfection appears easy, and I see that it is enough to acknowledge our nothingness, and like children surrender ourselves into the Arms of the Good God. Leaving to great and lofty minds the beautiful books which I cannot understand, still less put in practice, I rejoice in my littleness because "only little children and those who are like them shall be admitted to the Heavenly banquet."[6] Fortunately—"there are many mansions in my Father's House":[7] if there were only those—to me —incomprehensible mansions with their baffling roads, I should certainly never enter there . . .

VII

July 13, 1897.

Your soul is too great to cling to the consolations of earth, and even now its abode should be in Heaven, for it is written: "Where your treasure is, there will your heart be also."[8] Is not Jesus your only treasure? Now that He is in Heaven, it is there your heart should dwell. This sweet Saviour has long since forgotten your infidelities. He sees only your longing after perfection, and the sight makes glad His Heart.

Stay no longer at His Feet, I beseech you, but follow this first impulse to throw yourself into His Arms. Your place is there, and I see clearly — more clearly than in your former letters — that all other heavenly route is barred to you save the way your little sister treads.

I hold with you when you say that the Heart of Jesus is more grieved by the thousand little imperfections of His friends than by the faults, even grave, which His enemies commit. Yet it seems to me, dear Brother, it is only when those who are His own are habitually guilty of want of thought, and neglect to seek His pardon, that He can say: "These Wounds which you see in the midst of My Hands, I have received in the house of those who love Me." [9] But His Heart thrills with you when He had to deal with all those who truly love, and who after each little fault come to fling themselves into His Arms imploring forgiveness. He says to His Angels what the prodigal's father said to his servants: "Put a ring upon his finger, and let us rejoice."[10] O Brother! Verily the Divine Heart's Goodness and Merciful Love are little known! It is true that to enjoy these treasures we must humble ourselves, must confess our nothingness . . . and here is where many a soul draws back.

VIII

1897.

What attracts me towards our Heavenly Home is the Master's call—the hope of loving Him at last to the fulfilling of all my desire—the thought that I shall be able to win Him the love of a multitude of souls, who will bless Him through all eternity.

I have never asked God that I might die young—that to me were a cowardly prayer; but from my childhood He has deigned to inspire me with a strong conviction that my life would be a short one.

I feel we must tread the same road to Heaven—the road of suffering and love. When I myself have reached the port, I will teach you how best to sail the world's tempestuous sea—with the self-abandonment of a child well aware of a father's love, and of his vigilance in the hour of danger.

I long so much to make you understand the expectant love of the Heart of Jesus. Your last letter has made my own heart thrill sweetly. I learnt how closely your soul is sister to mine, since God calls that soul to mount to Himself by the *lift of love,* without climbing the steep stairway of fear. I am not surprised you find it hard to be familiar with Jesus—one cannot become so in a day; but this I do know, I shall aid you much more to tread this beautiful path when I lay aside the burden of this perishable body. Ere long you will exclaim with St. Augustine: "Love is my lodestone!"

IX

July 26, 1897.

When you read these few lines I shall perhaps be no more. I know not the future; yet I can confidently say that my Spouse is at the door. It would need a miracle to keep me in exile, and I do not think that Jesus will work that miracle—He does nothing that is of no avail.

Brother, I am so happy to die! Yes, happy . . . not because I shall be free from suffering: on the contrary, suffering combined with love seems the one thing worthy of desire in this vale of tears; but happy to die because far more than on earth I shall help the souls I hold dear.

Jesus has always treated me as a spoilt child. . . . It is true that His Cross has been with me from the cradle, but for that Cross He has given me a passionate love . . .

X

August 14, 1897.

I am about to go before God, and I understand now more than ever that one thing only is needful — to work for Him alone, and do nothing for self or creatures. Jesus wishes to own your heart completely. Before this can be, you will have much to suffer . . . but oh! what joy when comes the happy hour of going Home! I shall not die — I do but enter into Life . . . and whatsoever I cannot tell you here upon earth I will make you understand from the heights of Heaven. . . .

---

[1] Matt. 26:39.

[2] Isa. 9:6.

[3] This letter and the following are addressed to a Seminarist. [Ed.]

[4] John 14:2.

[5] Ps. 102[103]:8, 14, 13.

[6] Cf. Matt. 19:14.

[7] John 14:2.

[8] Luke 12:34.

[9] Cf. Zach. 13:6.

[10] Cf. Luke 15:22.

PRAYERS OF SOEUR THÉRÈSE, THE LITTLE FLOWER OF JESUS

AN ACT OF OBLATION AS A VICTIM OF DIVINE LOVE

This Prayer was found after the death of Sister Teresa of the Child Jesus and of the Holy Face in the copy of the Gospels which she carried night and day close to her heart.

O my God, O Most Blessed Trinity, I desire to love Thee and to make Thee loved—to labour for the glory of Holy Church by saving souls here upon earth and by delivering those suffering in

Purgatory. I desire to fulfill perfectly Thy Holy Will, and to reach the degree of glory Thou hast prepared for me in Thy Kingdom. In a word, I wish to be holy, but, knowing how helpless I am, I beseech Thee, my God, to be Thyself my holiness.

Since Thou hast loved me so much as to give me Thy Only-Begotten Son to be my Saviour and my Spouse, the infinite treasures of His merits are mine. Gladly do I offer them to Thee, and I beg of Thee to behold me only through the Eyes of Jesus, and in His Heart aflame with love. Moreover, I offer Thee all the merits of the Saints both of Heaven and of earth, together with their acts of love, and those of the holy Angels. Lastly, I offer Thee, O Blessed Trinity, the love and the merits of the Blessed Virgin, my dearest Mother—to her I commit this Oblation, praying her to present it to Thee.

During the days of His life on earth her Divine Son, my sweet Spouse, spake these words: "If you ask the Father anything in My Name, He will give it you."[1] Therefore I am certain Thou wilt fulfill my longing. O my God, I know that the more Thou wishest to bestow, the more Thou dost make us desire. In my heart I feel boundless desires, and I confidently beseech Thee to take possession of my soul. I cannot receive Thee in Holy Communion as often as I should wish; but, O Lord, art Thou not all-powerful? Abide in me as Thou dost in the Tabernacle—never abandon Thy Little Victim. I long to console Thee for ungrateful sinners, and I implore Thee to take from me all liberty to sin. If through weakness I should chance to fall, may a glance from Thine Eyes straightway cleanse my soul, and consume all my imperfections—as fire transforms all things into itself.

I thank Thee, O my God, for all the graces Thou hast granted me: especially for having purified me in the crucible of suffering. At the Day of Judgment I shall gaze on Thee with joy, as Thou bearest Thy sceptre of the Cross. And since Thou hast deigned to give me this precious Cross as my portion, I hope to be like unto Thee in Paradise and to behold the Sacred Wounds of Thy Passion shine on my glorified body.

After earth's exile I trust to possess Thee in the Home of our Father; but I do not seek to lay up treasures in Heaven. I wish to labour for Thy Love alone—with the sole aim of pleasing Thee, of consoling Thy Sacred Heart, and of saving souls who will love Thee through eternity.

When comes the evening of life, I shall stand before Thee with empty hands, because I do not ask Thee, my God, to take account of my works. All our works of justice are blemished in Thine Eyes. I wish therefore to be robed with Thine own Justice, and to receive from Thy Love the everlasting gift of Thyself. I desire no other Throne, no other Crown but Thee, O my Beloved!

In Thy sight time is naught—"one day is a thousand years."[2]
Thou canst in a single instant prepare me to appear before Thee.

* * * * * * *

In order that my life may be one Act of perfect Love, I offer myself as a Victim of Holocaust to Thy Merciful Love, imploring Thee to consume me unceasingly, and to allow the floods of infinite tenderness gathered up in Thee to overflow into my soul, that so I may become a very martyr of Thy Love, O my God! May this martyrdom, after having prepared me to appear in Thy Presence, free me from this life at the last, and may my soul take its flight—without delay—into the eternal embrace of Thy Merciful Love!

* * * * * * *

O my Beloved, I desire at every beat of my heart to renew this Oblation an infinite number of times, "till the shadows retire,"[3] and everlastingly I can tell Thee my love face to face.

MARY FRANCES TERESA OF THE CHILD JESUS AND OF THE HOLY FACE.

The ninth of June, Feast of the Most Blessed Trinity, In the year of grace, 1895.

A MORNING PRAYER

O my God! I offer Thee all my actions of this day for the intentions and for the glory of the Sacred Heart of Jesus. I desire to sanctify every beat of my heart, my every thought, my simplest works, by uniting them to Its infinite merits; and I wish to make reparation for my sins by casting them into the furnace of Its Merciful Love.

O my God! I ask of Thee for myself and for those whom I hold dear, the grace to fulfil perfectly Thy Holy Will, to accept for love of Thee the joys and sorrows of this passing life, so that we may one day be united together in Heaven for all Eternity. Amen.

AN ACT OF CONSECRATION TO THE HOLY FACE

Written for the Novices

O Adorable Face of Jesus, since Thou hast deigned to make special choice of our souls, in order to give Thyself to them, we come to consecrate these souls to Thee. We seem, O Jesus, to hear Thee say: "Open to Me, My Sisters, My Spouses, for My Face is wet with the dew, and My Locks with the drops of the night."[4] Our souls understand Thy language of love; we desire to wipe Thy sweet Face, and to console Thee for the contempt of the wicked. In their eyes Thou art still "as it were hidden . . . they esteem Thee an object of reproach."[5]

O Blessed Face, more lovely than the lilies and the roses of the spring, Thou art not hidden from us. The tears which dim Thine Eyes are as precious pearls which we delight to gather, and, through their infinite value, to purchase the souls of our brethren.

From Thy Adorable Lips we have heard Thy loving plaint: "I thirst." Since we know that this thirst which consumes Thee is a thirst for love, to quench it we would wish to possess an infinite love.

Dear Spouse of our souls, if we could love with the love of all hearts, that love would be Thine. . . . Give us, O Lord, this love! Then come to thy Spouses and satisfy Thy Thirst.

And give to us souls, dear Lord . . . We thirst for souls!—Above all for the souls of Apostles and Martyrs . . . that through them we may inflame all poor sinners with love of Thee.

O Adorable Face, we shall succeed in winning this grace from Thee! Unmindful of our exile, "by the rivers of Babylon," we will sing in Thine Ears the sweetest of melodies. Since Thou art the true and only Home of our souls, *our songs shall not be sung in a strange land.*[6] O Beloved Face of Jesus, while we await the Eternal Day when we shall gaze upon Thine Infinite Glory, our only desire is to delight Thy Divine Eyes by keeping our faces hidden too, so that no one on earth may recognize us . . . Dear Jesus, Heaven for us is Thy Hidden Face!

VARIOUS PRAYERS

"If you ask the Father anything in My Name, He will give it you." — John 16:23.

O Eternal Father, Thy Only-Begotten Son, the dear Child Jesus, belongs to me since Thou hast given Him. I offer Thee the infinite merits of His Divine Childhood, and I beseech Thee in His Name to open the gates of Heaven to a countless host of little ones who will for ever follow this Divine Lamb.

"Just as the King's image is a talisman through which anything may be purchased in his Kingdom, so through My Adorable Face — that priceless coin of my Humanity — you will obtain all you desire." Our Lord to Sister Mary of St. Peter.[7]

Eternal Father, since Thou hast given me for my inheritance the Adorable Face of Thy Divine Son, I offer that Face to Thee, and I beg Thee, in exchange for this *coin* of infinite value, to forget the ingratitude of those souls who are consecrated to Thee, and to pardon all poor sinners.

PRAYER TO THE HOLY CHILD

O Jesus, dear Holy Child, my only treasure, I abandon myself to
Thy every whim. I seek no other joy than that of calling forth Thy
sweet Smile. Vouchsafe to me the graces and the virtues of Thy
Holy Childhood, so that on the day of my birth into Heaven the
Angels and Saints may recognise in Thy Spouse: *Teresa of the
Child Jesus.*

PRAYER TO THE HOLY FACE

O Adorable Face of Jesus, sole beauty which ravisheth my heart, vouchsafe to impress on my soul Thy Divine Likeness, so that it may not be possible for Thee to look at Thy Spouse without beholding Thyself. O my Beloved, for love of Thee I am content not to see here on earth the sweetness of Thy Glance, nor to feel the ineffable Kiss of Thy Sacred Lips, but I beg of Thee to inflame me with Thy Love, so that it may consume me quickly, and that soon *Teresa of the Holy Face* may behold Thy glorious Countenance in Heaven.

PRAYER

Inspired by the sight of a statue of The Blessed Joan of Arc

O Lord God of Hosts, who hast said in Thy Gospel: "I am not come to bring peace but a sword," [8] arm me for the combat. I burn to do battle for Thy Glory, but I pray Thee to enliven my courage. . . . Then with holy David I shall be able to exclaim: "Thou alone art my shield; it is Thou, O Lord Who teachest my hands to fight."[9]

O my Beloved, I know the warfare in which I am to engage; it is not on the open field I shall fight. . . . I am a prisoner held captive by Thy Love; of my own free will I have riveted the fetters which bind me to Thee, and cut me off for ever from the world. My sword is Love! with it—like Joan of Arc—"I will drive the strangers from the land, and I will have Thee proclaimed King"—over the Kingdom of souls.

Of a truth Thou hast no need of so weak an instrument as I, but Joan, thy chaste and valiant Spouse, has said: "We must do battle before God gives the victory." O my Jesus! I will do battle, then, for Thy love, until the evening of my life. As Thou didst not will to enjoy rest upon earth, I wish to follow Thy example; and then this promise which came from thy Sacred Lips will be fulfilled in me: "If any man minister to me, let him follow Me, and where I am there also shall My servant be, and . . . him will My Father honour."[10] To be with Thee, to be in Thee, that is my one desire; this promise of fulfilment, which Thou dost give, helps me to bear with my exile as I wait the joyous Eternal Day when I shall see Thee face to face.

PRAYER TO OBTAIN HUMILITY

Written for a Novice

O JESUS! When Thou wast a wayfarer upon earth, Thou didst say: — "Learn of Me, for I am Meek and Humble of Heart, and you shall find rest to your souls."[11] O Almighty King of Heaven! my soul indeed finds rest in seeing Thee condescend to wash the feet of Thy Apostles — "having taken the form of a slave."[12] I recall the words Thou didst utter to teach me the practice of humility: "I have given you an example, that as I have done to you, so you do also. The servant is not greater than his Lord . . . If you know these things, you shall be blessed if you do them."[13] I understand, dear Lord, these words which come from Thy Meek and Humble

Heart, and I wish to put them in practice with the help of Thy grace.

I desire to humble myself in all sincerity, and to submit my will to that of my Sisters, without ever contradicting them, and without questioning whether they have the right to command. No one, O my Beloved! had that right over Thee, and yet Thou didst obey not only the Blessed Virgin and St. Joseph, but even Thy executioners. And now, in the Holy Eucharist, I see Thee complete Thy self-abasement. O Divine King of Glory, with wondrous humility, Thou dost submit Thyself to all Thy Priests, without any distinction between those who love Thee and those who, alas! are lukewarm or cold in Thy service. They may advance or delay the hour of the Holy Sacrifice: Thou art always ready to come down from Heaven at their call.

O my Beloved, under the white Eucharistic Veil Thou dost indeed appear to me Meek and Humble of Heart! To teach me humility, Thou canst not further abase Thyself, and so I wish to respond to Thy Love, by putting myself in the lowest place, by sharing Thy humiliations, so that I may "have part with Thee"[14] in the Kingdom of Heaven.

I implore Thee, dear Jesus, to send me a humiliation whensoever I try to set myself above others.

And yet, dear Lord, Thou knowest my weakness. Each morning I resolve to be humble, and in the evening I recognise that I have often been guilty of pride. The sight of these faults tempts me to discouragement; yet I know that discouragement is itself but a form of pride. I wish, therefore, O my God, to build all my trust upon Thee. As Thou canst do all things, deign to implant in my soul this virtue which I desire, and to obtain it from Thy Infinite Mercy, I will often say to Thee: "Jesus, Meek and Humble of Heart, make my heart like unto Thine."

---

[1] John 16:23.

[2] Ps. 39[40]:4.

[3] Cant. 4:6.

[4] Cf. Cant. 5:2.

[5] Cf. Isa. 53:3.

[6] Cf. Ps. 136[137]:4.

[7] Sister Mary of St. Peter entered the Carmel of Tours in 1840. Three years later she had the first of a series of revelations concerning devotion to the Holy Face as a means of reparation for blasphemy. See *Life of Léon Papin-Dupont,* known as "The Holy Man of Tours."

[8] Matt. 10:34.

[9] Cf. Ps. 143[144]:1, 2.

[10] John 12:26.

[11] Matt. 11:29.

[12] Phil. 2:7.

[13] John 13:15-17.

[14] Cf. John 13:8.

MOTTO OF THE LITTLE FLOWER

From St. John of the Cross

"LOVE IS REPAID BY LOVE ALONE"

"MY DAYS OF GRACE"

Birthday . . . . January 2, 1873
Baptism . . . . January 4, 1873
The Smile of Our Lady . May 10, 1883
First Communion . . May 8, 1884
Confirmation . . . June 14, 1884
Conversion. . . . December 25, 1886
Audience with Leo XIII. November 20, 1887
Entry into the Carmel . April 9, 1888
Clothing . . . . January 10, 1889
Profession. . . . September 8, 1890
Taking of the Veil. . September 24, 1890
Act of Oblation . . June 9, 1895

[ENTRY INTO HEAVEN — September 30, 1897]

SELECTED POEMS OF SOEUR THÉRÈSE, THE LITTLE FLOWER OF JESUS

MY SONG OF TO-DAY

Oh! how I love Thee, Jesus! my soul aspires to Thee —

   And yet for one day only my simple prayer I pray!
Come reign within my heart, smile tenderly on me,
    To-day, dear Lord, to-day!

   But if I dare take thought of what the morrow brings,
   It fills my fickle heart with dreary, dull dismay;
I crave, indeed, my God, the Cross and sufferings,
    But only for to-day!

   O sweetest Star of Heaven! O Virgin, spotless, blest,
   Shining with Jesus' light, guiding to Him my way!
Mother! beneath thy veil let my tired spirit rest,
    For this brief passing day!

   Soon shall I fly afar among the holy choirs,
   Then shall be mine the joy that knoweth no decay;
And then my lips shall sing, to Heaven's angelic lyres,
    The eternal, glad To-day!

June, 1894.

MEMORIES

Selected Stanzas

"I find in my Beloved the mountains, the lonely and wooded vales, the distant isles, the murmur of the waters, the soft whisper of the zephyrs . . . the quiet night with its sister the dawn, the perfect solitude—all that delights and all that fires our love."—St. John of the Cross.

I hold full sweet your memory,
My childhood days, so glad, so free.
To keep my innocence, dear Lord, for Thee,
Thy Love came to me night and day,
    Alway.

. . . .

I loved the swallows' graceful flight,
The turtle doves' low chant at night,
The pleasant sound of insects gay and bright,
The grassy vale where doth belong
    Their song.

. . . .

I loved the glow-worm on the sod;
The countless stars, so near to God,
But most I loved, in all the sky abroad,
The shining moon of silver bright,

At night.

. . . .

The grass is withered in its bed;
The flowers within my hands are dead.
Would that my weary feet, Jesu! might tread
Thy Heavenly Fields, and I might be
   With Thee!

. . . .

My rainbow in the rain-washed skies —
Horizon where my suns arise —
My isle in far-off seas — pearl I most prize —
Sweet spring and butterflies — I see
   In Thee!

. . . .

In Thee I have the springs, the rills,
The mignonette, the daffodils,
The Eglantine, the harebell on the hills,
The trembling poplar, sighing low
   And slow.

. . . .

The lovely lake, the valley fair
And lonely in the lambent air,
The ocean touched with silver everywhere —
In Thee their treasures, all combined,

I find.

. . . .

   I go to chant, with Angel-throngs,
The homage that to Thee belongs.
Soon let me fly away, to join their songs!
Oh, let me die of love, I pray,
   One day!

. . . .

   I hear, e'en I, Thy last and least,
The music from Thy Heavenly Feast;
There, deign receive me as Thy loving guest
And, to my harp, let me but sing,
   My King!

. . . .

   Unto the Saints I shall be near,
To Mary, and those once treasured here.
Life is all past, and dried is every tear;
To me my home again is given—
   In Heaven.

   April 28, 1895.

I THIRST FOR LOVE

In wondrous Love, Thou didst come down from Heaven
  To immolate Thyself, O Christ, for me;
So, in my turn, my love to Thee is given—
  I wish to suffer and to die for Thee.

  Thou, Lord, didst speak this truth benign:
"To die for one loved tenderly,
Of greatest love on earth is sign";
  And now, such love is mine—
    Such love for Thee!

  Do Thou abide with me, O Pilgrim blest!
  Behind the hill fast sinks the dying day.
Helped by Thy Cross, I mount the rocky crest;
  Oh, come, to guide me on my Heavenward Way.

  To be like Thee is my desire;
  Thy Voice finds echo in my soul.
Suffering I crave! Thy words of fire
  Lift me above earth's mire,
    And sin's control.

  Chanting Thy victories, gloriously sublime,
  The Seraphim—all Heaven—cry to me,
That even Thou, to conquer sin and crime,
  Upon this earth a sufferer needs must be.

For me upon life's dreary way
   What scorn, what anguish, Thou didst bear!
Let me but hide me day by day,
   Be least of all, alway,
      Thy lot to share.

Ah, Christ! Thy great example teaches me
   Myself to humble, honours to despise.
A little one — as Thou — I choose to be,
   Forgetting self, so I may charm Thine Eyes.

My peace I find in solitude,
   Nor ask I more, dear Lord, than this:
Be Thou my sole beatitude,
   And ever — in Thee — renewed
      My joy, my bliss!

Thou, the great God Whom earth and Heaven adore,
   Thou dwell'st a prisoner for me night and day;
And every hour I hear Thy Voice implore:
   "I thirst — I thirst — I thirst — for love alway!"

I, too, Thy prisoner am I;
   I, too, cry ever unto Thee
Thine own divine and tender cry:
   "I thirst!" Oh, let me die
      Of love for Thee.

For love of Thee I thirst! fulfil my hope;
  Augment in me Thine own celestial flame!
For love of Thee I thirst! too scant earth's scope:
  The glorious Vision of Thy Face I claim!

 My long, slow martyrdom of fire
 Still more and more consumeth me.
Thou art my joy, my one desire,
  Jesu! may I expire
   Of love for Thee.

 April 30, 1896.

TO SCATTER FLOWERS

O Jesus! O my Love! each eve I come to fling
    My springtide roses sweet before Thy Cross divine;
By their plucked petals fair, my hands so gladly bring,
    I long to dry Thine every tear!

  To scatter flowers! — that means each sacrifice:
  My lightest sighs and pains, my heaviest, saddest hours,
My hopes, my joys, my prayers — I will not count the price —
    Behold my flowers!

With deep untold delight Thy beauty fills my soul,
   Would I might light this love in hearts of all who live!
For this, my fairest flowers, all things in my control,
   How fondly, gladly would I give!

   To scatter flowers! — behold my chosen sword
     For saving sinners' souls and filling Heaven's bowers:
The victory is mine — yea, I disarm Thee, Lord,
   With these my flowers!

   The petals in their flight caress Thy Holy Face;
     They tell Thee that my heart is Thine, and Thine alone.
Thou knowest what these leaves are saying in my place:
   On me Thou smilest from Thy Throne.

   To scatter flowers! — that means, to speak of Thee —
     My only pleasure here, where tears fill all the hours;
But soon, with Angel Hosts, my spirit shall be free
   To scatter flowers.

June 28, 1896.

WHY I LOVE THEE, MARY!

Last Poem written by Soeur Thérèse

Concluding Stanzas

Henceforth thy shelter in thy woe was John's most humble dwelling;
The son of Zebedee replaced the Son Whom Heaven adored.
Naught else the Gospels tell us of thy life, in grace excelling;
It is the last they say of thee, sweet Mother of my Lord!

But oh! I think that silence means that, high in Heaven's Glory,
When time is past, and to their House thy children safe are come,
The Eternal Word, my Mother dear, Himself will tell thy story,
To charm our souls — thy children's souls — in our Eternal Home.

Soon I shall hear that harmony, that blissful, wondrous singing;
Soon, unto Heaven that waits for us, my soul shall

swiftly fly.
O thou who cam'st to smile on me at dawn of life's beginning!
Come once again to smile on me . . . Mother! the night is nigh.

I fear no more thy majesty, so far removed above me,
For I have suffered sore with thee: now hear me, Mother mild!
Oh, let me tell thee face to face, dear Mary! how I love thee;
And say to thee for evermore: I am Thy little child.

May 1897.

NOTE. — The above poems are reprinted from the translation of the
Little Flower's poems made by Susan L. Emery, of Dorchester,
Mass.,
U.S.A., and published by the Carmel of Boston. [Ed.]